Sponsored by
the American Society
for Training and Development

ORGANIZATIONAL CAREER DEVELOPMENT

Thomas G. Gutteridge
Zandy B. Leibowitz
Jane E. Shore

Foreword by
Stephen K. Merman

ORGANIZATIONAL CAREER DEVELOPMENT

*Benchmarks
for Building a
World-Class
Workforce*

 Jossey-Bass Publishers
San Francisco

Substantial discounts on bulk quantities of Jossey-Bass books
are available to corporations, professional associations, and other
organizations. For details and discount information, contact the
special sales department at Jossey-Bass Inc., Publishers.
(415) 433-1740; Fax (415) 433-0499.

For sales outside the United States, contact Maxwell Macmillan
International Publishing Group, 866 Third Avenue, New York,
New York 10022.

Manufactured in the United States of America

The paper used in this book is acid-free and meets the
State of California requirements for recycled paper
(50 percent recycled waste, including 10 percent
postconsumer waste), which are the strictest guidelines
for recycled paper currently in use in the United States.

10% POST
CONSUMER
WASTE

The ink in this book is either soy- or vegetable-based and during the
printing process emits fewer than half the volatile organic compounds
(VOCs) emitted by petroleum-based ink.

Library of Congress Cataloging-in-Publication Data

Gutteridge, Thomas G.
    Organizational career development : benchmarks for building a
world-class workforce / Thomas G. Gutteridge, Zandy B. Leibowitz,
Jane E. Shore.
        p.   cm. — (The Jossey-Bass management series)
    Includes bibliographical references and index.
    ISBN 1-55542-526-7 (acid-free paper)
    1. Career development.   2. Personal management.   I. Leibowitz,
Zandy B., date.   II. Shore, Jane E., date.   III. Title.
IV. Series.
HF5549.5.C35G88   1993
658.3′12 — dc20   93-29
                                                                  CIP

FIRST EDITION
HB Printing   10 9 8 7 6 5 4 3 2   *Code 9338*

*The Jossey-Bass
Management Series*

CONTENTS

Part Two: The State of the Art

     People Developers,   184

9.   Career Development Successes:
     What Works and Why   187

     Conclusion: Challenges and Recommendations
     for the Twenty-First Century   196

     Appendixes:
         A.   ASTD Survey Questionnaire and Results   207
         B.   Interview Questionnaire for Case Studies
              and Best Practices   232
         C.   Australian Survey Results   235
         D.   Singapore Survey Results   240
         E.   Readings in Organizational Career
              Development   245

     References   255

     Index   259

FOREWORD

The new catchword of the 1990s is "world class." In the business world, to be world class means to have the organizational capability to do business more quickly, less expensively, and with higher quality than any of your competitors.

When the authors of this book began looking at career development systems a decade ago, almost no one fully appreciated the fact that aligning an individual's skills, values, and interests with an organization's competitive requirements is a crucial strategy for any world-class organization seeking to survive economic uncertainty and unending change. To deal with the varied scenarios that our world faces, a player in today's business environment requires new and different kinds of capabilities. Two in particular are sorely needed: the ability to monitor the future accurately and the capacity to maintain a workforce that responds quickly to volatile customer needs and competitive conditions.

The authors of this book are acutely aware of these needs, and they have closely observed the evolution of career development in the past decade. By combining an academic/research focus with a consulting/applications perspective, they have been able to share many useful and diverse viewpoints. With this book, these authors have launched the challenging long-term project of benchmarking best career development practices in organizations at home and abroad. Their work will help the entire field move toward a productive future in which practitioners and organizations will be learning and improving continuously.

Significantly, this book offers an international perspective that will have several notable effects on the field. To begin with, the authors have positioned career development as a global business issue—one that requires leadership from the world's most successful organizations. Moreover, they have skillfully communicated the reality of career development as a business strategy that brings a competitive advantage to organizations in any setting that are seeking to enlighten their business with the benefits of a fully integrated human resources system. Third, the results reported in this book depict career development leadership roles in locations other than the United States. American practitioners seeking to improve their systems will gain much by studying best practices in other cultures. Finally, this work opens the door to the creation of an evaluation system that will pinpoint the contributions of career development interventions to large-scale organizational change.

This book is intended for several types of readers, but particularly for those who are called on to help an organization implement a career development system. I would recommend that any organizational task force chartered to inquire into such a system use this book as a tool to get up to speed quickly and to identify systems to use as models. The book is equally valuable for those in academic and research arenas, enhancing appreciation of career development theory as it is applied in real-world settings.

Finally, I would recommend this book for executive leaders and line managers who are seeking justification for career development as a way to capitalize on the core competencies of their workforces. Career development is a primary concern for any manager. The question of how to staff an organization to meet customer requirements is continually perplexing. We are indeed indebted to these authors for keeping us current on the

state of the practice and for providing this valuable compen-
dium of pointers toward exciting future possibilities.

February 1993   Stephen K. Merman
                     *1992 president of the American Society
                     for Training and Development*

PREFACE

As we approach the twenty-first century, the development of people takes center stage as a crucial business strategy. In fact, as John Naisbitt and Patricia Aburdeen stated in their book *Megatrends 2000*, "In the global economic boom of the 1990s, human resources are the competitive edge for both companies and countries. In the global economic competition of the information economy, the quality and innovativeness of human resources will spell the difference." (1990, p. 39).

Thus, for a growing number of organizations in the United States and abroad, the statement "People are our most important resource" is far more than an obligatory line in an annual report. Because so many companies are running toe to toe in the technology race, savvy organizations see leveraging their workforces' talents and skills as the chief means of staying competitive. Innovative workplace strategies that receive front-page attention as enhancers of organizational effectiveness — such as quality teams and self-managed work teams — rely for their success on the foundation of an empowered, well-developed workforce.

Organizational career development — consciously linking people's career plans with the organization's workforce needs — has blossomed in the last several decades as a strategy for improving workforce effectiveness. In the late 1960s, this strat-

egy was viewed mainly as a good way to help individual employees realize their personal goals. More and more, however, it has
been seen as a tool to help organizations adjust to new and often
problematic business realities, including globalization and
downsizing. In less than three decades, in fact, the field of
organizational career development has changed so quickly that
there has been little time or opportunity to document and take
stock of this growth and its implications. Yet because of the field's
widely perceived relevance to overall business success, human
resources (HR) practitioners are increasingly interested in gaining a better understanding of the state of organizational career
development practice as we head toward the year 2000.

In the early 1990s, the American Society for Training and
Development (ASTD) undertook to sponsor our proposal for
such an investigation, the results of which are the subject of this
book. ASTD shared our sense that the time was right to build
and expand on earlier systematic explorations of the field. The
landscape had changed dramatically, and particularly significant shifts had occurred over the last decade—among them
those described in the following paragraphs.

*"People development" is more closely aligned than ever before with
the strategic business needs of organizations.* Because technological
advances are continuous and ubiquitous, it is increasingly likely
that bottom-line margins of success will be gained through HR-
related advantages. Simply stated, this means that while everyone is automating, not everyone has the skills or experience to
exploit successfully the advantages that automation confers.
Moreover, competencies in the workplace increasingly demand
skills that are not related to technology—traits such as effective
communication skills, teamwork, critical thinking, and the ability to react to change, all of which tend to come with a well-
developed workforce.

People development has thus become part of the culture
in many organizations, "the way we do things around here." And
in today's "lean and mean" business climate, development is a
necessary survival strategy: it helps companies position themselves so they can adjust to rapid changes in their environment.
A sudden shift in product line, for instance, may require retrain-

ing, whereas delayering may call for job enrichment activities. Development processes enable companies to meet such challenges quickly and effectively.

More and more, organizational career development has taken a systems *approach.* Early efforts typically involved isolated interventions such as career and life planning workshops. Over time, it became clear that the effectiveness of such one-shot activities was limited. For a long-lasting effect on people and work flows, many HR practitioners realized that a systematic approach to organizational change was needed. Simultaneously, natural links between career development activities and other HR initiatives and practices began to emerge.

As with any human behavior system, changes in one part of a system have a ripple effect elsewhere. For example, providing career information may cause employees to use an existing job-posting system more often, and the effectiveness of a performance appraisal discussion may be enhanced if an employee and supervisor meet regularly to talk over career issues. This type of synergism increasingly characterizes career development activities.

The focus of career development has shifted radically, from the individual to the organization. In the late 1960s, the focus was on addressing *individual* employees' goals through career counseling and career planning workshops. By the 1980s, the emphasis had changed: organizational career development was seen as a tool for addressing *business* needs in a vastly changed corporate environment. In the 1990s, the focus is on a balance between the two — on individual and organizational alignment. This outlook construes organizational career development as a strategic process in which maximizing individuals' career potential is a way of enhancing the success of the organization as a whole.

Concepts of career development have broadened to encompass new organizational realities. Many of today's employees grew up in an era of unprecedented economic growth and opportunity, and they have tended to equate success with upward mobility, viewing anything short of a promotion as a career failure or penalty. But as economic conditions have shifted, organizations have responded by eliminating layers of management, and the flattened structures that have resulted now offer less and less room at the top. To accommodate the large numbers of talented workers left in the middle, organizations have had to think more creatively about what growth and success really mean. There is increasing recognition that career success can come in the form of a lateral move, "growing in place" through job enrichment.

Because our economy has globalized, we now need to view career development in a worldwide context. Career development concepts and technologies travel across national boundaries, in part as a result of the growth of multinational corporations but also because of the explosion of information technologies. As participants in the global economy become more interdependent, models of innovation in career development are as likely to be found overseas as in the United States.

This book explores these large transformations as they are reflected in organizational life today and as they bear on developmental practices. Specifically, we aim to answer two questions: What is the *state of the practice* of organizational career development in the 1990s? and What is the *state of the art*? The first question was explored in a 1978 survey sponsored by the American Management Association (Walker and Gutteridge, 1979); the second, in a 1983 ASTD-sponsored series of case studies (Gutteridge and Otte, 1983). Our own research effort melds these two approaches, updates their findings, and takes a first-time look at the international scene.

Audience

We believe that the findings in this book will be useful to several audiences. Practitioners—HR managers, consultants, executives, and career development specialists—will be able to benchmark their experiences against those of other organizations and to learn from their successes and mistakes. Our survey of the state of current practice illuminates the challenges faced by any organization seeking to implement a career development system. In addition, our study of best practices sheds light on possible paths to success and points the way toward exciting future developments in the field. Researchers, academicians, and students of human resources, organizational development, and industrial psychology will benefit from learning about a wide variety of approaches currently being used in organizational career development.

Overview of the Contents

We have organized this book in two major parts, preceded by the opening chapter that describes our study as a whole. Part One looks at the state of the practice, describing and interpreting the results of our survey of U.S. and overseas organizations.

Chapter Two focuses on U.S. data, presenting the results of the survey of one thousand large corporations as well as U.S. government agencies. The survey examines organizations' career development practices, assessment of practices, and general attitudes regarding career development. It comments on the implications of the results for today's flattened organizations. In addition, the chapter compares these current survey results with those of the 1978 survey of U.S. organizations. Given the dramatic changes in the business environment over the last decade, the two sets of results were surprisingly similar. These similarities have important and cautionary implications for today's practitioners.

Chapter Three explores organizational career development across Europe and also presents results of the same survey. A key driver in Europe is to motivate and retain scarce talent. The focus, however, will probably move in the next decade beyond its current emphasis on high-potential managers.

Chapter Four presents the Australian survey results and highlights the need to link career development to business strategy. Particularly in the private sector, partnerships between organizations and employees will likely strengthen, as will linkages with other HR functions.

In Chapter Five, career development in Singapore is explored (including survey results), with an emphasis on the need for management support for development efforts. Despite widespread support for career development as a concept, it is still a relative newcomer and the existence of actual systems is rare.

Chapter Six closes Part One by offering useful comparisons of the survey data from abroad and at home. The similarities and differences have interesting implications for practitioners. The chapter has a chart that compares each of the five survey samples on critical dimensions.

Part Two highlights the state of the art in organizational career development through a series of case studies of career development systems as well as examinations of specific best practices. In Chapter Seven, we present profiles of twelve organizations' successful career development systems that illuminate their "macro" focus. Both here and overseas, there are certain key elements that are found to make systems function effectively at various stages of implementation.

Chapter Eight surveys best practices in six organizations, using an operational, or "micro" perspective. Whether job posting, succession planning, or accountability mechanisms, these practical approaches help organizations achieve their career development objectives.

Chapter Nine weaves together all the book's findings to explore nine common themes, or success factors. It examines what works across diverse organizations and why and how practitioners can benefit from these learnings.

Finally, the Conclusion looks toward the future. How are organizations changing and what are the implications for career development in the twenty-first century? What challenges will practitioners face? The book closes with a series of recommendations for organizations to enable them to build a more competitive workforce through their development systems.

Acknowledgments

This book, like organizational career development, reflects a partnership of many different people. Writing it would not have been possible without the generous, eager participation of many individuals and organizations. Indeed, it was inspiring to witness time and again the high level of interest and enthusiasm for the study from practitioners all across the field. Many were themselves participants in the study, willing to share their career development experiences so as to build the overall knowledge base. To the many study participants, both named and unnamed throughout this text, we offer our heartfelt thanks.

The American Society for Training and Development sponsored the study. Conceptual Systems, Inc., provided the support and resources to carry out the research and to document and disseminate the findings. ASTD's Career Development Professional Practice Area referred us to several of the case study and best-practice organizations. The Southern Illinois University College of Business and Administration provided support throughout the study.

We are most grateful for the contributions of Alastair Rylatt, Violet S. K. Seah, C. Brooklyn Derr, and Erik Jansen. Their chapters enabled us to provide expert views of the international context of career development. We truly appreciate their willingness to share their time and knowledge and to allow others to benefit from their vast experience in the field.

In addition we would also like to thank the following people for their effort in producing the Australian contribution: Janelle Moy from Educe Consulting Services Pty. Ltd. for her support in producing the 1992 Australian Institute of Training and Development study; Eugene Fernandez from Eugene Fernandez and Associates for coauthoring the Australian Best Practices Series with Alastair Rylatt; and finally, Jacki Hunt from Baxter Healthcare, Michelle Sloane from Westpac, and Enid Murphy from Overseas Telecommunications Company Ltd. for their time and support in producing the case histories. We also appreciate those who provided the excellent writing assistance with several other case studies and best practices: Yeo Ngoh Kim for National Computer Board (NCB), John Duncan for Amoco Production Company (APC), and Ken Ideus for BP Exploration (BPX). We were also very fortunate to have the expert writing and editorial contributions of Martha Cooley.

Martin Kaufman conducted and recorded several of the case study interviews and provided insightful analysis of some of the survey data. Edward Roke was tremendously helpful in both the survey design and the data interpretation. Jon Camitta and Jodie Franklin entered copious amounts of survey data. The survey sampling and mailing process was ably assisted by Janet Shauer, Melissa Covaleski, Laura Ackerman, and Cynthia Gilliam.

Jill Dudley graciously and lovingly provided critical administrative and clerical support at every phase of this study. Janet Shauer and Linda Vincent oversaw the production of the final manuscript, and managed to do so both calmly and competently. Linda Mint, Gina Van Daniker, and Melissa Covaleski used their superb skills to design and produce a number of the book's visuals, as did Kathy Foster with large portions of the text.

Finally, our thanks go to the Jossey-Bass editors and staff for their support and encouragement from the book's inception through its publication.

February 1993

Thomas G. Gutteridge
Storrs, Connecticut

Zandy B. Leibowitz
Silver Spring, Maryland

Jane E. Shore
Washington, D.C.

THE AUTHORS

Thomas G. Gutteridge is dean and distinguished professor of management at the School of Business Administration at the University of Connecticut. He received his B.S. degree (1965) in industrial engineering from General Motors Institute and his M.S. (1966) and Ph.D. (1971) degrees in industrial administration from the Herman C. Krannert Graduate School at Purdue University.

Gutteridge's teaching and research interests are in the area of career development, human resources management, and industrial relations. Gutteridge is a consultant in the career development and human resource planning field as well as a labor arbitrator for the American Arbitration Association and the Federal Mediation and Conciliation Service. He is a member of the American Society of Training and Development and the Human Resource Planning Society. Gutteridge is coauthor of a monograph titled "Career Planning Practices" for AMACOM, contributor to the ASTD monograph titled "A Guide for Career Development Inquiry," and coauthor of ASTD's *Organizational Career Development: State of the Practice* (1983, with F. L. Otte). He has also authored a number of publications regarding the labor market characteristics and career patterns of college graduates and displaced technical professionals as well as articles on organizational human resource planning and career development practices in such publications as *California Management Review*, *Industrial and Labor Relations Review*, and *Academy of Management Journal*.

Formerly Gutteridge was dean and professor of management at the College of Business and Administration at Southern Illinois University, Carbondale, for nine years and professor and administrator at the School of Management at the State University of New York, Buffalo, for thirteen years. He also has six years of private-sector work experience, primarily in the personnel and labor relations areas, and was an instructor at Purdue University. He is a past member of the ASTD board of directors and has served as director of the Career Development Division of ASTD. He has also served as president of the Niagara Frontier Chapter of the American Society of Personnel Administration.

Zandy B. Leibowitz is a psychologist who specializes in designing human resource and career development systems for organizations. She is currently adjunct associate professor in the Counseling and Personnel Services Department at the University of Maryland and is on the faculty of the University of Michigan Executive Education Center. She is a principal in Conceptual Systems, Inc., a consulting firm based in Silver Spring, Maryland. She received her B.A. degree (1970) in psychology, her M.A. degree (1972) in counseling, and her Ph.D. degree (1974) in counseling psychology, all from the University of Maryland.

Her clients include a variety of public and private organizations such as Amoco, AT&T, BellCore, Bell Labs, Kodak, Corning Incorporated, Nationwide Insurance, NASA's Goddard Space Flight Center, Washington Health Care Corporation, Fannie Mae, Baxter Healthcare, Boeing, Ciba-Geigy, and the National Football League. She has spoken extensively to groups such as the Human Resource Planning Society, the American Society for Training and Development, and the American Management Association. Her publications in the areas of career development, human resources, adult development, and self-management are extensive. Two of her recent publications are the books *Adult Career Development* (1992) and *Designing Career Development Systems* (1986). She is also the coauthor of a micro-computer-based career development system, *CareerPoint*. She has served as the executive director of ASTD's Career Development Professional Practice Area. She received ASTD's Walter Storey Career Development Award for her outstanding contributions to the field.

Jane E. Shore is senior career development consultant with Fannie Mae in Washington, D.C. She received her B.A. degree (1976) in psychology and social work from Antioch College and her M.A. degree (1992) in counseling from the University of Maryland, College Park.

Shore has over fifteen years of experience in human resource program design, career development consulting, training and development policy, and employment and outplacement counseling. Her recent work has been mainly in the design and implementation of career development systems and related human resource programs. Clients have included Corning, Martin Marietta, World Bank, MITRE Corporation, MCI, U.S. General Accounting Office, MetPath Inc., and Washington Hospital Center. She has designed studies and published in the areas of workplace training policy, new employee development, managerial accountability for development, and computers in human resources. Shore is coauthor of two recent *Training and Development* articles on managers as people developers and new employee transitions, coauthor of a chapter on new employees in *Career Development: Theory and Practice* (1992), contributor to *Using Computers in Human Resources* (1991), and author and coauthor of a number of publications of the National Institute for Work and Learning on workplace education and training policy. She has spoken on career development and other human resource areas to such groups as the American Society for Training and Development, Training Officers Conference, National University Continuing Education Association, and the Washington Deming Study Group.

Formerly Shore was a senior consultant with Conceptual Systems, Inc., in Silver Spring, Maryland. Shore received ASTD's 1991 Career Development Student Research Award for her research in organizational career development. In 1992, she served as a regional representative of ASTD's Career Development Professional Practice Area. She is a member of ASTD, the National Career Development Association, and the American Counseling Association.

CONTRIBUTORS

C. Brooklyn Derr is professor of human resource management at the David Eccles School of Business at the University of Utah, Salt Lake City. He is also adjunct professor at the International Institute of Management Development (IMD) in Lausanne, Switzerland, where he recently spent three years in residence working with some of Europe's largest multinational corporations. Derr teaches human resource management and management development courses. He has also taught at the European Institute of Business Administration (INSEAD) in Fontainebleau, France, and at the Ecole Supérieure de Commerce in Lyon, France. In addition, he has taught at Harvard University and at the University of California, Los Angeles. He received his B.A. degree (1967) in political science from the University of California, Berkeley, and his Ed.D. degree (1972) in organizational behavior from Harvard University.

Derr is the author of four books and over thirty-five published articles. His works include the book *Managing the New Careerists* (1986) and the audiotape *Career Success Maps* (1989). He has done research in the area of career and management development, and has served as consultant to a variety of business, governmental, and educational organizations.

Erik Jansen is assistant professor in the Department of Management at the David Eccles School of Business, University of Utah.

Jansen teaches human resource management and career development in the M.B.A. program and the philosophy of science in the Ph.D. program. He received both his A.B. degree (1970) in psychology and his M.A. degree (1976) in industrial psychology from San Diego State University. He received his Ph.D. degree (1986) in business administration from the University of Southern California.

His research focuses on motivation, careers, and reward systems. He has done research and consulting with Fortune 500 firms in aerospace, oil and gas, information processing, telecommunications, financial services, and health care. He has studied human resource practices in China, Japan, and Europe and has published in the *Academy of Management Review* and the *Journal of Business Venturing*.

Alastair Rylatt, director of Excel Human Resource Development, is one of Australia's leading trainers, strategists, and counselors in human resource consulting. Examples of his internationally known clients include Avis, Australian Institute of Management, Caltex Oil, Coca-Cola, Harlequin Mills and Boon, and McDonnell Douglas. Since 1987 he has completed around 150 projects involving approximately 650 public, private, and tertiary-sector organizations. He received both his B.Bus. degree (1984) in business administration and his Grad. Dip. Employment Relations degree (1987) from the University of Technology, Sydney.

One of Rylatt's major interests is improving the quality of learning in Australian organizations. He is the founder and leader of the Australian Human Resources Institute Career Development and Skill Formation Network, the president of the Accelerative Learning Society of Australia (N.S.W. Division), and a committee member of the Australian Institute of Management Organizational Change Group. His other memberships include the American Society for Training and Development, Australian Institute of Training and Development, Australian Consortium on Experiential Education, and Career Planning and Adult Development Network.

Rylatt pioneered the 1991 Australian Institute of Training

and Development study of Australian career development practices. In May 1989, he received a certificate of recognition from the Australian Institute of Training and Development for his ongoing and pathfinding achievements in the industry. From 1983 to 1987 he implemented career and management development activities in the Australian government.

Violet S. K. Seah is research and publications executive at the Singapore Institute of Management (SIM), Singapore's national management organization. She received her B.S. degree (1982) with honors in sociology and social research from the University of Northumbria at Newcastle, United Kingdom.

Some of the research projects she has handled include studies on productivity movement, attitudes of the Singaporean workforce, studies on organizational practices and managers' personalities, computer security and abuse, service management, and various aspects of training in Singapore organizations. Seah writes and edits for the *Singapore Management Review*, the official journal of SIM. The articles she has written for the *Singapore Management Review* include "Computer Security and Computer Abuse in Singapore," "Organisation Types: What Type of Company Do Singaporeans Prefer to Work For?" and "Service Management in Singapore Companies."

Before joining SIM, she was a research officer with the National Productivity Board and Singapore Computer Systems.

ORGANIZATIONAL CAREER DEVELOPMENT

CHAPTER 1

Organizational Career Development: A Study of Changes in the Field

Since the mid 1970s, career development has been transformed from an isolated tool for individual growth to a key strategic asset for far-sighted organizations. Yet despite this profound change, there have been almost no recent systematic investigations of this exciting field. As a new century approaches — and as the popular media devote increasing attention to issues of worker empowerment, the creation of "learning organizations," and the realities of a global economy — examining the role and effects of career development at home and abroad seems a timely and useful undertaking.

Getting Started: Basic Concepts and Terms

In using the term "organizational career development," we are referring to a planned effort to link the individual's career needs with the organization's workforce requirements. It is a process for helping individuals plan their careers in concert with an organization's business requirements and strategic direction. The process and its underlying concepts are graphically portrayed in Figure 1.1.

Along with the concept of alignment between the individual and the organization, three interrelated assumptions characterize the field of organizational career development to-

1

Figure 1.1. Career Development System — Linking Organizational Needs with Individual Career Needs.

Individual Career Needs

How do I find career opportunities within the organization that:

- Use my strengths

- Address my developmental needs

- Provide challenge

- Match my interests

- Match my values

- Match my personal style

ISSUE:

Are employees developing themselves in a way that links personal effectiveness and satisfaction with the achievement of the organization's strategic objectives?

Organizational Needs

What are the organization's major strategic issues over the next two to three years?

- What are the most critical needs and challenges that the organization will face over the next two to three years?

- What critical skills, knowledge, and experience will be needed to meet these challenges?

- What staffing levels will be required?

- Does the organization have the bench strength necessary to meet the critical challenges?

Source: © 1992, Conceptual Systems, Inc.

day. First, development is generally seen as an ongoing process, not a one-time event. Ideally, it is integrated with diverse HR structures, policies, and procedures of the organization. That kind of integration brings significant strategic advantages. Many organizations are finding that when they mesh career development systems with other HR initiatives, the result is a healthy impetus for continuous improvement.

Second, all three groups — employees, managers, and organizations — have specific roles to play in a career development system. Employees are responsible for assessing themselves, creating plans within the context of organizational realities, and carrying out certain development activities. Managers support their employees and play a crucial role in helping them understand the organization's needs and requirements. The organization itself is responsible for providing tools, resources, and structures to support the process.

Third is the concept of a *system* itself— "systems thinking" is central to organizational career development. What is a system? Russell Ackoff (1981, pp. 15–18) offers these useful descriptions:

- Essential elements of a system derive from the interactions of its parts.
- Every part of a system has properties that it loses when they are separated from the system as a whole.
- If each part of a system, considered separately, is made to operate as efficiently as possible, the system as a whole will not operate as effectively as possible.

The development process links *current job performance* and *future development*. It begins with the current job and then relates that job to future goals and plans for reaching those goals. Development thus includes multiple options extending beyond simply getting promoted — such as improving skills, enriching the present job, staying current, and preparing for future directions.

With this general framework in mind, Gutteridge (1987,

pp. 60–61) has described organizational career development practices in six areas:

1. Employee self-assessment tools, such as career planning workshops, workbooks, or computer software.
2. Organizational potential assessment processes, such as promotability forecasts and assessment centers.
3. Internal labor-market information exchanges, including career information handbooks, resource centers, and so on.
4. Individual counseling and career discussions between employees and supervisors, HR staff, or specialized career counselors.
5. Job matching systems such as job posting, skills audits or inventories, and replacement or succession planning.
6. Development programs, including internal and external programs and seminars, tuition reimbursement, job rotation, enrichment, mentoring systems, and so on.

The Context of This Study

Our study of organizational career development in the 1990s grew out of two earlier efforts. In 1978, under the auspices of the American Management Association, Walker and Gutteridge surveyed a random sample of 225 American companies, asking questions about their career planning and development practices. The resulting study was published in 1979. The survey questions dealt with factors leading to the implementation of career development activities, the nature and prevalence of various practices, and evaluations of effectiveness; our current survey is built around similar questions.

The major conclusion of the 1979 study was that "career planning programs for salaried personnel are not nearly as common or as advanced as might be thought. While there is widespread support for career planning as a concept, there is a wide gap between the ideal and the reality of current practices" (Walker and Gutteridge, 1979, p. 1). As Walker and Gutteridge discovered, although numerous organizations reported a wide variety of career planning activities in 1978, few had integrated career development systems.

The 1979 study documented the pervasiveness of career development programs in organizations; however, a detailed exploration of the *content* of such programs had still not occurred. The effort sponsored in 1983 by ASTD (and conducted by Gutteridge and Otte) was an attempt to analyze, in even greater detail, forty organizations known to have career development activities in place. The forty case studies were conducted through structured telephone interviews based on a premailed interview guide and focusing in particular on the (then) emerging techniques of career counseling, workshops, and workbooks.

Study Methodology

In 1990, we undertook to update and broaden those earlier studies. By integrating the methodologies used in 1979 and 1983, we have been able to examine both the state of the practice and the state of the art. We investigated the state of the practice through a broad-based, large-scale survey that was designed to give us a snapshot of current practice. We captured the details of various state-of-the-art efforts (that is, the best practices or systems) through structured but open-ended telephone interviews with targeted organizations. In both cases, the earlier scope of inquiry was extended to include overseas organizations.

Our survey included five separate samples: a random sample of 1,000 U.S. corporations; 96 federal agencies; and targeted samples of corporations outside the United States: 850 in Australia, 1,000 in Singapore, and 550 throughout various European countries. Most (though not all) of our international respondents were organizations headquartered overseas; in some cases, they were overseas operations of U.S.-based corporations. (Career development as practiced by multinationals increasingly involves international assignments as a key feature — a trend that is sure to continue.)

The U.S. corporate survey (presented with results in Appendix A) was mailed in 1990 and 1991 to a random sample of

750 companies from the Corporate 1000 (Gibbons, 1990a) and 250 from the Financial 1000 (Gibbons, 1990b).* This ensured diversity of industry and geographical representation even though we did not stratify our sample. It also allowed us to focus on large organizations, where we believed career development activities were more likely to occur. This is not, however, to discourage smaller organizations from making use of our findings. While large organizations may have more visible career development systems (and thus provide researchers with richer data), all the practices and activities we uncovered can be — and are — used successfully by mid-sized and smaller organizations. The challenge, no matter what the size of a company, is the same: to tailor the variety of available development tools and resources toward particular business goals, opportunities, and limitations.

Wherever possible, we mailed our questionnaire to a personnel or HR executive (as indicated in standard business directories). We aimed for high-level officials, such as HR vice presidents, as we felt they would have the broadest organizational perspective. Where we lacked names, we used ASTD lists (chiefly in the 1990 membership directory) to obtain names of appropriate HR practitioners, such as managers of training and development or employee development specialists. Again, we aimed for the highest level available. In several cases, we mailed to personal contacts at organizations. (In a few instances, we had no name to mail to even after telephoning the organization, so we addressed the survey to "Director of Personnel" or "Personnel Department.")

We followed up our initial survey mailing with a postcard reminder and also did a targeted telephone followup with our contacts and with individuals from the ASTD lists, believing that these two groups would be most likely to respond to an ASTD-sponsored survey of career development.

---

* *The Corporate 1000* is a quarterly directory of up-to-date information on the top one thousand public corporations in the U.S. It covers manufacturers, service businesses, and utilities. *The Financial 1000* provides current information on the one thousand leading commercial banks, insurance companies, Wall Street firms, and thrifts.

Ultimately, we received 256 responses—a healthy 26 percent response rate. In some cases, respondents returned their surveys anonymously (both the initial returns and responses to the followup); thus, although we had a good sense of our sample, it is impossible for us to know exactly which organizations responded.

Our survey was not an unbiased, scientifically designed inquiry. It was biased toward large organizations, and it was not stratified by industry or location. Some of our respondents described corporatewide career development systems; others described career development within a particular division or unit. Moreover, we assumed that our respondents were likely to be connected with a program or to have a strong interest in career development, and this has undoubtedly skewed the responses somewhat, even though we encouraged those without programs to reply as well. Despite these caveats, however, we feel that our survey results offer a reasonable representation of career development trends within large organizations, and they allow us to make meaningful generalizations about the state of the practice as a whole today.

Our U.S. survey was also mailed to training and development professionals in 96 federal government agencies (listed in ASTD's *1990 Membership Roster of the Interagency Advisory Group of the Committee on Development and Training*). We followed up with telephone reminders and ended up with 27 responses. This survey's results are also presented in Appendix A; the results of both surveys are discussed in detail in Chapter Two. Our international surveys were identical in content (with very minor wording and spelling changes) to the U.S. survey. The samples and methodologies used are outlined in Chapters Three, Four, and Five.

In all cases, the questions asked were similar but updated versions of those used in the 1978 survey. They were designed to address the following issues:

- The current extent of career development activities within the responding organization.
- The scope, resources, and responsibilities involved.

- The level or group of employees at which career development is targeted.
- The issues or needs driving career development in the
  organization.
- Whether and how career development is tied to HR structures and strategic planning efforts.
- How the effectiveness of the career development effort is
  assessed.
- General attitudes and predictions about organizational career development.

Our examination of the state of the art included case
studies of career development *systems* as well as an exploration of
specific best *practices*. We sought to explore the critical systems
dimension as well as particular interventions or techniques. We
identified organizations for our case studies and best-practices
inquiry by drawing on our knowledge of various career development efforts, recommendations from professional colleagues,
and references to model programs in the literature. Interviewees
(in most cases one per organization) were typically career development or HR managers or specialists—the people charged
with carrying out a career development effort. In one case an
organization wanted to be profiled but requested anonymity in
line with corporate policy. We refer to this organization as "a
major telecommunications company."

In several cases, interviewees withdrew their participation
in our study because of downsizing or layoffs that reduced or
even abolished the career development activities they had described. This constitutes unfortunate evidence that career development can be a casualty of today's business environment despite the fact that it is increasingly enlisted as an asset.

Appendix B contains the interview guide for the case
studies and best-practices inquiry. Our goal was to have respondents tell the story of their programs—why and how they
were implemented, their salient features or components, and
how their results were measured. What we asked for, and grate-
fully received, were honest accounts of lessons learned: successes, mistakes, and advice. The results are shared in Part Two.

PART ONE

The State
of the Practice

CHAPTER 2

Career Development in the United States: Rethinking Careers in the Flattened Organization

In 1990 and 1991, we surveyed 1,000 large U.S.-based organizations and 96 U.S. government agencies regarding their career development activities. Our goal was to paint a general, broad-brush picture of the field—to find out how much and what kind of career development is actually occurring in American organizations. We also wanted to determine how organizations assess the impact of their developmental efforts and how they view the field overall.

This chapter presents highlights of our survey, with a particular focus on the corporate results. We received only a small number of responses from government agencies and are wary about generalizing from them; thus, we refer to findings from the government survey only when they differ markedly from the corporate findings. (Results of both surveys are in Appendix A.)

The Context of Career Development

In this section, we present the results that relate to the context in which career development occurs: demographics, the characteristics of various development systems, the prompts or "drivers" of career development, and organizational attitudes and philosophy.

Demographics

Although there was substantial diversity of industry representation among our respondents, well over half of them were from
either the Midwest or the Northeast. It is unclear whether these
distributions reflect those of the original sample or of the respondent group. Approximately 30 percent of respondents
were from manufacturing; 25 percent in financial, insurance, or
real estate companies; and 19 percent in energy, including
public utilities. Not surprisingly, then, multinationals were the
largest group of respondents: over 40 percent described their
organizations as international.

In terms of the total size of organizations, more than one-
third of all respondents had between 1,000 and 5,000 employees; 35 percent had between 5,000 and 25,000 employees. Over
half had annual budgets of over $1 billion; 40 percent had
budgets of between $100 million and $999 million. Thus, our
typical respondent organization was a large, multinational manufacturing organization headquartered in the Midwest, with an
annual budget of over a billion dollars.

Prevalence of Career Development Systems

In our survey we defined an organizational career development
system as "a system of processes and practices designed to link
an individual employee's career goals with the organization's
human resource needs." To clarify, we added that "examples of
career development programs and activities would include
workshops, manager-employee career discussions, resource centers, career planning software, and succession or replacement
planning."

As Figure 2.1 shows, nearly 70 percent of our survey
respondents had or were launching career development systems
(as defined in our survey). Of this group, most organizations had
systems in place for either less than one year or more than six
years. Our speculation is that this rate of prevalence is higher
than would be found in large U.S. organizations overall and that

Figure 2.1. Prevalence of Career Development Systems.

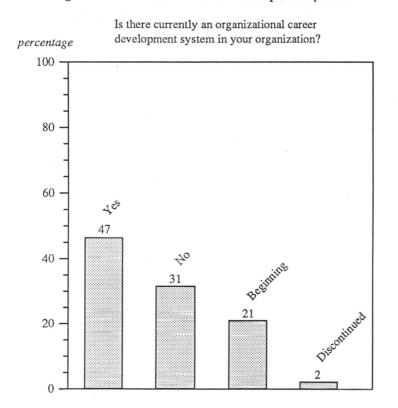

it reflects the self-screening involved in choosing to be survey participants.

Of the total respondent group, 31 percent did not have a career development system, and a very small number had a system but had discontinued it. Three main reasons were given for not having career development systems: insufficient support by top management (54 percent), insufficient budgetary resources (37 percent), and lack of HR capability or interest (27 percent).

The findings we discuss here derive from the 70 percent— the respondents who either had a career development system or were starting one. However, all respondents—whether in this group or not—were asked to answer two questions, one about the future of career development within their organization and one about how the field has changed.

"Drivers" of Organizational Career Development

What was driving career development in those organizations that had or were starting systems? We asked respondents to name the top three factors influencing the development of career programs in their organizations, and their answers surprised us. They most often named (1) a desire to develop or promote from within, (2) a shortage of promotable talent, and (3) an organizational commitment to career development (see Figure 2.2). Interestingly, despite the realities of a changing business climate, the top two factors related to upward mobility. In marked contrast, only 8 percent of all respondents named a desire to motivate employees under conditions of limited growth as one of the top three factors, and a mere 2 percent listed a desire to improve worker productivity.

One-third of all government respondents said that career development was driven by organizational commitment, while 27 percent cited employee interest in career planning. The top two responses in the corporate sample were not cited by any respondents in the government sample. Thus, development of "bench strength" was not a concern among government respondents, but responsiveness to employee desires was apparently a stronger concern than for corporate respondents.

Attitudes Toward Career Development

We asked a series of twenty-two questions relating to overall attitudes about career development. The responses fell into four categories: general management attitudes, perceived effect on supervisory responsibilities, perceived general effects, and attitudes about administration of career development programs (see Table 2.1). Several general themes emerged from the responses:

Figure 2.2. Factors Driving Career Development.

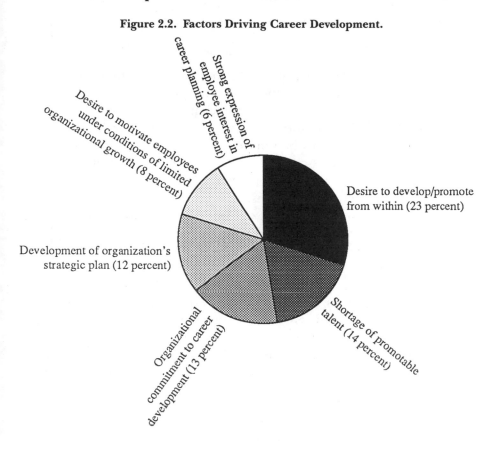

- Organizations, managers, and employees all view career development as important.
- Career development is related to the business needs of the organization.
- Supervisors play an important but problematic role in career development.
- Career development has many of the positive effects generally associated with it but not the negative ones.

Some thought-provoking disparities emerged when we compared the reported "drivers" of career development and people's attitudes toward it. While only a few respondents cited

Career Development: Why Companies Do It—Or Do Not

Our survey showed that many American companies undertake career development because of concerns relating to upward mobility. The traditional model of career success—climbing the corporate ladder—can be hard to relinquish even when there is ample evidence that it no longer reflects career realities in the United States. The fact is that not everyone gets to move up in today's leaner, flatter organizations.

A growing number of American employers are devising creative, satisfying solutions to the question of how to help their employees achieve career success and enhance organizational competitiveness at the same time. Among these solutions are lateral career moves that build skills, job enrichment, retraining, rotational assignments, and temporary but high-visibility assignments on task forces.

Why do some companies shy away from developmental activities? Here are several possible reasons:

- Lack of awareness of links between development, motivation/empowerment, and productivity.
- Lack of understanding of the process and how it can be undertaken.
- Lack of senior management support (which again reflects loyalty to the notion of success as upward mobility).

The primary challenge for HR practitioners, then, is to educate top managers about the career development process and its benefits and to secure their buy-in right from the start.

motivating employees or improving worker productivity as reasons for implementing career development systems, many said that career development is important to senior managers as an employee development tool, that it enhances job performance, and that it should be tied to the organization's strategic plan. We speculate that assumptions about the benefits of career development, even favorable assumptions, are not what pushes companies to design and implement a system; however, once a career development system is in place, top management and HR practitioners see its benefits and develop positive attitudes toward it. It remains unclear what specific factors actually push managers over the edge; our guess is that the impetus is very specific to an organization's culture and business needs.

Implementation of Career Development Systems

How have companies structured their career development systems? Here we look at some of the survey results that relate to implementation — the who, how, where, and what of career development activities. In this realm, too, some interesting surprises emerged.

Nearly half of the respondents used a task force or advisory group to design or implement their career development system. They rated the effectiveness of such groups as above average (3.6 on a 5-point scale).

Virtually all the systems that our respondents have implemented deal with exempt salaried employees; 59 percent also cover nonexempt salaried employees, and only 36 percent cover hourly workers. We asked respondents to indicate which salaried groups their programs targeted. Again, the emphasis on upward mobility was obvious: nearly three-quarters of programs target "fast-track" management candidates or "high-potential" employees, and 56 percent target management trainees. This was in line with our earlier findings about an emphasis on building bench strength. Interestingly, two arguably larger and faster-growing employee groups — plateaued employees and preretirees — garnered much lower numbers (29 and 18 percent, respectively) as targets of career development programs.

Table 2.1. Attitudes About Career Development.

	Agree or Strongly Agree (Percentage)	Disagree or Strongly Disagree (Percentage)
General Management Attitudes		
Senior management believes career development raises employee expectations.	89	11
Senior management feels career development is a fad.	16	84
Managers believe career development is not really anything new.	74	26
Senior management believes career development is an important part of employee development.	80	20
Managers believe career development is not needed.	14	86
Only a small percentage of employees are really interested in career development.	20	80
Perceived Effect on Supervisory Responsibilities		
Career development means an increased burden for supervisors.	85	15
Few supervisors are equipped to hold employee career discussions.	84	16
Supervisors feel that employee career development is not part of their job.	52	48
Perceived General Effects		
Career development programs must be tied in with the organization's strategic business plan.	85	15
Career development generally disrupts an organization.	13	87
Turnover increases as a result of employee participation in career development programs.	13	87
Career development strains the capacity of other human resources systems.	23	77
Career development increases anxiety for many employees.	30	70
Career development enhances job performance of employees.	89	11
Career development equips employees to use personnel systems more effectively.	84	16

Table 2.1. Attitudes About Career Development, Cont'd.

	Agree or Strongly Agree (Percentage)	Disagree or Strongly Disagree (Percentage)
Career development allows improved utilization of employee talents.	93	7
Career development helps employees deal with a low-growth environment.	82	18
Attitudes Regarding Administration of Career Development Programs		
Job requirements and career information need not be provided in a career development program.	17	83
Career development is best introduced on a pilot, experimental basis.	59	41
Employees' participation in a career development program should be voluntary.	84	16
Employees should be able to keep confidential their records and other outputs of career development activities.	78	22

Concern for addressing workforce diversity was suggested in the proportion of programs targeting minority employees and women — roughly 50 percent for each group. Moreover, 17 percent targeted older workers, and the same percentage targeted handicapped employees. Interestingly, over twice as many government programs (that is, three-quarters) targeted new employees as did corporate programs. Our guess is that this situation will change: with the current (and projected) reality of an increasingly smaller population of new entrants to the U.S. labor market, a reduced skills base, and greater workforce diversity, American companies will have to pay more attention to the new employee. As organizations have known for some time, it is very costly — not to mention demoralizing — to hire and lose an employee within a year; therefore, proper orienting and training of new entrants (which bear directly on length of tenure) become quite important.

Responses to questions about the structure of career development systems suggested that staffing was lean: 54 percent had less than one staffperson devoted full time to career development; 21 percent had one full-time person; only 10 percent had five or more full-time staff. Slightly over half of all systems were both centralized and decentralized, and almost all organizations placed the career development function inside the HR department.

Generally, career development is seen as a shared responsibility. We asked respondents to indicate where their organization's career development efforts focused—on the individual, the organization, or somewhere in between. They placed the focus almost in the middle, with a slight emphasis on the organization. We also asked how their organizations apportion responsibility for career development among the employee, the manager, and the organization; employees have the largest responsibility (just over half), managers just over one-quarter, and organizations just under one-quarter (see Figure 2.3).

Figure 2.3. Responsibility for Career Development Systems.

System focus

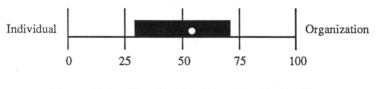

Mean = 50.4   SD = 22   Median = 50   Mode = 50

Respondents view career development as:

51 percent employee's responsibility

25 percent manager's responsibility

24 percent organization's responsibility

Taken together, these answers suggest that responsibility for career development is generally seen as a balance, that individuals are primarily responsible for their own career development, and that career development systems are designed to meet organizational needs. This attitude underscores the fundamental concept of individual/organizational alignment: meeting individual career needs is good for business.

Types of Career Development Practices Used

What specific types of career development practices were our survey respondents using? Again, the results suggest a focus on traditional modes. Using Gutteridge's six categories, we first calculated the frequency of various types of practices.

Development programs, 59 percent.
Job matching systems, 53 percent.
Individual counseling or career discussions, 46 percent.
Organizational potential assessment processes, 45 percent.
Employee self-assessment tools, 28 percent.
Internal labor-market information exchanges, 24 percent.

We then rank ordered these by averaging the prevalence of specific practices within each category. The top category, development programs, focuses largely on training and development programs and seminars as well as tuition reimbursement (although it also includes other items such as job enrichment and redesign and mentoring systems). Job matching systems such as job posting and succession planning were next.

The fact that these were the top two categories accords with corporations' emphasis on internal promotion and development of bench strength. Yet we questioned whether such efforts could succeed, given the low use of other tools. How, we wondered, can development and job moves be targeted effectively if employees are not assessing themselves and lack access to relevant career and organizational information? Are the organizations that use these tools and techniques really doing what we mean by career development? These questions arose again when we examined the prevalence and effectiveness of specific career development practices (see Table 2.2).

Perceived Effectiveness of Career Development Practices

The top three reported practices — tuition reimbursement, in-house training and development programs, and external seminars and workshops — are traditional training and development activities, and they are not necessarily tied to any career development focus or strategy. The next two highest (employee orientation programs and job posting) are also not always linked to a development strategy. We surmised that the reason that only roughly half of our respondents rated external seminars and workshops and employee orientation programs as effective was that these practices were not targeted as part of a career development plan. That is, they were more or less one-shot in nature and were not promoted as features of a broader developmental strategy, one that identified individual goals in the context of organizational challenges and opportunities.

We were further surprised at the low prevalence and effectiveness ratings of other tools that we thought had become relatively common and accepted components of career development systems. For example, only 34 percent of respondents were using career planning workshops; only 15 percent had stand-alone career workbooks; and only 13 percent had computer

Table 2.2. Prevalence and Effectiveness of Career Development Practices.

Most Common Career Development Practices	Prevalence (Percentage)	Effectiveness Rating* (Percentage)
Tuition reimbursement	95	71
In-house training and development programs	92	62
External seminars and workshops	91	50
Employee orientation programs	86	49
Job posting	83	61

*Composite of "effective" and "very effective" ratings.

software. Moreover, only half of those using workshops rated them as effective or very effective, and less than half of those with computer software considered it effective.

While a strikingly high percentage reported that supervisors or line managers were doing counseling or holding career discussions, less than one-quarter described them as effective. One possible reason for this perception of ineffectiveness is that only 44 percent of responding organizations were training their supervisors in career discussions. Of that group, less than half rated the training as effective or very effective. What seems to be missing in many organizations is an emphasis on accountability for development and a concomitant dedication of resources to training.

Two other practices that can be effective development strategies (especially in an era of declining promotional opportunities)—job rotation and job enrichment or job redesign—were used by 54 and 41 percent of respondents, respectively. Yet these, too, were rated effective or very effective by less than half.

Some of the foregoing practices were notably more prevalent and effective in the government sample. Fifty-six percent reported the use of career planning workshops (with a 67 percent effectiveness rating). Almost twice as many as in the corporate sample had preretirement workshops, and 44 percent had computer software (with an 86 percent effectiveness rating). Sixty-seven percent of supervisors or line managers were doing counseling or career discussions (with a 40 percent effectiveness rating); of the 44 percent doing supervisory training, 57 percent rated it effective or very effective. Well over three-quarters reported that they had job rotation, and almost two-thirds rated it effective or very effective. And while only one-third had job enrichment or redesign, 80 percent of that group rated it effective or very effective.

Finally, our survey results suggest that many of the respondents had a variety of HR systems in place, such as promotion and transfer practices (used by all respondents), job description and evaluation (used by 97 percent), and performance appraisal (also used by 97 percent). These offerings are common in large organizations; however, the degree to which they were linked to career development varied greatly. For example, while 83 percent of respondents said that they linked performance appraisal to career development, just under half linked career development with job description and evaluation. As we will see next, this question of *integrating* different practices looms large as a factor in the success of an organization's developmental efforts.

Outcomes: Respondents' Assessments

Considering the increasing emphasis on accountability and measurement throughout the HR field, our findings about the evaluation of career development programs were disturbing (see Figure 2.4). Almost one-quarter of respondents reported doing no evaluation at all, and nearly two-thirds relied on informal verbal feedback. These responses suggest that the organizations had few formal means of assessing whether their career development systems were achieving their objectives and how to modify and improve them accordingly.

Government respondents were somewhat more inclined to do evaluation. Only 13 percent said that they did none; 56 percent reported the use of questionnaires, 31 percent used interviews or focus groups, and 19 percent used data analysis. Nearly 70 percent used informal verbal feedback.

We asked respondents to give their own assessments of the effectiveness of their career development systems. Again, there was a significant difference between the corporate and government samples, with effectiveness ratings higher in the latter. As Figure 2.5 indicates, less than one-third of respondents in the corporate sample rated their systems as effective or very effective; this percentage was a full 20 points higher in the government sample. A large proportion of corporate respondents (42 percent) were lukewarm about the effectiveness of their programs; only 29 percent in the government sample rated them as in between. Finally 29 percent rated them somewhat or very ineffective, compared to 21 percent in the government sample.

After amassing our initial survey results, we cross tabulated a number of variables with effectiveness ratings to see if this would shed any light on the low ratings. The two variables

Figure 2.4. How Career Development Systems Are Evaluated.

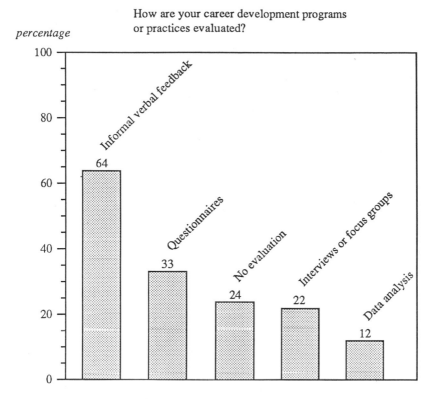

percentage

How are your career development programs or practices evaluated?

that were significant were the length of time a career development system had been in place and the amount of staff devoted full time to career development. Programs older than two years were more likely to be perceived as effective than those less than two years; and, not surprisingly, somewhat or very effective systems were more likely to have more than one full-time staffperson. These findings underscore the notion that systems take time to develop and require adequate resources to be successful.

Implications

We have already observed a certain "disconnect" between respondents' ratings of system effectiveness and their reactions to

Figure 2.5. Assessment of Career Development System Effectiveness.

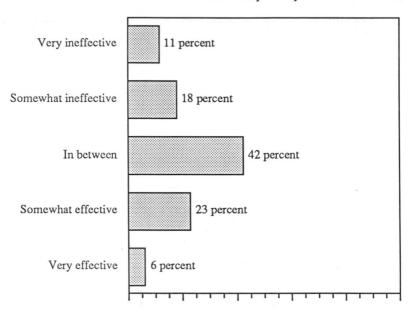

Overall, how effective is your
career development system?

open-ended questions about the outcomes of their career development activities. While respondents did not rate their systems very highly in terms of effectiveness, they still expressed the belief that their systems had positive outcomes for their organizations in terms of building employee skills and morale and increasing the efficacy of HR and strategic planning. And while most responding organizations were doing little in the way of formal evaluation, they did recognize the need for greater accountability, formality, and systemization.

As it happens, these responses square with observations made by another group of organizations we queried in detail about organizational career development: the twelve companies featured in the case studies presented in Chapter Seven of this book. While we do not want to jump the gun in describing those organizations' systems (which are at the forefront of the field and

Assessing Career Development: Reports from the Field
(Open-ended data from the survey)

Major impacts of organizations' career development efforts:

- Enhanced employee retention
- Enhanced employee skills and morale
- Employee empowerment
- Demonstration of organizational commitment of employees
- Improved HR planning and selection
- Better strategic advantage

What respondents said they would have done differently:

- More training and buy-in of managers
- Better funding and commitment of resources
- More systemized implementation, evaluation, and accountability

What is being planned:

- Expansion and refinement of current programs
- Greater systemization and integration

What has changed in the last decade:

Shift toward greater employee responsibility
- View of career development as results-oriented element of strategic business plan
- Increased formality and systemization
- Greater efficiency and range of tools

reflect advanced thinking, not the current state of the practice as a whole), it seems useful to introduce some of the caveats and suggestions offered by HR practitioners in those organizations. We found, as we attempted to capture the implications of our survey findings for real-world practice, that their observations served us well. In particular, the following four observations were common to all twelve organizations.

1. Involve top management early and obtain its visible, up-front support for career development.
2. Set guiding principles right from the start. Base these on sound knowledge of the organization's culture, business strategy, and success criteria.
3. Grow career development systems from the line up, and involve a diverse cross section of employees and managers in system design, implementation, and evaluation.
4. Maintain flexibility so that different business units can make the system work for their own needs and contexts.

At this point, we have taken a close look at the current status of career development in the United States, drawing on recent survey results that focus on the context, implementation, and outcomes of various systems. How (if at all) do these fresh results differ from those of the 1978 survey? And what do the variances suggest about the state of the practice? These questions are the subject of the next section.

From 1978 to the Present: How Much Progress Has Been Made?

The state of the practice of career development in the United States in 1978 was explored through a questionnaire mailed to 1,117 members of the Human Resources Division of the American Management Association (Walker and Gutteridge, 1979). Responses came from 225 companies. The survey was designed to provide a profile of career planning practices that would aid practitioners in designing and implementing career management programs. Walker and Gutteridge concluded (p. 4) that "many companies view career planning practices as a desirable and necessary component of human resource management. Most companies provide the basic elements: career counseling and communications. Workshops, workbooks, and special career planning techniques are relatively recent but appear to be growing. . . . In several years, a follow-up survey should indicate widespread use of the practices described and should provide a better reading of their effects."

Our own survey was very similar in content to the 1978 survey. It was reformatted, and several questions were added that focus on current concerns such as plateauing, strategic alignment, and evaluation. Some wording changes were made. For example, the term "career planning" was changed in most places to the broader term "career development." This alteration reflects the now widely accepted notion that where careers are concerned, the individual and the organization are linked; individual career planning must be complemented by an ongoing organizational commitment of resources and provision of relevant information.

The similarity in content of the two surveys allowed us to compare their data. (For the purposes of this discussion, "the current survey" refers to the U.S. corporate sample only.) We had predicted that the two sets of survey results would be markedly different, given downsizing, delayering, plateauing, diversity, global competition, and other business realities as well as the observable growth of organizational career development tools and technologies—but we were wrong. Overall, our most striking finding was how similar the results of the two surveys were, how little has changed in the state of the practice since the late 1970s.

We will not explore every similarity between the two surveys; rather, we will highlight those that seem most significant and will focus on several important differences. To begin with, respondents to the current survey were from larger organizations with larger annual budgets. They represented the banking, financial, and insurance industries more heavily than did the 1978 respondents, half of whom were from manufacturing. (Much of the difference in industry breakdown could reflect the

fact that one-fourth of our current sample was chosen from the
Financial 1000.) Naturally, any comparison of annual budgets
would have to take into account the considerable impact of over
a decade of inflation.

Companies in the 1978 survey were not asked whether
they had career planning systems, but they *were* asked which
factors influenced the development of their career programs.
The desire to develop or promote from within was clearly the
top factor in both surveys, and the second highest factor, a
shortage of promotable talent, was also the same in both. These
two related factors make more sense to us as major prompts of
career development in 1978 than in the early 1990s. Perhaps
these concerns persist in part because it takes time for attitudes
to catch up with organizational or economic realities. That is,
even though the reality is that there are and will be fewer opportunities to move up the organizational ladder, many people still
view career development in terms of this obsolete criterion.

That said, we found some evidence of the effect of new
realities on responses to the question of influences on the
development of career programs. Concern about turnover was a
much greater issue in 1978 than in recent years, and motivating
employees under conditions of limited growth was a lesser issue
in 1978 than currently. We would expect turnover to be a lesser
concern in an economic downturn and, concomitantly, for
plateauing to be a greater concern. However, it is unclear why a
desire to improve worker productivity was a significant factor
(one of the top five) in 1978 but not at all significant in the
current survey.

The importance of the organization's role in career development was evident in both surveys. "Organizational commitment to career development" was the third highest factor in the
current survey, and "management's desire to aid career planning" was the third highest in 1978.

What about actual practices used? Because of changes in
the survey wording and the categorization of practices, it is
somewhat more difficult to compare findings about career planning and development practices. However, it is safe to say that
the respondents' prediction, in 1978, that workshops, work-

books, and other career planning techniques would be in widespread use was not supported by the results of the later survey.

In 1978, the only practices reported by half or more of the respondents were counseling by personnel staff or supervisors and employee communications on career-related topics: educational assistance, company conditions and economic information, career paths and ladders, training and development options, and job posting and job vacancy information. Specifically, 89 percent said they had informal counseling by personnel staff, 56 percent had career counseling by supervisors, and 25 percent trained their supervisors in career counseling (one-third planned to provide such training). Also, a little over half said they had job posting and communication of vacancies. Only 11 percent had workshops dealing specifically with life and career planning, although 17 percent planned to introduce such workshops within a year. Thirty-four percent had retirement workshops. Sixteen percent reported use of self-analysis and planning workbooks, and 42 percent had job performance and development planning workbooks.

The current survey revealed a significant increase, as predicted, in the amount of career counseling provided by supervisors or line managers (from 56 to 83 percent) and in the amount of training for this (25 to 44 percent). This increase is obviously good news, given the recognized importance of the manager's role in career development. However, it is also true that the current survey revealed widespread dissatisfaction with how the manager's role was actually played. Thus, although the practice is more common, the role itself remains problematic.

The use of career planning workshops more than tripled (from 11 to 34 percent), but the number of workshops was still low, and only half of the 34 percent found them effective or very effective. (The 1978 survey did not ask about the effectiveness of specific practices.) Usage of career workbooks increased only slightly, with less than half of all respondents rating workbooks as effective or very effective. The use of computer software (not queried in 1978) was reported by only 13 percent of respondents, and only 48 percent rated it effective or very effective.

The only practice that grew significantly and was viewed

positively was job posting, which increased from 54 percent in 1978 to 83 percent in the 1990s (with 61 percent rating it as effective or very effective). Its growth and effectiveness are probably related to the shift in many corporate cultures toward greater openness and communication.

In general, the relatively low overall effectiveness ratings in the current survey are an echo of the results in 1978, when 54 percent of respondents described their programs as partially effective and 29 percent as moderately effective. Open-ended comments made in 1978 (similar to those in the current survey) suggest that it was too early either to judge program success or to give a highly positive rating.

Responses to general attitude statements were similar in both surveys. They emphasized the importance and perceived benefits of career development as well as the problematic role of supervisors. The percentage of people stating that career development is burdensome to supervisors actually rose from 63 to 74 percent. This could reflect the fact that career development systems, as well as expectations of the role that supervisors will play in them, have grown at the same time that there are more employees per supervisor in many organizations because of delayering. Clearly, this points to the need for more (and better) training of managers in their multiple roles as coaches, information sources, and so forth.

Interestingly, many of the predictions made in 1978 about future plans for career development are similar to those made in the current survey. Both sets of respondents envisioned expanded, more formalized programs with greater integration and an increased role for managers. The latter prediction has come true, as has another 1978 prediction that employees would be given more information on job opportunities and requirements.

When current survey respondents were asked what had changed noticeably in the last decade, they cited increased formality and systemization and greater efficiency and range of tools. Overall, these predictions and assessments seem to indicate a unanimity of opinion on where the field is and should be headed and on how long it takes to build and refine a career

Career Development Practices: An Unfulfilled Promise?

Generally speaking, it appears that career development practices have not yet fulfilled the promising potential predicted by survey respondents in 1978. Perhaps this is because the effectiveness of even the best career development systems apparently increases over time; systems in place longer tend to be rated more effective. It also may be the case that some practices simply have not been around long enough to work well. Also, without evaluations, any practice is going to be more difficult to improve—another problem identified in the current survey.

What can organizations do to enhance the effectiveness of a planned or existing career development practice? Here are a few basic suggestions:

- Keep the big picture of the career development system in view at all times; avoid piecemeal thinking.
- Get plenty of formal and informal feedback from people across the organization.
- Focus on the organization's specific business objectives and assess outcomes on the basis of those aims.
- Pilot and implement initiatives on a unit-by-unit basis.
- Keep the effort visible and highlight success stories.

development system. More than a decade after the first survey, organizational career development is evidently still a work in progress.

Thus far, we have reported on the results of data collected in the United States. While the state of organizational career development in our own nation is of obvious interest, the realities of a globalized economy, multinational employees, and fierce foreign competition make it important for American practitioners in the field to be aware of what is happening abroad. An important element of our current study, therefore, is its expansion across international borders. The next three chapters examine results of surveys carried out in Europe, Singapore, and Australia.

CHAPTER 3

Career Development in Europe: Motivating and Retaining Scarce Talent

C. Brooklyn Derr
Erik Jansen

Over the years, European companies have offered a variety of HR programs to develop individual employees and improve their performance, but traditionally they have associated career development with high-potential managers (Derr, 1987; Evans, Farquhar, and Landreth, 1989). In the coming decade, this situation is likely to change. With the emergence of a new perspective, Europeans will be making new associations between organizational career development and diverse HR programs and practices.

The demographics of most European countries make the shortage of talent a critical HR issue for the mid 1990s. Moreover, new employee values (such as a balanced lifestyle and a high quality of work life) require employers to be much more open and flexible if they are to attract and retain talent that matches the organization's requirements. And the organizational landscape in Europe is changing by virtue of economic recession, global competition, and transformations in Eastern Europe in the wake of the Soviet Union's collapse.

Joint venturing, decentralization, and globalization all affect individual employees. In particular, the emergence of flat, organic cluster or network organizations and the elimination of redundancy challenge the image of a career as a long-term contract with a single organization. For American workers at multinational corporations, globalization has changed foreign assignments from a career detour to a career requirement.

All these forces challenge HR practitioners' definitions of careers and how they are developed. In this chapter we report on current organizational career development practices in Europe and explore career-related issues of the future.

State of the European Field

Between 1946 and 1964, the post–World War II baby boom produced an ample supply of well-educated, talented young Europeans. Since 1965, however, the labor pool as a whole has been declining. The baby bust (well known throughout the West) will have a dramatic effect on the availability of European labor in the 1990s and the early twenty-first century.

Germany leads Europe in this projected shortage of labor. In the 1990s, new job seekers under age twenty-five are expected to decrease by a rate of 3.5 percent annually in Germany, and demographers project that there will be 40 percent fewer people between the age of fifteen and nineteen in 2000 than there were in 1985. The Netherlands, Italy, and the United Kingdom each will experience a 25 to 30 percent shortfall of teenagers between 1985 and 2000 (France's shortfall is likely to be only 9 percent, largely because of its immigration policies) (Vandernerive, 1990). In sum, the pool of young job seekers will shrink, increasing the need to export work and import labor.

In businesses in the countries of the Organization for Economic Cooperation and Development (OECD), there is less concern about a declining birth rate per se than about the declining level of workforce skills and education. For example, according to the Institute for Employment Research, in the United Kingdom in the 1990s (as compared to the 1980s) the demand for engineers and scientists will increase 19 percent, for managers 10 percent, and 8 percent for skilled technicians. HR planners point out that these demands will exist in tandem not only with a declining supply of workers but also with a declining supply of talent. Although the number of young people entering European universities remains relatively high, the number entering technical and scientific specialties is dropping (Green, 1990).

Projected shortages of employees in general and of talented employees in particular vary among countries and industries, but the overall trend points to a crucial HR management issue. The recruitment and retention of valuable employees will be a key concern throughout the 1990s. Not surprisingly, a recent fifteen-country survey of 1,530 European managers (Derr and others, 1992) reported that individual employees were expected to become significantly more important over the next five years. In such a context, a central issue is ensuring future leadership for organizations.

The traditional concern with high-potential employees has been to get the best and the brightest to the top. This limited focus on identifying, selecting, training, and developing future leaders will be as critical in a context of scarcity as it has been in a context of plenty, if not more so. However, leaders now must ask whether HR programs and practices should focus on new categories of high-potential employees. The best and the brightest may include project and program heads, entrepreneurs, and technical or functional specialists and professionals. Organizational success may depend on these people as surely as on a talented management team.

This is not to suggest that developing traditional future leaders and managers is no longer a critical issue. In light of changing demographics and organizational conditions, it remains as urgent as always. The fundamental questions are these: How can organizations find and keep an adequate supply of future managers over a long period? Should companies continue to "grow" their own top managers internally or concentrate on recruiting them from the outside?

To further complicate the picture, the values of the workforce also appear to be shifting. Berney (1990) calls current European MBAs the "quality generation" because money seems less important to them than the quality of time they spend with their family and friends and the quality of their work life. Derr and Laurent (1989) found that European executives had diverse definitions of career success. Young, talented European MBAs appear to place more value on balancing their personal and professional lives, doing interesting and challenging work, having autonomy and freedom on the job, and positively contributing to their society than on climbing the company or professional ladder. Because demand is likely to exceed supply, especially for talented employees, accommodating these emerging values is likely to become an HR priority.

The emphasis on recruiting, retaining, and motivating talent has policy and management implications. To cite an obvious example, companies can no longer assume that talented women will arrive with total career dedication; it will be to

---

Facing the Talent Shortfall in Europe

In the coming decade, how will European HR managers cope with their organizations' people shortages? Here are some potential solutions.

- More attention will be paid to the match between an organization's needs and an individual's capabilities during the recruitment and selection processes, increasing the chances that the employee will stay with the company over the long term.
- More attention will be paid to retaining, motivating, and effectively using an organization's existing employees, not just dealing with high-potentials.
- New or underused sources of talent will be sought, including women (as well as men who wish to be active parents), young talent in the so-called Third World; in-country minorities; and members of the baby-boom generation.
- More partnerships will be created among government, industry, and education to increase the numbers of technical and scientific graduates, women in needed specialties, and minorities.

the organization's advantage to offer flexible career management to young parents. As another example, companies recruiting so-called Third World and minority talent must reexamine
the underlying cultural assumptions of their management development programs. Diversity and its management will become an important issue during the 1990s and beyond.

Derr and colleagues (1992) found that roughly 90 percent
of 1,530 European HR managers believe that understanding
individual values and ways of motivating is critical; only knowledge of organizational change was ranked as more important.
Changing values, a more diverse workforce, and labor-market
shortfalls all point to an expansion of career development beyond "star performers" to focus on "solid citizens": individuals
whose differences must be acknowledged and accommodated.

The Context of Career Development in Europe

Our survey of career development in Europe was done in the
late fall of 1991; 125 questionnaires were distributed to HR
directors in large European multinational corporations, and 70
questionnaires were returned (for a response rate of 56 percent).
As with the U.S. sample, European respondents tended to come
from very large organizations; nearly one-third were from organizations of 10,000 to 25,000 people, another one-third from
companies of 50,000 or more. The companies represented a
range of industries (see Figure 3.1), and the markets they served
were largely international (see Figure 3.2). Table 3.1 presents the
location of the firms' headquarters.

Prevalence of Career Development Systems

Over three-quarters of all European respondents reported that
they currently had a career development system in place, about
one-quarter of them for two years or less and slightly over half
for five years or more. Five or more staff were allocated full-time
to career management activities in about 37 percent, a little under
half had two or fewer, and 19 percent reported that no full-time
staff were specifically designated for career management.

Figure 3.1. Survey Sample by Industry.

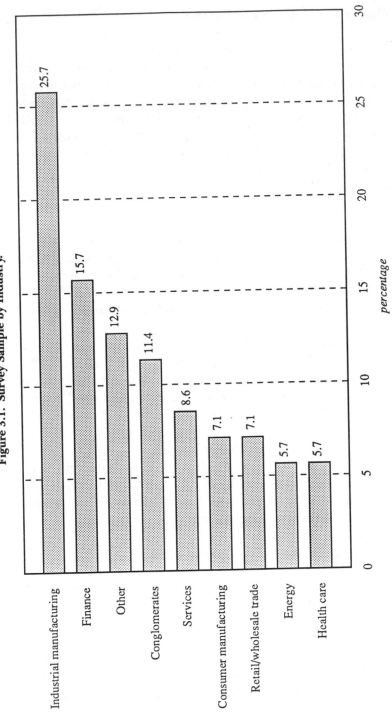

Figure 3.2. Markets Served by Survey Sample.

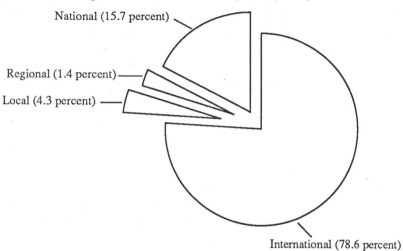

National (15.7 percent)

Regional (1.4 percent)

Local (4.3 percent)

International (78.6 percent)

"Drivers" of Organizational Career Development

Various factors influence the establishment of career develop-ment programs in Europe. Figure 3.3 reports what HR manag-ers consider the three top factors. The most important was the organization's strategic plan (about 58 percent reported that this was one of the top three factors, and one-third reported that it was the most influential). When asked an open-ended question about their organizations' plans for future career development

Table 3.1. National Origin of Headquarters.

Location of Headquarters	Firms (Percentage)
United Kingdom	38.6
Switzerland	15.7
Sweden	15.7
Germany	7.1
The Netherlands	7.1
Norway	2.9
Finland	2.9
France	2.9
Other	7.1

practices, respondents mentioned linkages to strategy and business planning as among the top three new initiatives. Hence, the strategic context of European practices should not be underestimated.

About one-half of the organizations indicated that one of their three top factors included the organization's commitment to career development, and nearly one-quarter named this number one. This would seem to indicate that career development is becoming part of the culture and value system of many European organizations. European firms appear to see career development as important to their employees, and to managing the implicit psychological contract with their employees, the set of mutually held assumptions and expectations that bind the employee and the employer. This finding corroborates the research cited above, which stresses a new emphasis on individual employee needs.

Some of the factors that were negligible in importance were concern about turnover, equal employment opportunity program commitments, survey/needs assessment findings, the desire for a positive recruiting image, and the desire to avoid unionization. In general, this indicates that the primary emphasis has been one of goal congruence: managing the goals of individuals in the strategic context of the organization's goals. The future talented workforce in Europe may be shrinking, but those who add value congruent with the company's strategic objectives will be more valued and enjoy greater career development opportunities.

Attitudes Toward Career Development

Various attitudinal questions were asked about career development within the European organizations (see Table 3.2). One set of questions referred to positive, purposive aspects of career development (senior management, strategy, the global improvement of performance, and HR system utilization). The strongest endorsement for any item in this set was expressed in terms of linking career development programs to the organization's strategic plan. Statements advocating career development to im-

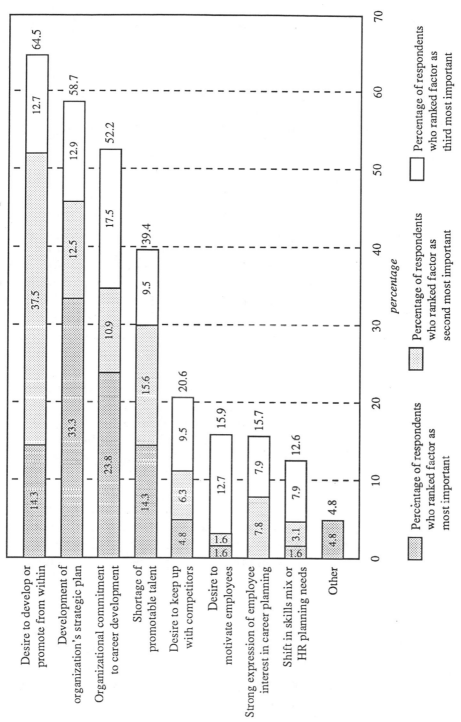

Figure 3.3. Factors Influencing Career Development in Europe.

prove employee skills and job performance were also strongly endorsed. There also is a strong perception, on the part of senior management, that career development is an important part of employee development and that career development raises employee expectations (which may have mixed consequences).

The second set of questions referred to a negative set of attitudes about career development. Our respondents strongly disagree with the following statements: "senior management feels that career development is a fad"; "managers believe career development is not needed"; and "career development generally disrupts an organization." These results, combined with the positive responses to the first set of questions, suggest that career development generally is perceived as being part of the value systems and cultures of these organizations.

A third set of questions fell somewhere between negative and positive. Managers tended to agree that participation should be voluntary (although almost one-fourth disagreed); that career development is best introduced on a pilot program (although close to half disagreed); and that "career development is not really anything new." These results suggest that career development is accepted and understood as not being a fad. It is interesting to note that HR managers still have conflicting opinions on how programs should be implemented—whether experimentally, voluntarily, or with confidentiality.

The data suggest some competing views of career development. Seventy-seven percent of all European survey respondents agreed or strongly agreed that their managers believe career development is not really anything new; however, less than 5 percent agreed that their managers believe career development is not needed. Thus, career development was apparently viewed as a traditional but necessary activity.

Almost 40 percent indicated that career development strains the capacity of other HR systems such as job posting, employee training, and tuition reimbursement. This finding is congruent with the fact that over 80 percent of respondents stated that career development equips employees to use

Table 3.2. Attitudes Toward Organizational Career Development.

Questionnaire Item	Strongly Agree (Percentage)	Agree (Percentage)	Disagree (Percentage)	Strongly Disagree (Percentage)	Means (Percentage)
Career development programs must be tied in with the organization's strategic business plan.	63.1	35.4	1.5	0.0	1.38
Senior management believes that career development raises employee expectations.	13.8	64.6	18.5	3.1	2.11
Senior management believes that career development is an important part of employee development.	35.4	58.5	4.6	1.5	1.72
Career development allows improved utilization of employee talents.	52.3	43.1	4.6	0.0	1.52
Career development enhances job performance of employees.	30.8	63.1	6.2	0.0	1.75
Career development equips employees to use HR systems more effectively.	6.3	74.6	19.0	0.0	2.13
Career development helps employees deal with a low-growth environment.	4.7	73.4	20.3	1.6	2.19

personnel systems more effectively. A small percentage felt that career development systems generally disrupt the organization.

Although most organizations reported disagreement with the statement that turnover increases as a result of employee participation in a career development program, a substantial minority (over 27 percent) agreed.

Finally, there is considerable diversity of opinion regarding supervisors. Nearly two-thirds agree that few supervisors are equipped to hold employee career discussions, and one-quarter indicated that supervisors don't feel career development is part of their job. There is almost an even split of opinion on whether or not career development means an increased burden for supervisors.

Implementation of Career Development Systems

High-potential employees (usually future general managers) remain the most common target group for career development programs; 88 percent of respondents targeted these employees, and 80 percent targeted new management trainees or future high-potentials. According to a Price-Waterhouse Cranfield study (1991), the most targeted group for recruitment by European firms was college graduates. Although recruitment targets differ from career development targets, the combined results of the Price-Waterhouse Cranfield study and ours suggest the continuation of a traditional pattern of recruiting young talent and then concentrating on those with high potential.

The European literature prominently discusses women as a key target group for future career development (see, for instance, Smith, 1990; "Women at Work," 1991; Thomason, 1991; Healy and Kraithman, 1991). Our results indicate that most European firms are not yet acting to take advantage of this segment of the labor market; only 30 percent of our European respondents targeted women. In the Price-Waterhouse Cranfield study, women were the second most-targeted recruitment after school graduates. (In Scandinavia, where 85 percent of all women work, women are not particularly targeted; however, in

Switzerland, Holland, and the United Kingdom, talented women are sought after.)

Although the European Community's (EC) social charter calls for plans to promote equal opportunities for women in all EC countries, this is not a salient issue in many countries. Women in the British workforce are experiencing difficulties in employment situations: sex discrimination claims increased 23 percent from 1988 to 1989 (Aikin, 1990), and in 1989 unemployment rates for women were almost double those of men across Europe (Eurostat, 1990). Although women are entering the workforce in increasing numbers, only about 40 percent of the 1990 workforce in Germany were women (with roughly the same percentages in Holland, the United Kingdom, and France), as compared to slightly over 60 percent in the United States.

Only 15 percent of our sample reported targeting minority employees; moreover, only Dutch, Swiss, and British respondents reported that they are actively trying to recruit minorities. Demographics suggest that pressures may be emerging to target women and minorities; if so, new career development practices are only beginning to gain momentum.

Structure of Career Development Systems

Career development systems function in the context of other HR systems and are linked in varying degrees to these systems (see Figure 3.4). It is not surprising that performance appraisal, recruitment practices, HR planning, and promotion and transfer practices were active in most firms and were linked to career development. In contrast, salary administration and job descriptions and evaluations were reported as often not linked to career development. Perhaps most surprising, in light of the importance previously attached to strategic planning and thinking, only two-thirds of all respondents reported that their organizational strategic planning was linked to career development.

Types of Career Development Practices Used

A wide variety of career development practices is currently in use in Europe, as Figure 3.5 illustrates. Of the possible options,

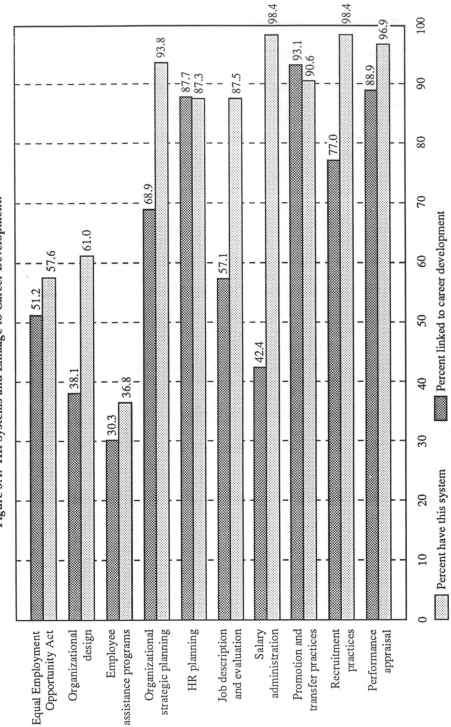

Figure 3.4. HR Systems and Linkage to Career Development.

Equal Employment Opportunity Act — 51.2, 57.6
Organizational design — 38.1, 61.0
Employee assistance programs — 30.3, 36.8
Organizational strategic planning — 68.9, 93.8
HR planning — 87.7, 87.3
Job description and evaluation — 57.1, 87.5
Salary administration — 42.4, 98.4
Promotion and transfer practices — 93.1, 90.6
Recruitment practices — 77.0, 98.4
Performance appraisal — 88.9, 96.9

Percent have this system
Percent linked to career development

Figure 3.5. Employee Self-Assessment Tools.

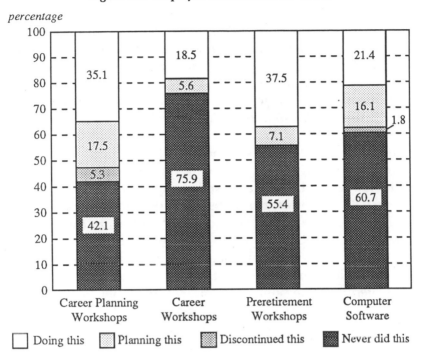

percentage

| | Doing this | | Planning this | | Discontinued this | | Never did this |

few companies report using dual-career couple programs, and less than half of the respondents are using mentoring programs or job enrichment and design.

To facilitate matching talented individuals to their internal labor markets, organizations reported that they distributed information on job and career opportunities internally. About one-third provided general information about career ladders or dual tracks; about one-quarter provided career information handbooks; and roughly 17 percent had career information or resource centers where employees could seek advice. Job posting was the most frequently used practice—nearly three-quarters of all respondents offered it—and 34 percent systematically offered information in other ways. About two-thirds did not plan to offer internal staffing information through alternative formats or systems.

Respondents reported that they attempted to match available jobs with interested and competent employees through informal canvassing of general personnel managers (about 56 percent), succession planning for high-potential positions (about 75 percent), internal staffing committees or conducting skills inventories (about one-third each), and other kinds of internal placement systems (about three-quarters).

Almost all respondents said that supervisors or line managers engaged in career counseling discussions with their subordinates. In over 80 percent of the firms, HR staff also conducted career counseling sessions with employees. However, only about half of the companies we surveyed had senior career advisers on their staffs. Even fewer firms used specialized career counselors: roughly 40 percent used internal career counselors and roughly 20 percent used external counselors.

How effective are managers in their developmental responsibilities? The median effectiveness of supervisors or line managers was rated only 3.33 on a 5-point scale. Significantly, only slightly under half of our sample provided supervisor training for career discussions. About another 21 percent were planning such programs, and roughly 31 percent had no such plans and had never done such training. It is interesting to note, however, that those organizations without such training rated it as quite effective (3.83 on a 5-point scale). Like their American counterparts, European organizations seem to be somewhat ambivalent about the manager's role: they see it as useful but not necessarily effective.

Perceived Effectiveness of Career Development Practices

Fifteen percent of the respondents reported that their career development systems were very effective, about 43 percent rated them as somewhat effective, and 15 percent rated them as ineffective. Roughly one-quarter indicated that they were in between. Different respondents based these judgments in different sources of information. The most frequently mentioned evaluation sources were informal verbal feedback, questionnaires, focus groups, and data analysis of productivity, performance, mobility, or costs. Only 11 percent indicated that no evaluations were done.

The most effective practices (as perceived by HR managers) tended to be the processes that assess organizational potential: psychological testing, assessment centers, and job assignments. For most organizations that have been managing high-potential employees, these practices should be well understood and developed. Career resource centers, specialized counselors (both internal and external), and programs for dual-career couples were viewed as being very effective by a minority of organizations using them. Although it is impossible to tell whether they are so viewed because a more select group is using them to good advantage, these programs and practices could well be used effectively by other organizations. In-house training and development programs were viewed as the most effective of all career development practices; career planning workshops were also rated highly.

A substantial minority viewed the following programs and practices as ineffective: computer software; career ladders and dual-career ladders; informal canvassing for job matching; internal placement systems; programs for dual-career couples; and employee orientation programs.

Outcomes: Respondents' Assessments

Almost 30 percent of our survey respondents in Europe said that career development had become more individualistic, more tailored to individual differences and new values and lifestyles, and (above all) required open and frequent communication with employees (especially the more talented ones) about their career aspirations. They stated that it is no longer possible to assume that all talented, valuable employees are interested in climbing the career ladder and getting ahead in traditional ways.

Flexibility in career development with regard to the changing organizational landscape was described by nearly 15 percent of the respondents. They indicated that career development had become more adaptive and placed a greater emphasis on employee responsibility in response to such structural revolutions as decentralization, downsizing, mergers, joint ventures, and requirements for work across boundaries.

In support of responses to attitudinal questions, nearly 15 percent of the respondents said that top management views career development as a more legitimate and important concern than in the past. Again, this theme supports arguments that career development is firmly entrenched in the values and cultures of many of these organizations. The importance of such legitimacy should not be underestimated: when asked what they would have done differently in designing their organization's career development system, 16 percent of those who responded said they would have obtained more top-level support, and 1 percent said they would have had more up-front employee involvement, communication, and employee ownership of their career development programs. Clearly, while legitimacy and support from both management and employees are increasing, they should not be taken for granted.

Thirteen percent of all respondents reported that in the last ten years, their companies had become more active in integrating their career systems, making them more systematic and better managed. Systematization and flexibility may therefore be taking place at the same time. One possibility is that traditional career development systems for high-potentials are becoming far more integrated and centralized while other types are becoming more decentralized and adaptive. Another possibility is that career information systems are changing, minimizing this distinction between centralized and decentralized and between structure and flexibility. As management information systems, cluster organizations, and networks replace traditional organizational forms, information can be highly structured, flexible, and available at the center and the periphery simultaneously.

Implications

Among our European respondents, the focus on high-potentials was strong. Nearly 10 percent of those answering an open-ended question about the future said that they planned to increase and improve their management and succession planning systems for high-potential employees. This theme was expressed more broadly by over 12 percent of the respondents, who said that they planned to do a better job matching talented individuals with organizational opportunities, mostly by using competency-based analysis.

Numerous respondents plan to make their current career development systems more effective, better integrated, and more supportive of the goals of top management. One future agenda item was a need to focus on systems that adapt to flatter, decentralized organizations; another was to create better career information systems and bases. As noted earlier, this supports an image of organization in which flexibility can be systematized and institutionalized without losing its ability to respond to changing business circumstances.

A few respondents indicated that they had future plans to help senior managers at the business unit and divisional levels create career development programs. The same relatively low percentage (6 percent) expressed a need to better train their line managers for career discussions with their people and to execute career development interventions. An equal percentage said that they need to focus more on line management competencies and skills.

Several respondents cited a trend in moving HR functions away from HR departments and specialists toward line managers, especially senior line managers who run divisions and strategic business units. (For further evidence of this trend, see Price-Waterhouse, 1991; Derr and others, 1992.) Recruitment, pay, workforce expansion and reduction, management development, organization development, and HR planning were among the functions most often cited as becoming line management responsibilities. Other creative ideas for the future included plans for programs for "solid citizens" and women managers, for better assessment tools, for more in-house career counseling, and for training programs that are tailored to both individual and organizational career needs.

Redefining Career Success

Given the dynamics of the labor market and global competition, the basic frameworks that individuals and organizations use to make sense of careers are likely to be questioned. Those who graduate from 1995 to 1996 may be among the first generation in recent history to negotiate a career in which they can balance their personal and professional lives. They may be able to demand interesting, challenging, and socially meaningful work and also achieve some degree of work autonomy. The challenges of achieving such a redefinition of career success will be complicated by global confrontations with other nations' work-related values—especially Asian values, which are typically based on principles of loyalty, discipline, education, savings, and hard work.

To remain valuable, individuals must learn, grow, and adapt continually. One might expect the fear of obsolescence to become more salient for many employees. Kanter (1989) has suggested that we are fast coming to the point where a career opportunity must be defined in terms of cutting-edge experiences that increase an employee's marketability within or outside the organization. Given the importance of close-to-the-customer service and cross-functional, cross-country, and cross-company teams, employees may well conclude that the best career opportunities result from moving laterally through decentralized positions; they may not want to deflate their value by pursuing traditional, upwardly mobile career paths. (Indeed, in many large multinationals, divisional management now has the power to block corporate efforts to transfer and reassign high-potentials for development.)

Several crucial questions will be asked by the workforce, by management, and by researchers who are trying to understand and reframe the meaning of career. Is it possible to stay with the same organization over the span of one's working life? How many transfers are optimal, for individuals and organizations, when we consider different regional and international markets and different organizational products and processes? How will career success be defined by talented employees in the coming decade (see Derr, 1986)? Is it possible to continue to think of a career as a ladder, or are the "career chunk" (Bailyn, 1982), the "career stage" (Dalton and Thompson, 1986), or "spiral career" (Driver, 1982) more timely career concepts future European workers?

The Face of the Future

The plans reported by our sample suggest that career development in Europe will become more tailored to individual needs, more legitimate (with more top-management support), more ingrained in organizational cultures, and more geared to the structural revolution as well as more devolved to the line. Career development will also become better integrated—flexibly linked to other HR and business systems with the help of accurate, quick-access information systems and new organizational forms such as clusters. Although high-potential management will continue to be crucial (and in many cases the backbone of career development interventions), the expansion of career development to management in general and to talented nonmanagers is likely to increase in Europe in coming years.

In view of the demographics of the European labor market and pressures associated with competition in a global economy, these planned directions are congruent with the needs that European organizations will face. In part because young people and other talented employees sense that they will be valued in the future (despite current economic problems), organizations are emphasizing new values and new definitions of career success.

As a result, we might expect emerging career development programs and practices to be offered to a wider range of talent and to cater to employee satisfaction and growth rather than solely to organizational productivity. In short, career development will be conducted at least as much to satisfy valuable individuals as to enhance organizational performance. Developmental options will, of course, be open especially to those employees who add value to the company.

These trends are only emerging, however. Our survey shows that current career development practices in seventy large European multinationals continue to focus primarily on the high-potentials and management trainees. The careers of these individuals are still carefully managed via succession planning, interviews, promotability forecasts, job rotations, psychological testing, and assessment centers. A few companies are earnestly seeking to expand their focus to include women (and, in Scandinavia, workers over forty-five). Very few firms report that their efforts extend to minority employees.

The devolution of career development to managers at the operational level must certainly cause talented employees to question the wisdom of hierarchically integrated, top-down career development systems. The legitimate role of corporate headquarters versus divisions in the design and management of career development systems is being questioned. Indeed, the crucial question for managers and employees alike may be this: Who manages what, and who offers the better career opportunities?

Finally, it is unlikely that professional success can be achieved in Europe in the future without some knowledge of key foreign markets, languages, and cultures. Organizations that do not provide meaningful cross-country experiences, including the chance to travel or live abroad, may be less attractive to talented employees.

CHAPTER 4

Career Development in Australia: Recognizing the Need for Linkage with Business Strategy

Alastair Rylatt

In Australia as elsewhere, the national economy has been undergoing major changes since the mid 1980s. A 1987 report produced by the Australian Council of Trade Unions/ Trade Development Council Mission to Western Europe urged a shift from protection (and attendant inefficiencies) to a new responsiveness to global free-market pressures. To accomplish this shift, argued the report, a productive, multiskilled workforce would be required.

The challenge of developing a workforce for the coming century has led to diverse economic and structural reforms in Australia. As of October 1991, for example, some 128 industry training advisory bodies existed in 18 major industries representing more than half of the private sector. (The role of an industry training advisory body is to discuss and implement competency standards, "award restructuring" [for improved skills and efficiency], and training initiatives after endorsement by the National Training Board.) Documented improvements have been made in the vital industries of hospitality, textiles and footwear, and automobiles, as well as in the public sector (particularly in communications and utilities).

Progress has, however, been somewhat hampered by various factors. The enormity of the national skills formation process has frustrated some bottom-up organizational career development initiatives, and the 1990 Training Guarantee Act has had little positive effect on career development. A report of the National Board of Employment, Education and Training in late 1991 made the following observations:

- Competencies were difficult to articulate (particularly in nontechnical tasks and occupations), and the lack of competency standards in vital industries could lead to inappropriate benchmarking.
- Some uncertainty existed about the linkage between national/industry and organizational/enterprise standards.
- There was a potential for new workplace rigidities caused by the proposed introduction of new credentialing requirements.
- Management and organizations did not fully grasp the importance of skills development, and there was some skepticism among employers about the complexity of the systems being created.
- It was difficult to adapt public education and training systems to workplace settings and to draw schools and universities into a national skills system; moreover, industry-responsive and community-based approaches might be slow to work.
- Some clarification was necessary with regard to the fact that career paths are more than simply vertical and that achieving higher skill levels involves far more than pay increments.
- The scope of the linkages between the many parts of a "change" agenda was not easy to grasp, and many people had unrealistic expectations about the time required—as well as the need—for more bottom-up organization-initiated change.

The Context of Career Development in Australia

The term "career development" has yet to become common in Australia; often it is used interchangeably with "career pathing," "employee development," "management development," "succession planning," and "performance management." Consequently, the philosophy of career development as a strategic tool linking the needs of the organization with the needs of the individual has not yet achieved universal acceptance or understanding. In addition, an accurate measurement of Australian investment in career development has not occurred, as existing records normally include only formal training and not broader, on-the-job learning and HR activities.

Since 1983, however, several trends have been observed. Performance management is used increasingly as a tool to ensure that employees and work teams are accountable for meeting business needs, and this has provided a basis for the concept of meshing short-term learning needs with longer-term business plans. Self-managed work teams and total quality management are used to accelerate on-the-job learning. Full-time career development staff are more and more common. Competency standards in nontechnical or salaried and professional areas are now more prevalent than they were a decade ago, and computerized skills inventories and job analysis are increasingly used— and linked. Finally, career planning courses, particularly in organizations undergoing downsizing and restructuring, are increasingly prevalent.

In addition, national policy has been addressing the linkages between postsecondary education and the world of work by assisting the development of a meaningful, coordinated partnership between education and vocational training—and by recognizing prior learning in this process. A national training framework, for example, is now being implemented to manage the education and training of career coordinators. Moreover, family and work-life issues are also being addressed via, for instance, the gradual introduction of organizationally sponsored child-care facilities and more flexible working methods, including permanent part-time work, job sharing, and flexible working hours.

Prevalence of Career Development Systems

Australian data were collected from 245 organizations in late 1990, during a severe economic downturn (and a concomitant tightening of resources for organizational career development). A postal questionnaire, modified from that used for the U.S. sample, was used. Of the questionnaires completed, 241 constituted valid cases for the purposes of this study (see Appendix C).

Survey respondents were typically senior HR decision makers and members of the Institute of Personnel Management of Australia (IPMA) or senior HR or training decision makers and members of the Australian Institute of Training and Development (AITD, New South Wales division). They were found in the top 100 Australian organizations throughout all states and territories. Of the 241 respondents, about 72 percent were businesses; the rest were public-sector organizations.

Private-sector respondents (particularly those in high technology, banking and finance, and manufacturing) were most likely to have introduced career development systems in their organizations. A little over half of all respondents had a career development system, and close to a quarter were in the process of launching one. The remaining respondents either had no system or had discontinued use of a previously existing system. Most organizations with a system had introduced it relatively recently (between four and six years earlier).

Table 4.1 compares Australian organizations with and without career development systems. Those with career development tended to fall in the upper ranges of annual sales or budgets (65 percent were concentrated in the three categories that exceeded $A100 million) and to employ fewer than 5,000 people (70 percent of all cases).

Over half had elements of both centralized and decentralized career development systems. Totally centralized systems were reported in about a third of all cases; only about 11 percent were totally decentralized. In over three-quarters of the organizations, a unit was assigned responsibility for career development, typically within a centralized HR area and often with only one (or a part-time) HR person devoted full time to career development (less than 20 percent had five or more staff people). Finally, these organizations were more likely to concentrate

Table 4.1. Australian Survey Respondents With and Without
Career Development.

Type of Organization	Without Career Development	With Career Development
Banking, finance, insurance, real estate	4	27
Energy (public utilities, petroleum, chemicals)	1	16
Government/military	23	16
Manufacturing (consumer)	2	14
Manufacturing (industrial)	6	11
Services (business services, food and hospitality, recreation, and repairs)	8	10
High technology	–	9
Retail/wholesale trade	3	5
Education/nonprofit	6	5
Medical/health care	1	4
Diversified/conglomerate	3	3
Other	2	6
Total	59 (n = 59)	126 (n = 126)

on salaried than nonsalaried employees as targets of career
development.

Both private- and public-sector organizations cited a
range of reasons for not having career development systems.
"Insufficient support by top management" was cited by close to
half as the major reason. The data also suggested that private-
sector organizations were more likely to have a career development system in place than public-sector organizations. Interestingly, a sharp contrast between sectors existed for only one
variable: fifteen government organizations cited lack of HR
capability or interest as the reason they lacked a career development system, in contrast to only five businesses.

"Drivers" of Organizational Career Development

Table 4.2 presents the factors that have most influenced the
introduction of career development programs in Australian

Career Development in Australia: Obstacles to Overcome

Why do some Australian companies lack career development systems? Here are some answers from the private sector:

- "Our company is decentralized, with a number of operating divisions and few corporate staff."
- "Our short-term organizational strategies aren't conducive to mid- and long-term manpower processes."
- "We're currently using an extensive organizational development process, emphasizing team development and cultural change rather than individual development."
- "Career development seems too cumbersome; we don't know how to make an assessment."
- "We have no systematic approach, but executive training is our basic approach to career development."

Some public-sector respondents commented:

- "We use a government skill center. We're considering in-house career development but not at present."
- "Career development hasn't been an issue to date. We're developing career paths through new classification, structures, and awards."

---

organizations. (From a given list, each respondent could choose three factors.) Interestingly, three factors were not identified by any of the respondents: encouraging early retirement, avoiding unionization, and the 1990 Training Guarantee Act (which requires structured training for organizations with annual gross payrolls of at least $A214,000).

Table 4.2. Factors Influencing Australian Career Development Programs.

Factor	Cited as Influential (Percentage)
Organizational commitment to career development	29.1
Development of organization's strategic plan	18.4
Desire to develop or promote from within	16.2
Shortage of promotable talent	8.9
Desire to improve worker productivity	6.7
Desire to motivate employees under conditions of limited growth	3.9
Concern about turnover	2.8
Equal employment opportunity program commitments	2.8
Desire to keep up with competitors	2.2
Survey or needs assessment findings	2.2
Shift in skills mix or HR planning needs	2.2
As a result of award structuring, structural efficiency principle	2.2
Strong expression of employee interest in career planning	1.7
Desire for positive recruiting image	0.6
Need to encourage early retirement	0.0
Desire to avoid unionization	0.0
1990 Training Guarantee Act	0.0
Total	100.00 (rounded off)

Attitudes Toward Career Development

The attitudes of respondents toward organizational career development were explored through twenty-two statements (see Table 4.3). Responses to the statements raised some discrepancies between ideal, as revealed here, and actual practice, as revealed in other questionnaire items. Here are several examples:

- Almost all respondents agreed or strongly agreed that career development must be linked with the organization's strategic business plan (statement 1), but this linkage existed in only a little over half of all responding organizations.
- Around 80 percent of respondents agreed or strongly

Table 4.3. Views of Career Development.

Statement	Strongly Agree	Agree	Disagree	Strongly Disagree	(n)
1. Career development programs must be tied in with the strategic business plan.	56.3%	38.8%	4.9%	0%	183
2. Senior management believes career development raises employee expectations.	12.2	59.4	26.7	1.7	180
3. Senior management feels that career development is a fad.	1.6	9.3	54.6	34.4	183
4. Senior management believes that career development is an important part of employee development.	30.6	61.2	8.2	0	183
5. Managers believe career development is not really anything new.	4.3	66.8	26.6	2.2	184
6. Managers believe career development is not needed.	0	8.6	64.3	27.0	185
7. Career development means an increased burden for the supervisor.	5.4	48.6	36.8	9.2	185
8. Few supervisors are equipped to hold employee career discussions.	17.2	62.9	19.9	0	186
9. Supervisors feel that employee career development is not part of their job.	4.4	44.3	48.6	2.7	183
10. Turnover increases as a result of employee participation in career development programs.	0.5	8.8	64.8	25.8	182
11. Only a small percentage of employees are really interested in career development.	0	17.4	66.3	16.3	184
12. Career development enhances the job performance of employees.	23.6	71.4	4.9	0	182
13. Career development increases personal anxiety for many employees.	1.1	17.9	73.9	7.1	184
14. Career development allows improved use of employee talents.	31.4	65.9	2.7	0	185
15. Career development strains the capacity of other systems.	4.4	28.3	58.3	8.9	180
16. Career development equips employees to use personnel systems more effectively.	6.9	71.8	21.3	0	174
17. Career development generally disrupts an organization.	10.4	69.8	19.8	0	182
18. Career development is best introduced on a pilot, experimental basis.	5.6	37.8	46.1	10.6	180
19. Job requirements and career information need not be provided in a career development program.	0	10.9	60.7	28.4	183
20. Employee participation in a career development program should be voluntary.	17.9	62.0	17.9	2.2	184
21. Employees should be able to keep confidential their records or other outputs of career planning activities.	23.6	54.4	19.7	2.2	178
22. Career development helps employees deal with a low-growth environment.	5.6	75.1	17.5	1.7	177

Source: Australian Institute of Training and Development. *Career Development Practices in Selected Australian Organisations: An Overview of Survey Findings*, p. 34. Chatswood: Australian Institute of Training and Development, 1991. Reprinted with permission.

agreed that career development generally disrupts an organization (statement 17).

- Although respondents suggested that their career development systems blended individual and organizational focuses, close to 80 percent agreed or strongly agreed that employees' records should be confidential (statement 21). A similar percentage agreed or strongly agreed that employee participation in a career development program should be voluntary (statement 20).

- Again, roughly 80 percent of respondents agreed or strongly agreed that career development helps employees deal with a low-growth environment (statement 22); however, only about 30 percent reported having career development programs that targeted plateaued employees.

In view of the pivotal role of supervisors in career development discussions and the current lack of programs to prepare them for this role, it is not surprising that respondents indicated that few supervisors are equipped to hold career discussions with employees and that supervisors feel that employee career development is not part of their job.

Responses of Australian organizations to three other statements are also worth noting:

- Opinion was divided on the introduction of career development on a pilot experimental basis (statement 18).

- Almost all respondents agreed or strongly agreed that career development enhances employee job performance (statement 12).

- Approximately 70 percent of respondents indicated that managers believe career development is not really anything new (statement 5).

Implementation of Career Development Systems

Salaried employees were covered by career development systems in all respondent organizations; approximately half also covered nonsalaried employees, and so-called casual employees (hourly workers) were covered in about 12 percent. The groups most frequently targeted for career development programs were fast-track management candidates or high-potentials, graduates, management trainees, new employees, and women. There was less evidence of practices that targeted employees with physical or mental disabilities, older workers, or preretirees.

Types of Career Development Practices Used

Survey respondents were given a list of thirty-one career development practices and asked to indicate the current status of each in their organizations. The results, provided in Table 4.4, indicate that a wide array of career development practices exists in Australian organizations.

The ten most frequently identified were these (percentages have been rounded off):

1. In-house training and development programs (95%)
2. External seminars or workshops (93%)
3. Counseling or career development discussions provided by supervisors or line managers (89%)
4. Tuition reimbursement (89%)
5. Counseling or career development discussions involving personnel staff (81%)
6. Interview process (organizational potential assessment) (72%)
7. Job assignment (66%)
8. Internal placement systems (63%)
9. Replacement or succession planning (62%)
10. Job posting (60%)

Emphasis was clearly placed on developmental, job matching, individual counseling, and organizational assessment processes. Although nearly 90 percent of organizations reported that individual counseling and career development discussions were conducted by supervisors and line managers, less than half gave them any training in career discussions. Strong linkages appear to exist between organizational career

Table 4.4. Status of Specific Career Development Practices.

	Planned (Percentage)	Occurring (Percentage)	(n)
Employee Self-Assessment Tools			
Career planning workshops	15.3	28.4	176
Career workbooks (stand-alone)	11.7	17.5	171
Preretirement workshops	5.3	35.1	171
Computer software	11.0	22.1	163
Organizational Potential Assessment Processes			
Promotability forecasts	15.5	48.8	168
Psychological testing	8.4	38.3	167
Assessment center	8.0	16.6	163
Interview process	9.8	72.3	173
Job assignment	9.4	66.1	171
Internal Staffing Information Exchanges			
Career information handbooks	12.3	33.3	171
Career ladder or dual-career ladders	9.6	27.1	166
Career resource center	6.5	14.3	168
Other career information formats	8.6	27.8	162
Individual Counseling or Career Discussions			
Supervisor or line manager	7.8	89.4	179
Senior career adviser	4.8	29.2	168
Personnel staff	5.1	80.9	178
Specialized counselor: (a) internal	3.6	19.8	167
(b) external	1.9	11.4	158
Job Matching Systems			
Informal cavassing	1.2	50.6	164
Job posting	2.4	60.2	166
Skills inventories or audits	29.2	45.0	171
Replacement or succession planning	18.7	62.0	171
Staffing committees	3.0	24.7	166
Internal placement systems	9.9	63.4	172
Development Programs			
Job enrichment or redesign	17.9	43.4	173
Job rotation	13.2	58.0	174
In-house training or development programs	2.8	94.5	181
External seminars or workshops	1.7	92.7	179
Tuition reimbursement	2.8	89.3	178
Supervisor training in career discussions	17.3	43.4	173
Dual-career couple programs	4.8	4.2	165
Mentoring systems	20.5	29.0	176

development practices and such HR practices as performance appraisal, promotion, and transfer practices and recruitment practices. Linkages were least evident with strategic planning, organizational design, employee assistance, salary administration, and equal employment opportunity activities.

Perceived Effectiveness of Career Development Practices

Australian respondents most frequently rated tuition reimbursement and in-house training and development programs as "very effective." Assessment centers, supervisor training in career discussions, preretirement workshops, and job posting all received "very effective" ratings from roughly 14 percent of respondents. Practices most frequently rated "very ineffective" included staffing committees, dual-career couple programs, career resource centers, and stand-alone career workbooks.

Influences on Effectiveness

Australian HR managers were asked what factors influence the effectiveness of career development practices in Australia. Their reactions to this quesion can be grouped into four general categories.

1. Planning, communication, and attitudinal factors

     Business reasons for system implementation
     Demonstrated commitment of senior management
     Access to role models or benchmarks
     Extensive data gathering and needs analysis prior to
          implementation
     Use of task forces that include staff and line management
          in design and implementation
     Development and communication of objectives
     Rigorous marketing
     Recognition by management and employees that career
          development is a long-term process

2. Organizational and systems factors

> Availability of a computerized HR information system
> Existence of formal linkages among the system and business plans, strategic planning processes, and HR systems
> Line management accountability for career discussions
> Flexible staffing and skills formation processes and counseling or mentoring processes

3. Implementation factors

> Adequate supervisor or management training in both the concept and benefits of career development systems and their implementation
> Availability of appropriate resources (counselors, software, workbooks, workshops, and so on)

4. Additional ongoing factors

> Continuity of implementation over time
> Continuous monitoring and evaluation to improve the system design and measure its effectiveness
> Reporting of system outputs (for example, impact on job performance, turnover, recruitment practices)

Outcomes

Evaluation of career development practices does not appear to be a high priority for most of the Australian organizations we surveyed. Seventy percent rely on informal feedback from participants, and close to 15 percent do not evaluate their programs or practices at all. The two most popular forms of formal evaluation were questionnaires to measure attitudes, learning, or behavior and analysis of data relating to productivity, performance, mobility, and costs. Just over half of the respondents rated their career development systems positively, but only about 7 percent considered them very effective.

Useful data on the state of career development systems emerged when participants elaborated on their overall ratings. Clear trends and themes included the following:

- Uncertainty about effectiveness because career development practices were still new.
- The importance of a linkage between career development practices, other HR activities, and the organization's business plan.
- The need for genuine support from senior managers.
- Problems with variations in system effectiveness within the organization.

Respondents that identified their career development systems as effective or very effective explained their ratings in terms of the increased evidence of promotion from within, the availability and continuity of development options and defined career paths, and reduced turnover. They also cited the participation of all employees in the process and, significantly, positive evaluation feedback.

Australian survey respondents were asked to identify the major positive or negative effects of their organizations' career development efforts. Of the 62 percent that responded, 95 percent identified a positive effect or benefit. The benefits identified by respondents were then classified using a model and structure provided in Merman and Leibowitz (1984). The results suggested a widespread awareness of possible benefits for both the organization and the individual. Organizational benefits include improved use of human resources, productivity, adaptability, stability, competitiveness, and compliance. Response frequencies suggested that the three main forces behind organizational career development were (1) the desire to promote and develop talent from within; (2) improved business performance; and (3) maintenance of a high-quality, adaptable workforce. Benefits for the individual that were noted most frequently included enhanced self-direction, employability, and personal and professional growth.

Respondents were asked to comment on what if anything

Perceived Negatives of Australian Career Development Efforts

What were some of the negative features of organizational career development efforts in Australia? Here are some comments from our survey respondents:

"Top-down support is lacking, particularly where long-term career development efforts are in conflict with short-term operational needs."

"We struggle with frustration and unreal expectations."

"Politics and self-interest still contaminate career development efforts."

"Business and HR systems aren't working together; succession plans are out of sync, or a changing environment frustrates our endeavors."

"Managers and employees are unwilling to discuss or negotiate career issues."

they would have done differently. Diverse responses were provided in 131 cases (see Table 4.5). Additionally, respondents were asked to indicate how organizational development had changed (if at all) in the last ten years. Their comments indicated that awareness of career development practices has increased, particularly in the last two years. Organizations are now recognizing the benefits of these practices and the need to link career development to corporate strategy. Approaches to career development and the tools used are becoming more sophisticated and formalized, and employees are increasingly aware of career development and multiskilling. An emphasis on individuals as well as on shared responsibility for career development was evident. (Interestingly, not all respondents were in agreement about changes in career development. About 15 percent reported that they detected little or no change in the field, and nearly 18 percent were unable to comment on any changes

Table 4.5. Desirable Changes in Career Development Practices.

Desirable Changes (in Retrospect)	Percentage	(n)
None	19.08	25
More supervisor or manager training	16.03	21
Formalized linkage between career development, performance management, and strategic plan	12.98	17
Too early to judge	12.21	16
Greater resources, workbooks, software, counselors, support staff, workshops	9.16	12
Increased management and individual accountability	5.34	7
More effective use of task forces in design, representation, and implementation	5.34	7
Earlier initiation of design	3.82	5
Continuous monitoring and evaluation	3.82	5
Better linkage to skills audits	3.82	5
Better marketing	3.05	4
More flexible staffing policy	3.05	4
Changed target group size	2.29	3
Total	100.00 (rounded off)	131

over the past decade.) Finally, flatter organizational structures have meant that opportunities for upward career moves are more limited. Respondents indicated that career development did not allow for an examination of alternative directions and enhanced development in current jobs.

What about the future? Of our Australia survey respondents, 154 identified 237 plans and initiatives for future career development practices. Those plans are shown in Table 4.6.

Implications

The future of organizational career development in Australia appears particularly promising in the private sector, where organizations are entering into a more assertive partnership with employees in the career development process. Practitioners will be seeking better linkages with HR and business planning activities, expanding into skills inventories or audits, mentoring systems, replacement or succession planning, job

Table 4.6. Planned Career Development Practices.

Career Development Practice	Percentage Planning Use
Decentralize responsibility: support and train line managers and staff to hold career development discussions	16.03
Formalize links and develop consistency between individual performance, expectations, and rewards with the framework of strategic business plans and HR systems	14.77
Conduct detailed needs assessment (within and outside the framework of award restructuring)	9.28
Target specific groups	8.02
Free up staffing and skills-formation processes	7.17
Continue as at present	5.49
Evaluate jobs, skills, and potential	4.64
Introduce regular evaluation of career development system	3.80
Expand career development to staff not currently involved	3.80
Introduce computerized management information system or HR system	3.80
Link career development to restructuring initiatives	3.80
Involve line and staff in career development design	3.38
Continuously develop succession planning	2.95
Introduce structured career planning process	2.95
Introduce more formalized organizational career counseling or mentoring process	2.53
Build a framework for implementing systems or competencies	2.53
Improve marketing of career development	2.11
No plans at present or career development a low priority	1.69
Don't know	1.27

enrichment or redesign, and supervisor training in conducting career discussions and overseeing self-managing work teams.

As elsewhere, in Australia there appears to be a "disconnect" between claimed benefits and documented evidence of success. Despite the large number of organizations responding to our survey, many did not actually have a career development system in place. There are two possible reasons for this. First, the absence of role models for best practices has made the benchmarking of excellence difficult. Second, some practitioners see career development as a collection of separate stand-alone activities (such as development methods and outplacement counseling) rather than as a wide-ranging, integrated HR management system.

Particularly disappointing was the performance of the public sector. Public-sector organizations were least likely to have career development systems in place. The lack of HR capability was cited as a major factor; however, other additional issues surfaced from followup field research. (In many cases, the difficulties being experienced were the ones that the private sector had been addressing.)

To begin with, senior public agency staff seemed not to be held accountable for delivering results. The guiding principle of "career service" (that is, recruitment and promotion by merit) has created some skepticism about career development activities, which have often been seen as providing favorable treatment to a chosen few. (Career development has been labeled, in some agencies, as "fast-track accelerated development," "replacement planning," and the "Crown Prince syndrome.") As a consequence, establishing targeted career development systems has been difficult. Moreover, HR functions within departments are frequently underfunded and often do not network well with other units to discuss career development implementation. Finally, constant demands on public servants to make efficiency gains seem to have generated an element of inertia.

Because organizational career development is about workplace learning and creating a culture that supports such learning, a multiplicity of activities and strategies must be used to accommodate diverse learning styles. A key element in the credibility of a change process in Australia, therefore, is effective role modeling of mentoring and coaching behaviors by senior managers. Another key element is the affirmation of appropriate organizational values. A career development policy must articulate the "code of practice" that the organization, the employee, and the manager will follow. Organizations must empower individuals to use their own talents and motivations in partnership with business requirements.

The lack of documentation of best practices is severely inhibiting implementation of effective career development practices in Australia. Career development practitioners need to undertake high-quality benchmarking so as not to promote a false sense of security. (Much of the current research goes on behind closed doors; best practices need to be documented and celebrated openly.) Professional bodies, industry, government, and higher educational institutions need to cooperate in order to help sponsor research, reward excellence, and provide leadership and vision.

As Australian organizations approach the twenty-first century, what development-related challenges are most pressing and how might private- and public-sector organizations best respond? Our findings, drawn from the survey results, fall into five categories. Each is briefly discussed below.

Disadvantaged Groups: Overcoming the Imbalance

Despite the fact that women, non–English-speaking employees, aborigines and Torres Strait Islanders, and physically and mentally disabled employees constitute 42 percent of the paid workforce, these groups remain poorly represented in upper-management positions in both the private and public sector. More flexibility in work patterns, hours, awards, and superannuation, job sharing, home-based employment, relocation support, and child-care facilities are urgently required to correct this problem.

HR Planning: Making It More Proactive

Organizations will need to allocate resources to motivate, retain, and retrain key personnel while providing career development resources to all staff, not just a select few. In addition, organizations will need to undertake the following activities:

- Motivating and empowering plateaued employees
- Involving older employees in career development
- Using accelerated-learning technology, such as self-management and on-the-job learning, to fast-track workplace learning

- Designing career development activities that are sensitive to cultural and learning diversity
- Developing employees in part-time jobs
- Implementing adult literacy programs
- Reintegrating career and quality-of-life issues
- Providing dual-career couple programs
- Providing internal or external resourcing and counseling for employees making career transitions
- Recruiting and training people from dysfunctional backgrounds for new careers
- Offering career planning programs for people in organizations undergoing downsizing or restructuring
- Developing international expertise by recruiting and rotating key people overseas

Development of Competency Standards

The challenge here is to develop standards that clearly articulate excellence of behavior. While headway is being made in Australia in developing competency standards in the trades, implementing such standards within professional or managerial occupations (on both an industry and an organizational level) often is difficult. To overcome this problem, Australian management needs to ensure that competency standards are flexible and frequently reviewed.

Relations Between Manager and Work Team: Greater Resourcing

The manager to work team relationship is a major factor in effective career development. However, in practice, this relationship is not being handled effectively in Australian organizations. The roles and responsibilities of managers and team members need to be clarified, and staff must be trained better and rewarded for demonstrating excellence.

Emphasizing Transition and Support

Australian career development practice suffers somewhat from structural paralysis. There appears to be little shared understanding of the scope and sequencing of the national and industry change agenda. This is particularly relevant to the disciplines of industrial relations and HR management; as a result, the current career development agenda has resulted in much confusion and concern.

The national agenda confronts a paradox. Should the current structured-change process driven by legislation and industry bodies continue to expand, or is there a need for a more flexible, free-market approach to skills formation and career development? The implementation of organizational career development now operates within a highly regulated arena. Although significant gains are being experienced in terms of developing consistency across industry and state boundaries, at the bottom line productivity improvements will result only if organizations are able to link career development activities aggressively with business requirements. And as Australia moves forward, it will need to shift its vision of productivity and growth to accommodate individual and organizational needs. In particular, Australian organizations will need to acquire a greater understanding of the fact that career development not only increases competitiveness but also adds value and meaning to individual lives.

CHAPTER 5

Career Development in Singapore: Seeking Management Support for Development Efforts

Violet S. K. Seah

In Singapore, little is known about organizations' career development practices, how they view career development, and how many have a career development system in place. To provide such data, the Singapore Institute of Management (SIM), in conjunction with the American Society for Training and Development (ASTD), conducted a survey of career development practices in 1991. Senior development or personnel executives in all 966 corporate members of SIM were sent a survey questionnaire; 252 completed questionnaires were returned for a response rate of 26 percent (see Appendix D).

The Context of Career Development in Singapore

The 70 companies that reported having career development systems covered a large spectrum of industries. Close to half were from service, manufacturing, retail and wholesale trade, banking, finance, and insurance. Half were multinationals, and 31 percent were local companies. About half were small companies with fewer than 100 employees, and about one-third were large companies with more than 500. Joint ventures and government ministries and statutory boards together made up 19 percent (see Appendix D).

Prevalence of Career Development Systems

The majority of Singapore organizations (37 percent) had had a career development system in place for more than six years, particularly the multinational and joint-venture companies. Another 23 percent had had a system for between three and four years; this included a fairly high proportion of local companies. Government ministries and statutory boards generally had had a system for less than two years (see Appendix D).

"Drivers" of Organizational Career Development

As Table 5.1 shows, the main reasons cited by respondents for implementing a career development system were the organization's commitment to career development, the development of the strategic plan, and the desire to develop and promote from within. As these responses suggest, organizations in Singapore were implementing career development systems largely to meet basic corporate requirements such as staffing needs and improved corporate performance.

Attitudes Toward Career Development

In Singapore there is widespread support of career development as a concept. Most respondents agreed that career development practices need to be tied in with the organization's strategic business plan and that senior management believes that career development is an important part of employee development (see Table 5.2). In addition, most agreed that career development has the potential to improve the utilization of employee talents and to enhance job performance. Similarly, the large number of respondents who disagreed that managers believe career development is not needed, that managers feel that career development is a fad, or that only a small number of employees are really interested in it all confirm support for career development as a concept.

However, despite this widespread theoretical support, only 28 percent of the 252 companies that responded to the

Table 5.1. Attitudes Toward Career Development.

Questionnaire Item	Strongly Agree (Percentage)	Agree (Percentage)	Disagree (Percentage)	Strongly Disagree (Percentage)	(n)
1. Career development programs must be tied in with the strategic business plan.	66	34	0	0	103
2. Senior management believes career development raises employee expectations.	24	59	13	4	103
3. Senior management feels that career development is a fad.	0	6	52	43	103
4. Senior management believes that career development is an important part of employee development.	53	47	0	0	103
5. Managers believe career development is not really anything new.	10	57	26	7	103
6. Managers believe career development is not needed.	0	0	55	45	103
7. Career development means an increased burden for the supervisor.	4	21	55	19	103
8. Few supervisors are equipped to hold employee career discussions.	15	58	21	6	103
9. Supervisors feel that employee career development is not part of their job.	3	32	52	13	103
10. Turnover increases as a result of employee participation in career development programs.	1	10	65	24	101
11. Only a small percentage of employees are really interested in career development.	2	16	60	23	102
12. Career development enhances the job performance of employees.	27	71	2	0	103

13. Career development increases personal anxiety for many employees.	3	29	62	6	103
14. Career development allows improved use of employee talents.	36	63	1	0	103
15. Career development strains the capacity of other systems.	1	20	69	10	103
16. Career development equips employees to use personnel systems more effectively.	6	90	4	0	100
17. Career development generally disrupts an organization.	0	8	70	23	102
18. Career development is best introduced on a pilot experimental basis.	1	35	48	17	101
19. Job requirements and career information need not be provided in a career development program.	1	8	68	23	103
20. Employee participation in a career development program should be voluntary.	8	58	28	6	103
21. Employees should be able to keep confidential their records or other outputs of career planning activities.	11	74	13	3	103
22. Career development helps employees deal with a low-growth environment.	4	65	28	3	99

Table 5.2. Reasons for Implementing a Career Development System.

Reason	Percentage
Organizational commitment to career development	32
Development of the strategic plan	26
Desire to develop or promote from within	22
Desire to motivate employees under conditions of limited organizational growth	6
Concern about turnover	3
Shortage of promotable talent	1
Survey or needs assessment findings	1
Desire to improve productivity	1
Desire for positive recruiting image	1
Others	1
No answer	6
Total	100

survey actually had a career development system in place. Over half had had one but discontinued its use, and 14 percent were intending to initiate a system. Among the reasons named for not having a system were:

> Lack of HR capability or interest (42 percent)
> Insufficient support by top management (16 percent)
> Insufficient budgetary resources (14 percent)
> Organization's needs not in line with career development (13 percent)
> Lack of manager or supervisor interest (5 percent)
> Lack of employee interest (4 percent)
> Other (such as company too small) (32 percent)

Implementation of Career Development Systems in Singapore

Almost all the companies with career development programs indicated that they were generally targeted at exempt salaried or nonsalaried employees. Only slightly more than half mentioned that their career development programs targeted nonexempts, and 7 percent targeted hourly workers.

Within the salaried employee group, the fast-track management candidates or high-potential employees were the main targets for career development (close to 80 percent of companies). This further confirms the fact that career development systems in most companies were set up to meet a human resources need—in this case, to minimize the turnover of high-potential employees. Apart from these employees, 66 percent of companies targeted management trainees and 54 percent targeted new employees (see Appendix D).

Structure of Career Development Systems

In almost half of respondents with a career development system, some components were centralized and others decentralized. Since most of these companies were American-based multinationals, this is not surprising; the companies are probably given a career development system by headquarters and authorized to adapt it to suit local needs (see Appendix D).

Career development in over 60 percent of those companies with a system operated from a specific unit or function. Nearly all were located inside the HR department, and about half had no staff working on career development activities full time. More than half did not have a task force or consultative committee to advise them on the design and implementation of their systems. Among those that did, the majority rated effectiveness as average.

It appears from these findings that career development is a rather low-key activity in most of the Singapore organizations we surveyed. Judging from the lack of staff support and advice for career development activities, the career development programs in these companies are probably an extension of the HR planning function as a whole. Indeed, career development appears to be strongly linked to the companies' training and personnel systems. In-house training and development programs were one of the most popular career development practices adopted, followed by job matching systems and organizational potential assessment processes. The popularity of these practices indicates that career development was more likely to be a management function initiated by the organization (career management) than an individual responsibility (employee career planning).

This observation is further supported by answers to two other questions. Respondents were asked to assign responsibility for career development to the three parties involved. The mean response was: the employee, 29 percent; the manager, 36 percent; and the organization, 35 percent. When asked whether their organizations' career development efforts emphasized the employee or the organization, respondents answered that they tended to focus slightly more on the organization.

Types of Career Development Practices Used

These ten career development practices are most frequently practiced in Singapore (see also Appendix D):

1. Counseling or career development discussions with supervisors or line managers (97 percent)
2. External seminars or workshops (97 percent)
3. In-house training and development (88 percent)
4. Job assignment (84 percent)
5. Employee orientation programs (78 percent)
6. Tuition reimbursement (78 percent)
7. Interview process (organizational potential assessment) (77 percent)
8. Promotability forecasts (70 percent)
9. Job enrichment or redesign (70 percent)
10. Replacement or succession planning (69 percent)

Employee self-assessment tools were the least adopted: on average, three-quarters of companies with a career development system did not use them. This reinforces the observation that career development in Singapore is viewed as the responsibility of the organization more than of the employee.

Potential assessment processes, usually used to assess an employee's suitability for promotion, can and should be more than simply a means of identifying promotable talent. They can also provide detailed feedback on the strengths and weaknesses of an individual employee. These inputs can then be used to construct an individual career development plan or to design a training program for an entire group of employees. The potential assessment processes most widely used included job assignments, interview processes, and promotability forecasts (all used by between 70 and 85 percent of respondents). Psychological testing and assessment centers were not popular among the companies surveyed (only roughly one-quarter used these).

Except for career ladders, the other practices grouped under the category of internal labor-market information exchanges, such as career resource centers and career information handbooks, were not popular. Practices in this category generally require a full-time career staffperson, which few of the companies with a system had.

Given the absence of full-time staff in most companies, career discussion and counseling were often conducted by supervisors and line managers. In fact, individual counseling and career discussions were used by almost all companies with a system, even though less than one-third offered supervisor training in career discussions. Significantly, some supervisors and managers also did not regard career counseling as part of their responsibility. To ensure that individual counseling is used effectively, therefore, companies in Singapore need to define the role of supervisors and managers clearly and provide them with training for counseling. Supervisors and managers themselves should be able to discuss their own career objectives with senior management. By providing an avenue for supervisors and managers to talk about their own objectives, the company also provides a model for these individuals to emulate when they counsel their subordinates (Gutteridge, 1987).

Within the category of job-matching practices, replacement or succession planning, job posting, and internal placement systems were the most widely used. As development need not always be equated with vertical mobility, many companies attempted to rotate jobs or enrich them by providing challenging goals that are meaningful and psychologically fulfilling. Examples of such tools are job rotation (60 percent usage) and enrichment or redesign (70 percent). Other popular activities were in-house training and external training (88 and 97 percent, respectively). Some organizations also provided tuition reimbursement schemes.

Mentoring and supervisor training in career discussions were used by less than half of companies. The least used practice was dual-career couple programs; only 13 percent had such a program. With an increase in women's participation in the workforce, however, this could change.

Survey respondents revealed strong connections between career development and diverse HR practices, particularly recruitment, promotion or transfer, and performance appraisal processes. Table 5.3 shows the extent of such linkages.

Perceived Effectiveness of Career Development Programs in Singapore

Two-thirds of respondents with career development systems evaluated their programs informally through verbal feedback. Slightly over one-third used data analysis of productivity and performance results; 30 percent used questionnaires and interviews of focus groups. Career development within most of these companies was thus very informally organized and, as noted, largely an extension of the HR planning function.

Only 7 percent of respondents rated their career development systems as very effective. (One percent considered their systems to be ineffective.) Respondents who rated their systems as very effective cited the greater sense of direction provided in managing their human resources more efficiently and the boost given to the company's image.

Outcomes: Respondents' Assessments

Our Singapore survey attempted to answer three basic questions about career development practices:

1. What are HR managers' views of organizational development?

Making It Happen:
Career Development in a Singapore Company

The National Computer Board (NCB), a Singapore company of over 900 mainly instructional technology professionals, instituted career development as a way of retaining employees and building their loyalty to the organization. Formalized in 1988, the system involves annual career discussions between all staff members and their managers and the implementation of development plans. The HR department briefs all new managers on the roles, techniques, and procedures involved in conducting a discussion and counseling. Career development is viewed as a shared responsibility of the organization, managers, and employees.

In addition, succession planning helps NCB identify and groom future leaders, and a scholarship program helps develop them. This assists the company in meeting one of its policy objectives, which is to promote people from within; in fact, each business unit is headed by someone who has been internally promoted. The top leadership of the organization actively supports and participates in the larger career development effort.

The effectiveness of career development at NCB has been demonstrated through job rotations among staff as well as the success of internal grooming and succession planning. The main area for improvement is ensuring that career discussions are made a priority and are held on time; maintaining a good fit between individuals and jobs is crucial for motivating the workforce as a whole.

NCB's advice to others about implementating a career development system? First, understand the needs of the organization. Then start small but with high visibility, and expand the system's scope gradually.

Table 5.3. Linkage of Career Development Practices with HR Systems.

HR Systems	In Place (Percentage)	Linked to Career Development (Percentage)
Recruitment practices	94	100
Promotion or transfer practices	94	100
Performance appraisal	99	100
HR planning	84	92
Job description or evaluation	90	89
Organizational design	56	85
Strategic planning	86	83
Salary administration	97	82
Employee assistance	64	82

2. To what extent have Singapore companies implemented a formal career development system?
3. What are the most widely adopted career development practices?

Our findings showed that despite general acceptance of the concept of career development, a wide gap existed between what managers believed and what they actually practiced. What they were saying, in effect, is that while it is nice to have career development as part of the HR management process, it is certainly not a necessity.

Managers may need to change their views on career development soon, however, once they realize that the workforce as a whole and employees' expectations are changing dramatically. Unless they are more employee oriented, they may not be able to recruit and retain the best employees in a tight labor market.

Except for a few large companies, most did not actually have a career development system even if they indicated that they had one. Most managers appeared to equate a detailed training plan with a formal career development system. Yet unless training efforts are expanded into an integrated career development system that is responsive to the career aspirations of a diverse employee group *and* the organization's own staffing needs, a training program alone cannot be considered a career development system (Gutteridge, 1987).

Among those Singaporean companies with systems, however, the response to organizational career development efforts has been positive. Respondents reported that their companies' efforts have resulted in:

- Increased staff motivation (because the company is doing something for them)
- Higher employee expectations
- Improved retention of good employees
- Better matching of organizational needs with employee expectations
- More effective succession planning efforts

Companies in Singapore need to consider career development a shared process; that is, an organization's career development system should provide a means for helping employees identify their career preferences within the organizational structure. Otherwise, the system will be designed without reference to employees' actual career interests, and this will negatively affect its usefulness.

Implications

Career development is a relative newcomer to the HR planning and development process in Singapore. It is still not widely accepted as an important component of HR management. The career development practices adopted are usually those that have been tried and tested; newer methods, such as employee self-assessment tools and psychological testing, which were deemed highly effective by the European sample of our survey, are seldom used in Singapore.

Nevertheless, over the last ten years, more Singapore companies have come to recognize the importance of career development, especially for employee retention in a tight labor market. With keener competition and an increased effort on the part of organizations to use HR more effectively, more companies are likely to consider the implementation of career development systems.

A number of significant changes in career development as it is practiced in Singapore could be anticipated through respondents' indications of what they were planning to do. The practices most frequently slated for implementation were these:

> Supervisor training in career discussions (20 percent)
> Skills inventories or audits (19 percent)
> Mentoring systems (18 percent)
> Job enrichment or redesign (17 percent)
> Job rotation (14 percent)
> Replacement or succession planning (13 percent)
> Career planning workshops (13 percent)
> Job assignment (12 percent)
> Career workbooks (10 percent)

Most respondents indicated that they were planning to implement supervisor training in career discussions, which shows that they were aware of the need to train supervisors in career counseling discussions. It is also interesting to note that some companies indicated that they were planning to implement career planning workshops and workbooks, which would encourage more individual employees to be involved in career planning. Here are some examples of respondents' comments on the future development of their systems:

> "We will continue to improve our existing program and to initiate new ones to enhance the effectiveness of career development."
> "Having started with the development of employees, we will expand our career development program to cover more levels of employees, including nonexempt staff members."
> "We will consider introducing other elements of career development, such as succession planning and job rotation."

"A more concerted effort to provide counseling will be under way here."

"We intend to develop career development into a full-fledged system throughout the HR division."

"We plan to intensify our effort in formulating a systematic process."

Judging from these comments, it appears that HR managers in Singapore are going to take career development more seriously. With more time devoted and more support from top management, career development will no longer have to remain in the back room of the HR department.

CHAPTER 6

Comparing Career Development at Home and Abroad

As the last three chapters have made clear, organizational career development is properly viewed in a global context. HR practitioners around the world share a wide range of concerns: maintaining competitive advantage, dealing with changed organizational structures, developing people from within to meet new challenges, and elaborating the role of managers in a career development partnership.

Indeed, more striking than the differences among samples were the overriding similarities in current practice and future priorities. These similarities were even more pointed in light of the fact that the U.S. corporate sample was random, whereas the other three were targeted largely at organizations that were members of training and development or HR associations.

All this is not to say, however, that there were not also some important differences in the results. This chapter will highlight both similarities and differences and will comment on important implications for the state of the practice.

Table 6.1 presents a comparison of the key results across samples. For ease of comparison, we have not included the U.S. government sample, as the response pool was so small. (Government respondents were, however, part of the overall Australian sample.) When reviewing and interpreting the data, keep in mind that the European sample represents 70 responses from a number of different countries; in contrast, each of the other three samples represents over 200 responses from one country.

Comparing the Context of Career Development

In all but the Singapore sample, well over half of all respondents indicated that they had or were starting a career development system. (This was true of only 42 percent of Singapore respondents, reinforcing observations made in Chapter Five that career development in Singapore is a relatively new phenomenon.) Nevertheless, the data on prevalence should still be read with caution because the international samples were targeted and the U.S. respondents were probably self-screened. In fact, the Singapore sample was the only one in which the majority of respondents neither had nor were starting career development systems.

There were notable similarities among samples in terms of the top three factors driving career development. We were surprised by the degree of similarity as well as by some of the responses themselves. Each of the four samples included a "desire to promote from within" and "organizational commitment to career development" among the top three factors. The strong emphasis on promotion was unexpected, given the very widespread recognition of flatter organizations, diminished opportunities for upward mobility, diversity, and so on—that is, of a dramatically transformed business context.

Importantly, the U.S. sample was the only one in which the development of the organization's strategic plan was *not* among the top three factors influencing career development. This relative deemphasis of the link between career development and business strategy, evidenced elsewhere in the survey results, may account for some of the differences in perceived effectiveness of career development systems in the United States and elsewhere.

Table 6.1. Comparison of U.S. and International Surveys.

Response category	U.S.	Australia	Singapore	Europe
Have or are starting CD system	68 percent	75 percent	42 percent	88 percent
Top three factors driving career development	1. Desire to develop or promote from within 2. Shortage of promotable talent 3. Organizational commitment to CD	1. Organizational commitment to CD 2. Development of organization's strategic plan 3. Desire to develop or promote from within	1. Organizational commitment to CD 2. Development of organization's strategic plan 3. Desire to develop or promote from within	1. Development of organization's strategic plan 2. Organizational commitment to CD 3a. Shortage of promotable talent 3b. Desire to develop or promote from within
Agree or strongly agree that:				
Senior management believes career development is an important part of employee development	80 percent	92 percent	100 percent	94 percent
Few supervisors are equipped to hold employee career discussions	84 percent	80 percent	73 percent	63 percent
CD programs must be tied in with the organization's strategic plan	85 percent	95 percent	100 percent	98 percent
CD allows improved use of employee talents	93 percent	97 percent	99 percent	95 percent

CD helps employees deal with a low-growth environment	82 percent	81 percent	71 percent	78 percent
Employees' participation in a CD program should be voluntary	84 percent	30 percent	66 percent	76 percent
Groups most frequently targeted in CD program	1. Fast-track management candidates or high-potentials 2. Management trainees	1. Fast-track management candidates or high-potentials 2. Management trainees	1. Fast-track management candidates or high-potentials 2. Management trainees	1. Fast-track management candidates or high-potentials 2. Management trainees
Have two or more full-time CD staff	25 percent	40 percent	33 percent	69 percent
Responsibility for CD	52 percent Employee 25 percent Manager 24 percent Organization	42 percent Employee 30 percent Manager 29 percent Organization	29 percent Employee 36 percent Manager 35 percent Organization	38 percent Employee 35 percent Manager 29 percent Organization
Top five CD practices	1. Tuition reimbursement 2. In-house training and development programs 3. External seminars or workshops 4. Employee orientation programs 5. Job posting	1. In-house training and development programs 2. External seminars or workshops 3. Counseling or career discussions by supervisors or line managers 4. Tuition reimbursement 5. Counseling or career discussions by HR staff	1. Counseling or career discussions by supervisors or line managers 2. External seminars or workshops 3. In-house training and development programs 4. Job assignment 5. Employee orientation programs	1. In-house training and development programs 2. Counseling or career discussions by supervisors or line managers 3. External seminars or workshops 4. Counseling or career discussions by HR staff 5. Interview process
Top two methods of evaluating CD system	1. Informal verbal feedback (64 percent) 2. Questionnaires (33 percent)	1. Informal verbal feedback (71 percent) 2. Questionnaires (35 percent)	1. Informal verbal feedback (67 percent) 2. Data analysis (31 percent)	1. Informal verbal feedback (67 percent) 2. Questionnaires (47 percent)
Rate CD system effective or very effective	29 percent	52 percent	62 percent	58 percent

Note: CD = career development; in some cases totals exceed 100 percent because of rounding off or multiple responses.

Table 6.1. Comparison of U.S. and International Surveys, Cont'd.

Response category	U.S.	Australia	Singapore	Europe
Benefits of CD system	Enhanced employee retention, skill, morale, and empowerment; demonstrated organizational commitment to employees; improved HR planning and selection; better strategic advantage	Improved utilization of human resources; productivity adaptability; stability; competitiveness; compliance; enhanced employee self-determination and employability; personal and professional growth	Greater sense of company direction; more efficient management of human resources; enhanced company image; improved employee motivation, expectations, and retention; better match between organizational and individual needs	Improved utilization of employee talents; enhanced job performance; training of employees to use personnel systems more effectively; preparation of employees to deal with a low-growth environment
Would have done differently	More training and buy-in of managers; better funding and commitment of resources; more systematized implementation, evaluation, and accountability	More training and accountability of managers; individual accountability; formal linkages to other HR systems; greater resources; better marketing and use of task forces; continuous monitoring and evaluation	More training; greater structure and formalization	More top-level support; increased employee involvement and ownership; greater systemization
Future plans for CD system	Expansion and refinement of current programs; greater systematization and integration	Support and training for line managers and staff; formalized HR system links; needs assessment and evaluation; expansion of current programs	Greater structure, formalization, and systemization; expansion of existing programs	Better link to business strategy; improve current programs, employee-organization matching, information systems, and management succession planning programs; more integrated and systemized; better training for managers

| How CD has changed in last decade | Shift toward greater employee responsibility; viewed as results-oriented part of strategic business plan; increased formality and systemization; greater efficiency and range of tools | Increased awareness of CD practices and their benefits and link to corporate strategy; more sophisticated and formalized approaches; increased employee awareness, expectations, and sense of shared responsibility; examination of alternative directions | Greater awareness of importance of CD for employee retention and more efficient use of human resources | More individualistic and dependent on new values; more respected, legitimate, and supported by top management; more systemized and integrated |

Note: CD = career development; in some cases totals exceed 100 percent because of rounding off or multiple responses.

Most respondents across the four samples articulated some version of the following beliefs:

- Senior management feels that career development is an important part of employee development and should be tied in with the organization's strategic plan.
- Career development allows for improved use of employee talents and helps them deal with a low-growth environment, but few supervisors are equipped to hold career discussions.
- Employees' participation in career development should be voluntary.

That is, career development is widely seen as important and beneficial to organizations and their employees, but most companies have problems in implementation, particularly the uncertain or inadequately supported role of managers.

There were some interesting differences in the Singapore profile. Of the four samples, Singapore respondents were in strongest agreement with statements about senior management's belief in career development and the importance of the link with strategy and in weakest agreement that programs should be voluntary. Perhaps this reflects the fact that career development is in an earlier, organization-driven stage of growth in Singapore, whose sociopolitical culture itself emphasizes institutional controls. It may also reflect the fact that employees there are generally accustomed to their employers being in charge of their careers. In any case, of the 70 Singapore respondents that currently had career development, over one-third had had it for more than six years.

A stronger focus on the role of the individual employee came through in the U.S. sample. At the same time, among American respondents there was a weaker perception of senior management buy-in to the importance of career development and of the strategic link than there was in the other samples, as well as a stronger belief that individual employees' use of career development systems should be voluntary. Also, more U.S. respondents saw a problem in most supervisors' ability to hold career discussions. Again, these findings seem to mesh with those on the perceived effectiveness of existing systems.

Comparing Implementations of
Career Development Systems

Along with the focus on upward mobility, all four sets of survey respondents said that the groups most frequently targeted in their career development systems were fast-track management candidates, high-potentials, or management trainees. Globally, it seems, organizations are still relying on a traditional definition of career development as they attempt to facilitate the movement of managers up the corporate ladder.

This traditional focus is underscored in responses to questions about the prevalence of various career development practices. All four samples listed in-house training and development and external seminars or workshops among the top five practices, and none included in the top five such self-assessment and career planning tools as career workshops or workbooks — practices that help "solid citizens" as well as high-potential employees and that are more geared to an environment in which up is not the sole direction of career growth.

Significantly, only the U.S. respondents did not include counseling or career discussions (with supervisors or line managers) among the top five practices. While direct causality cannot safely be inferred, we can speculate that this lack of inclusion is related to the stronger belief, among U.S. respondents, that few managers are equipped to hold career discussions. Perhaps the perceived lack of skill in this area is related in part to decreased opportunities for practice. This, in turn, would seem to reflect some ambivalence, on the part of senior managers, about the need for increased training in employee coaching or on-the-job coaching experience. While senior managers may support career development philosophically, they do not always back up their managers in practical ways. Is a Catch-22 at work here? We think there may well be.

We noted earlier that U.S. respondents placed more emphasis on individual employee responsibility, whereas Singapore respondents strongly emphasized the organization. This finding emerged again when we asked organizations to distribute responsibility for career development among employees, managers, and organizations. While all four samples' respondents clearly see career development as a shared responsibility, the U.S. sample gave employees over half of the responsibility, while the others gave lower percentages for employees (Singapore was the lowest, at 29 percent). Moreover, Singapore was the only sample in which over 30 percent of this responsibility was apportioned to the organization.

There was a wide range of responses to the question of the commitment of resources (staff) to career development. Respondents were asked to indicate how many staffpeople they had devoted full-time to career development. Only one-quarter of U.S. respondents reported two or more full-time career development staff; this was the lowest percentage of the four samples. The European sample had the highest: almost 70 percent. This divergence in responses could result from differences in organizational commitment to career development, beliefs about who is chiefly responsible, or how long the career development system has existed.

Comparing Outcomes

By now, we should perhaps not be surprised at differences between the U.S. sample and the others about the perceived effectiveness of career development systems. Respondents were asked to rate their system's effectiveness on a five-point scale. Only 29 percent of responding U.S. organizations rated their systems as effective or very effective, as opposed to 52 percent for Australia, 62 percent for Singapore, and 58 percent for Europe. On the basis of available data, we propose three factors that may account for the lower U.S. ratings:

1. Fewer staff available to support career development systems
2. A weaker link between career development and strategic business plans

3. Reduced incidence of managers holding career discussions with their employees

These factors may be interacting in complex ways, creating something of a chicken-or-egg dilemma for those trying to diagnose current obstacles. Moreover, while it is not possible to deduce this from the survey, it may also be that U.S. expectations of career development are higher simply because it has been in evidence longer.

An unfortunately uniform finding across all four samples was the lack of formal evaluations of career development systems. All four sets of respondents listed informal verbal feedback from participants as by far the most prevalent method. Questionnaires were the next most common method for all but the Singapore companies (data analysis was their second form).

The various groups cited a wide range of benefits to both the organization and individual employees, regardless of effectiveness ratings and notwithstanding the narrow focus of the initial drivers of career development. These benefits were largely in line with some of the attitude statements noted earlier. Commonly cited benefits included better planning and management of human resources; increased competitive or strategic advantage; and enhanced employee skill, motivation, and retention.

Asked what they would have done differently, respondents in all four samples typically named more systemization, accountability, and evaluation; more training and involvement of managers; and greater commitment of resources. These priorities were also reflected in statements about future plans: across the four samples, respondents indicated plans to increase systemization and to expand current programs. They also mentioned building linkages and providing better support and training for managers in their pivotal role in career development.

Finally, when asked to look at how the organizational career development field has changed over the last decade, respondents noted a greater awareness of the benefits and importance of career development to both individual employees and organizational strategy, as well as the greater range and sophistication of career development tools.

Thus, despite the traditional management-oriented focus of current practice, there was a consensus in the field internationally about the need to broaden and systemize career programs and to link them to business strategy so as to benefit both individuals and organizations.

As we have seen in this chapter, responses to the survey from American, Australian, Singaporean, and European samples were noticeably similar. Important differences were also evident, however, and one unanswered question is how much they reflect actual differences versus different sampling techniques. Perhaps future research will shed light on this question as the field of organizational career development continues to operate in a global context.

In the next chapter, we look in detail at twelve organizations with career development systems. Both the similarities and the diversity of these systems suggest that practitioners have been continuously learning and building on new understandings of organizational career development and reaping the benefits.

PART TWO

The State
of the Art

CHAPTER 7

Making It Work:
Profiles of Successful
Career Development Systems

Part One of this book underscores the view, held by many organizations at home and abroad, that career development activities need to be systemized. That is, their components must be linked by a common set of terms and assumptions, and the resulting system needs to be integrated with the organization's other HR activities and with overall business goals. For most HR practitioners and a growing number of line as well as senior managers, the systemizing of separate but related activities is seen as a way of leveraging or capitalizing on disparate strengths to increase their overall impact.

Successful career development systems typically entail an active partnership among employees, managers, and organizations, each with a particular set of roles and responsibilities to carry out if the entire system is to function effectively. Within this partnership, employees are responsible for initiating the self-assessment and development process; managers are charged with facilitating and encouraging this process; and organizations support the process by providing tools, resources, and ongoing endorsement and visibility.

To examine the state of the art of organizational career development, we interviewed individuals in diverse organizational settings, asking them about what might be called their strategic or "macro" focus. This perspective deals with the following:

- The business needs that impel the design of a career development system
- The system's evolution, components, and linkages
- The roles of the various partners or stakeholders
- The system's effects on organizational life

In this chapter we highlight this macro focus, presenting the central findings of our case studies of twelve organizations. (The interview guide that was used to conduct case study interviews is included in Appendix B.) Our goal was to spotlight successes and obstacles so that readers might gain from the experience of others. We have ordered the case studies in a general progression, from organizations in the early stages of development to those positioning or linking existing resources or activities, to those that have been in place as more or less integrated systems for several years. Our aim is to present, in an accurate and useful manner, the process through which a career development initiative evolves.

The organizations we chose for these case studies tended to be large, for larger companies typically have more resources to devote to career development and thus offer richer data to researchers. Access was also important: we chose organizations with which we were familiar so that we could amass as much current information and detail as possible. These twelve organizations are:

Amoco Production Company
BP Exploration
Overseas Telecommunications Company Ltd.
3M
NCR
Baxter Healthcare Pty. Ltd.
U.S. General Accounting Office (GAO)
Bechtel Group
Kodak Company
AT&T
Boeing
Corning

- Career development as a strategy for profitability and competitiveness
- Four-phase planning and implementation process involving middle and senior managers and more than 300 employees across the organization
- Career discussions and individual development plans supported by complementary HR practices
- Paradigm shift toward career development aligned with strategic business objectives

Background

Amoco Production Company (APC), a wholly owned subsidiary of Amoco Corporation, is a worldwide explorer and producer of oil and gas with approximately 14,000 employees. APC developed its career development system for two basic reasons: to improve profitability and competitiveness and to help employees define and pursue their individual visions of career success. The company believes that its overall capability will be enhanced when individual capabilities, interests, and aspirations are aligned with the organization's business objectives. APC's career development system is seen as a primary means of achieving this alignment.

Implementation

APC's process for implementing its system involved four integrated phases:

> Phase I
> > Initial input and study
> > Steering committee formation
> > Advisory group formation

Phase II
   Assessment of current and future state
   External research
Phase III
   Design
   Development
Phase IV
   Customization
   Implementation

Phase I. In 1988, an all-employee survey identified several issues affecting employee and organizational capability: employee involvement, recognition and reward, and career development. Since 1988, a series of organizationwide task forces has addressed each issue. The third in this series, the organization effectiveness (OE) steering committee, met for the first time in November 1990. Its charter was to design, develop, and implement a system that became known as Amoco Career Management (ACM).

The OE steering committee was composed of middle to senior-level managers (fifteen in all) who represented all segments of the organization. The group was chaired by an executive vice president and supported by two subject-matter experts from the HR division. Each committee member was charged with establishing an employee advisory group. In this way, over 300 employees were actively involved in the committee's work.

The committee met monthly, two days at a time, throughout the project. Advisory groups met on average once or twice a month. Phase I ended in January 1990.

Phase II. The steering committee's work began in Phase II, when it initiated a self-education process to learn about the current state of career development within APC, best practices in the industry, and related HR practices. The committee also studied in some detail the competitive environment within which APC was operating. Finally, the committee exhaustively solicited and incorporated information, concerns, and recommendations from employees.

All of this input was conceptually aligned with a vision of the future state of career development that was shared and disseminated throughout the company. Phase II ended in August 1991.

Phase III. Based on the work in Phase II and the identification of a desired future state, the OE steering committee began the ACM design phase in August 1991. The committee reorganized into four design teams:

1. Self-assessment and training
2. Overall process and accountability
3. Career discussion and individual development planning
4. Information

Eventually a fifth subcommittee (the complementary practices team) was formed to assess and offer recommendations for improvements to other HR practices. This group looked specifically at promotion guidelines, job classification and evaluation, and dual or nonsupervisory career ladders. To ensure needed expertise and adequate employee and organizational involvement, each subcommittee added members who were not from the steering committee.

Phase IV. When the steering committee neared the end of the design phase, an external consultant was hired to help package and roll out the ACM process. (To that point, no consultants had been involved.) Hiring the consultant inaugurated the final phase in February 1992.

To support this effort, the steering committee identified a four-person implementation team. This team, headed by a steering committee member, contained one HR professional, one training and organization development professional, and one former engineer who had migrated into the technical training area. These four members served full time on the implementation team and kept the steering committee informed of their progress at monthly meetings.

Essentially, the implementation team brought to life the

design recommendations of the steering committee's design subcommittees. They also spearheaded an effort to customize the ACM process for international and field locations.

The ACM implementation process is outlined in Figure 7.1.

Needs Assessment

The steering committee used two methods to determine needs: (1) employee focus groups and advisory groups to identify employee issues, and (2) company strategic and business plans to identify company needs. The following employee needs were identified:

- More input into personal career direction and more say in decisions that affect careers
- Greater ability to make and be recognized for business contributions
- More knowledge about how the career development process works
- Greater opportunity for both professional and personal development

Company needs included achieving strategic and business objectives and improved strategic staffing—getting the right person in the right job at the right time.

At the outset, the steering committee decided that the improved career development process should apply to all Amoco employees worldwide. (Although this approach has not been altered, no final decision has been reached on whether to use a pilot approach.) Preimplementation publicity entailed a series of one-page bulletins spaced about one month apart. These were designed to clarify the purpose of the emerging system, its elements, and its intended outcomes.

System Components

The key feature of ACM is individual career discussions between employees and their supervisors. This discussion is then

Figure 7.1. ACM Development Process.

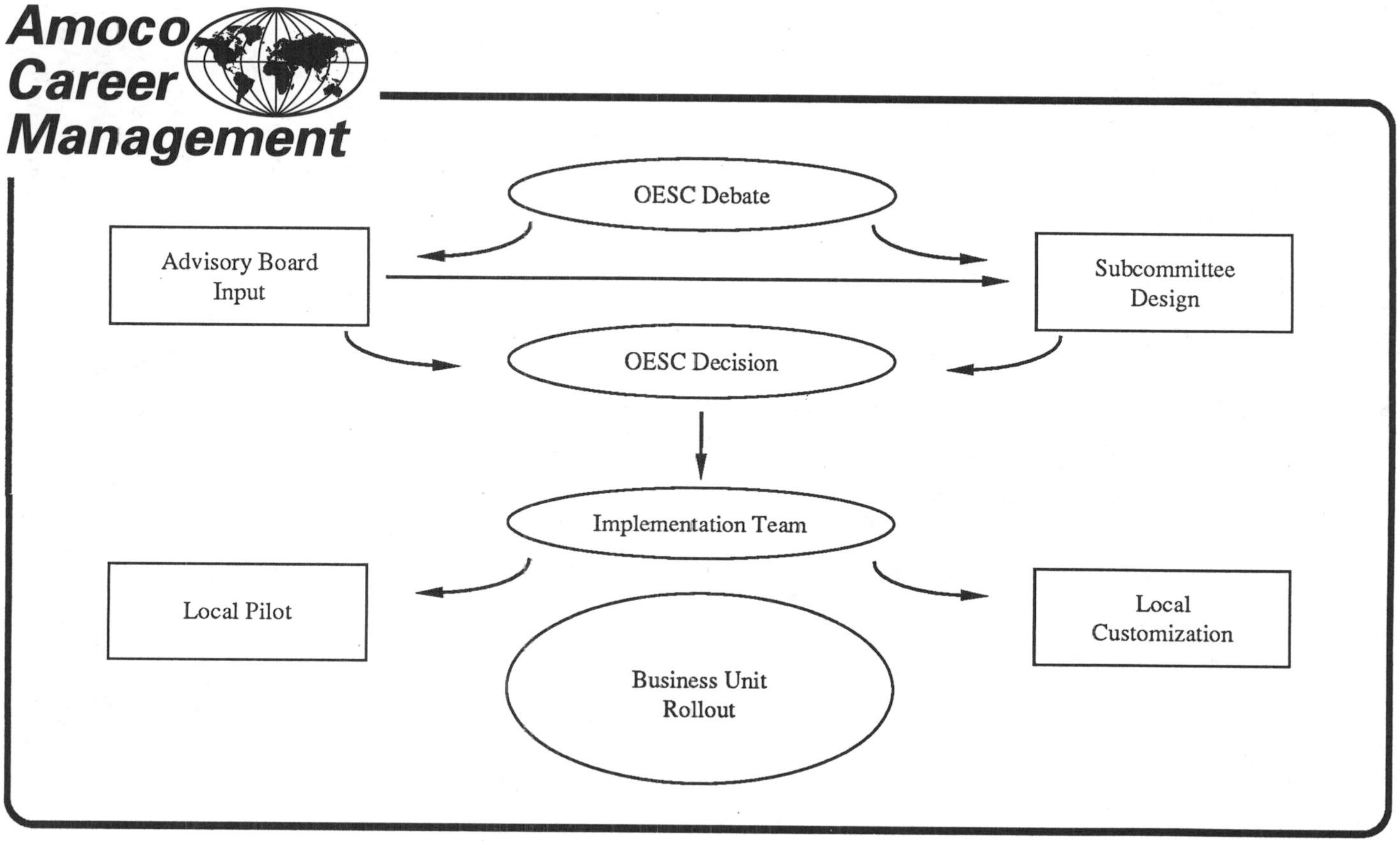

Source: Amoco Production Company. Reprinted with permission.

documented by an individual development plan. Supporting features are employee and supervisory training, job posting or canvassing (internally referred to as self-nomination), and management feedback and review. The features and process of ACM are diagrammed in Figure 7.2. These features were chosen because they accord with the steering committee's beliefs about the roles that employees, supervisors, and the company play in an effective career development system.

- Employees are responsible for assessments of self and organization, personal goal setting, and action planning.
- Supervisors are responsible for providing perspective, advice, and support.
- The company is responsible for providing an environment conducive to effective career development, establishing strategic direction, and fostering professional growth.

Results

If ACM is working as planned, employees will have the information and support to identify their personal career vision, develop an action plan to achieve that vision, and attain or pursue desired opportunities. The individual development plan format is designed to take employees through a process that helps them identify their vision of career success, understand how that vision fits with company needs and expectations, produce a development plan, and gather feedback from their immediate supervisor and other levels of management as appropriate. This process should benefit the company as well as the individual, through better alignment of employee competencies with business goals and creation of a more motivated workforce. One major issue to date is that the process requires a significant commitment of time, especially on the part of supervisors.

The ACM process is viewed as a system because its elements are integrated with each other and with other Amoco strategic and HR initiatives and practices, in particular performance management and continuous improvement. Additionally, efforts are under way to align ACM more closely with

Figure 7.2. Amoco Career Management.

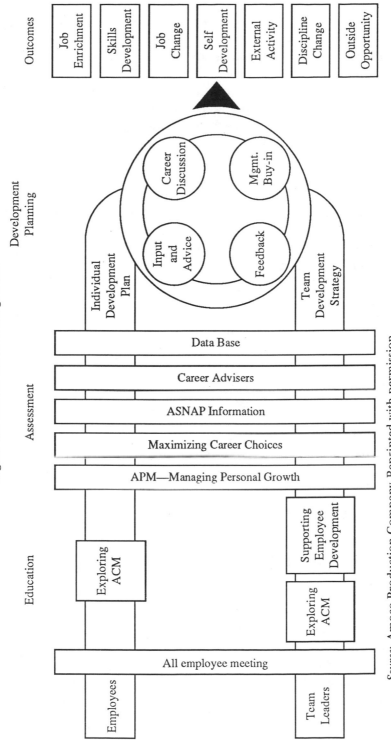

Source: Amoco Production Company. Reprinted with permission.

succession planning, diversity, and promotion and reward systems.

The focus of these efforts is not on upward mobility; rather, it is on development, contribution, and impact. Work in this area is still under way; the key issue is paradigm shift. Career and performance management systems, continuous improvement, and several other related processes are designed to promote competitive advantage, not simply individual advancement. Older HR systems were designed for an older paradigm in which career success was defined by the frequency and rapidity of promotions. In some cases these systems still reward and foster such thinking. An effort is under way to reassess such systems and bring them into alignment with current strategic objectives.

[BP] BP EXPLORATION

- Development as a business strategy
- Local and global design teams
- Line-driven process
- Consistent message to all employees regarding career development and their responsibilities

Background

BP Exploration (BPX), one of three main business streams of the BP Company, began revising its career development processes in the late 1980s as part of a corporate change effort. The company needed to find ways to adjust to a destabilized, low-growth industry environment and move away from a traditional "career ladder" mentality. Career development was seen not only as a response to strong employee interest but also as a means of bolstering the organization's strategic plans for a more flexible, responsive workforce.

BPX implemented career development through local and international design teams using a pilot approach. It targeted all staff, moving away from a focus primarily on management-track employees. Needs were determined through dialogues with and within local organizations. A program and approach were piloted in one location and then extensively reviewed by the global team. Career development, as an initiative, was publicized through companywide briefs, and programs were publicized through efforts of individual business units.

System Components

The key features of BPX's career development system (or personal development system, as it is now called) include:

- Career discussions between managers and staff
- Employee and manager workshops
- A career development handbook
- Personal development planning centers

The system emphasizes networking and ongoing personal responsibility for career and personal development. It also makes use of job rotations—shifting assignments to support individual career plans and stimulate motivation.

One of the pluses of the system is that it offers a consistent corporate message about careers and personal development with everyone taking part. The system is linked to other HR processes, such as performance appraisal and staff development. Initially viewed as being owned by HR, it has now progressed so that line managers have near-total responsibility and ownership.

Results

BPX's career development system has become part of the business process, although management feels that the link between career development and business planning has to be strengthened further. The system's most important effect to date has been changing the view of who is responsible for career development, placing greater emphasis on the individual. Another effect has been a broadening of the focus from management-track employees to all employees. There is greater awareness, throughout BPX, of the importance of personal development planning for all employees.

The system has been evaluated via informal verbal feedback from participants as well as interviews, questionnaires, upward feedback for supervisors and managers, and reviews of individual plans. System designers and implementers say that one way BPX could have developed its system differently in the early stages is by building an infrastructure in tandem with and in support of the new processes. Future plans call for a continued focus on a flexible structure for implementation and for strengthening the alignment between personal and business goals; the emphasis here is on building dual success—both personal and organizational.

BPX believes that its plans are in line with changes in the field as a whole. Formal ladders and traditional career structures have declined, and there is a greater emphasis on flexibility in skill and knowledge acquisition and less emphasis on long-term, one-company careers with automatic progression for time in grade.

OVERSEAS TELECOMMUNICATIONS COMPANY LTD.

- Planned development process for salespeople in a rapidly changing industry
- Linkage between business and HR strategies
- Plans to increase involvement and development of managers
- Focus on continuous improvement

Background

In the telecommunications business since 1946, the Overseas Telecommunications Company (OTC) of Australia has enjoyed the status of a government-owned monopoly. (In 1989, OTC was converted from a statutory authority to a wholly government-owned public company.) It has thus been cushioned from many of the changes occurring in the industry globally and in the

Australian economy in particular and has continued with its expansion planning.

OTC's head office is in Sydney, and it currently has eight international liaison offices. There are 2,250 employees, of which 1,500 are technicians and engineers. OTC has recently been marketing its services overseas, garnering major contracts in Laos, Vietnam, Cambodia, Hong Kong, the former Soviet Union, and the Philippines.

Since the late 1980s, OTC's financial performance has been impressive. In January 1992, the company merged with Australia's domestic carrier, Telecom, another government-owned business with 72,000 employees. (This merger formed the Australian and Overseas Telecommunications Corporation.)

Facing a climate of deregulation, intense competition, mergers, and increased global business activities, OTC adopted in 1990 a development strategy for its sales force. The so-called Account Management Accreditation Scheme (AMAS) was designed to help fifty account managers (based in Australia and abroad) position OTC as the preferred provider of telecommunications solutions.

The perceived benefits of this scheme to OTC are:

- Improved customer satisfaction
- Better-defined process of development for account managers within the framework of corporate goals
- Focused development of account managers to a level of superior customer contact skills, business acumen, and applications knowledge
- Improved retention and reduced turnover of staff
- A standardized framework to assess and evaluate skills development

For account managers, the perceived benefits include:

- Improved opportunities for job satisfaction
- A clearer understanding of organizational direction and values

- Improved opportunities for development
- Improved credibility in the marketplace

Implementation

The needs assessment for the AMAS occurred in two stages. Stage 1 involved a skills audit, in early 1990, of seven functions within the sales group: commercial account manager, national account manager, regional sales manager, manager of telesales, manager of sales support, manager of customer network planning, and sales executive. Stage 2 extracted two sales functions as the initial focus of the AMAS: the national account managers, responsible for major corporate customer groups, and the commercial account managers, responsible for smaller customers.

This process was pioneered by an advisory group known as the stakeholders, including senior business and sales managers, marketing executives, and HR managers. They helped define the roles of national and commercial account managers. An analysis of the behaviors, skills, and attitudes associated with these roles provided a skills profile for a model account manager. This skills profile in turn created a framework for determining clear standards of expected behaviors, the basis for a needs analysis, priorities for training requirements, and tailoring of development activities to individual needs.

The AMAS was publicized to staff through presentations, inclusion of the AMAS outline in induction programs, and distribution of AMAS policy to other divisions within OTC. It was carefully promoted as a developmental process rather than a staff appraisal process. A preassessment required both the sales manager and the account manager to evaluate the account manager's level of competence against an inventory of skills, behaviors, and attitudes that reflected the skills profile. The account manager's skill requirements were then discussed and agreed on during a counseling session.

The existing process is shown in Figure 7.3. Overall, the AMAS is considered a serious attempt to implement a career development system that is linked to business and HR strategy, including the company's performance review scheme.

Results

The AMAS is a new system, and its success cannot yet be assessed fully. Nevertheless, end-of-year evaluations indicate that the overall performance of account managers has improved in varying degrees as a result of added on-the-job experience and training. Major successes so far have been the actual introduction of the scheme in the first year and data gathering to improve the process. In addition, the effects of the AMAS on employees, managers, and OTC as a whole have been positive. Already, various divisions and work groups within the company have shown a keen interest in adopting similar processes. Employees are now able to develop individualized career development plans in consultation with their managers, and the sales training coordinator, who is not part of AMAS, helps clarify the system for various managers and participants.

At this early stage, the AMAS appears to serve as a model for an entire systems approach to organizational career development within OTC. Every effort is being made to review and acknowledge progress in an ongoing manner by constructing solid communication lines among participants, managers, and system administrators. OTC also recognizes the importance of maintaining the enthusiasm of target audiences and enlisting the support of new managers.

In hindsight, AMAS designers feel that progress could have been accelerated by involving line managers more in the initial design and supplementing the process with resources and training to assist managers in performing their coaching and counseling role. Formal skills development of managers began in 1992 in the areas of counseling and coaching.

Opportunities exist to expand career development throughout OTC. Past change processes, such as total customer service and total quality management, have generated positive career development outcomes. Also, as part of the review process for the AMAS, for example, the skills audit will include clear measurement of standard behaviors.

Figure 7.3. The AMAS Process.

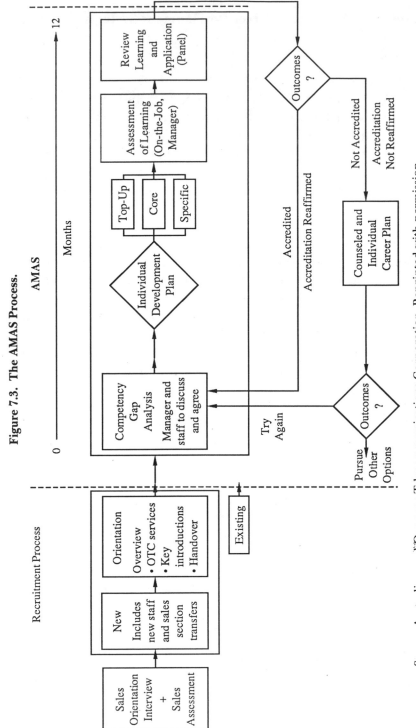

Source: Australian and Overseas Telecommunications Corporation. Reprinted with permission.

- Linkage and integration of existing tools and resources
- Leveraging of internal talent
- Focus on development and lateral mobility
- Outcomes: enhanced communication and productivity

Background

Management at 3M has actively addressed the career development needs of its employees for a number of years. Since the mid 1980s, the company's career counseling group has offered individual career counseling, tests and assessment, and career workshops; through an HR review process, employees have been assessed by their supervisors and the supervisors' managers. Data on job suitability and career potential are gathered, computerized, and used for internal searches for candidates.

The relatively new career resources department is now systemizing and coordinating career development interventions. The company has historically focused more on appraisal and HR planning than on specific elements of employee career development, and the new interventions emphasize the balance between the needs of the organization and those of the employee.

System Components

The major new career development interventions at 3M are:

- The job information system
- The performance appraisal and development process
- A personal career management manual
- Supervisor and employee workshops
- The "consensus review" process
- Career counseling
- Career modules
- Partner relocations

- Tuition refunds
- Outplacement

Together they constitute an effective career development system.

Job Information System (JIS). For several years, 3M's national employee opinion polls had shown that employees wanted more information on career opportunities. Thus, the climate was clearly right for the job information system, piloted in late 1989. Employees' reactions were quite positive, and the pilot program was extended. The system has since been implemented across the company (see Chapter Eight). Its piloting involved many months of planning on the part of a task force composed of HR, line, and staff personnel.

Performance Appraisal and Development Process (PADP). The PADP process involves employees at all levels (exempt and non-exempt) and within all functions. It was instituted for exempt employees in 1989 and for nonexempts in 1990. (When it was extended to nonexempts, meetings and training were offered to this population.)

Each employee receives a copy of an employee input worksheet that is used for the coming year. Employees record how they see the content of their jobs and define the four or five major result areas and expectations for the year. The worksheet also includes a job improvement plan and a career development plan.

Employees then meet with their supervisors to review the worksheet and agree on job content, major result areas and expectations, and a development process for the coming year. The worksheet can be modified as needed throughout the year. The process is designed to focus on performance strengths and improvement areas (in addition to job content and results achieved), based on "how-to" factors related to goal achievement. At the end of the year, the supervisor completes the performance appraisal, drawing on the performance elements and result areas that were previously established and discussed.

Before the PADP process was implemented, the 3M appraisal process did not focus on specific planning requirements for development. This process has reinforced the concept that the employee has primary responsibility for job and career development while the supervisor serves as a key resource, providing counseling, advice, and coaching.

Significantly, the PADP process has helped facilitate supervisor-employee communication at 3M. Performance discussions are held at varying intervals (normally at least once a quarter), and employees are encouraged to take the initiative in informal discussions with their supervisors as needed.

Personal Career Management Manual. A personal career management manual is distributed to each employee. It outlines the shared responsibilities of employees, supervisors, and the organization with regard to career development. The manual also defines available corporate career development resources and provides a matrix of possible employee career concerns.

Supervisor Workshops. A one-day workshop helps supervisors understand the complex career environment in which they operate and to sharpen their skills and their understanding of the various roles they play (counselor/coach, referral agent, and so on). Supervisors' responses have been very positive, and a process of workshop followups is planned. The workshop has reinforced the idea that people development is an essential part of a supervisor's job. This strong development focus is also emphasized through the peformance appraisal process. Although general performance is included in all employees' appraisals, additional ones have been created for supervisors. The first of these added factors is "employee development and managing."

Employee Workshops. As early as 1978, 3M had career growth workshops designed to help employees look at their own careers. Revised in 1990, the employee workshop is now a two-day offering called "Career Directions" that emphasizes self-assessment, goals, and action plans and the benefits of lateral as well as promotional job experiences. An optional third day focuses on internal job-seeking skills, preparing resumes, interviews, and so on; also included is information on effectively using the JIS.

Some supervisors initially feared that the workshop would actually encourage people to leave their jobs. In fact, however, most employees who have gone through the workshop report that they are now more satisfied in their current career paths and have an increased awareness of how to manage their careers more realistically. Job enrichment is a big emphasis; the basic approach is that "career development begins with your current assignment."

Employees as asked followup questions after participating in the workshop, and their action plans are tracked (with supervisor involvement). To aid employees and supervisors alike, the HR area contains a library of career-related videos, and business books on career topics are also available in various 3M libraries. While the company is not currently using career development software, career-related computer services are being investigated.

Consensus Review Process and Succession Planning. This sequential process culminates with group vice presidents meeting with their respective divisional vice presidents to discuss elements of performance and the potential of their managers. The process affects ratings and the HR review process and thus has implications for job moves, development, and promotion. It is an important information-sharing tool as well as another source of feedback on performance for managers. The process begins with directors holding meetings with their managers, executive directors with their directors, and divisional or staff vice presidents with executive directors.

Tied closely to the consensus review process is an executive-level succession planning program that has been in place for six to seven years. This highly successful program is being considered for extension to the middle-managerial level.

Career Counseling. While employees are encouraged to go to their supervisors first to discuss career issues, professional career counseling is also available. (In addition, an HR manager is also assigned to every division as a resource.) The counseling function includes a number of assessment tools. Employees may be referred to career counseling from supervisors, employee assistance counselors, or an HR manager, or they may go on their own. Counseling is typically used as a followup to the employee workshop, for an employee seeking to develop an educational plan, for critiques of resumes and interviewing skills, for consideration of career alternatives following a disability, or for an employee seeking a job or career redirection.

Career Modules. Acting as internal consultants, career development staff have developed modules on topics of interest and have presented them around the company. A popular module deals with plateauing. Module presenters include information on the career resources department and available internal career development resources.

Partner Relocation. The career development staff coordinates the corporatewide partner relocation program. This has become an important feature because of dual-career couples, although the program also addresses options for nonworking partners.

Tuition Refund. This program has been in place for many years. It covers the costs of courses and fees that are related to an employee's current job as well as all courses and fees in a job-related or career-related degree program.

Outplacement. Internal outplacement is coordinated through 3M's Employees in Transition program. Employees whose jobs are eliminated automatically participate in a career transition workshop and also receive individual transition counseling. This approach has retained the productivity of thousands of employees over the last eight years. External outplacement of terminated employees is also provided on request from management.

Results

As it attempts to integrate employee and organizational needs more accurately and realistically, 3M has experienced improved productivity as well as greater employee involvement in meeting corporate goals. Supervisors have gained confidence in career guidance and further credibility in improved communication with employees. Career development services and programs at 3M are addressing a real need. Career development and current job improvement are separate but interrelated, and because the company has addressed each specifically, it has maximized the benefits of both.

An AT&T Company

- Goal: to improve internal movement of information systems personnel
- Needs assessment and benchmarking by a task force
- Focus on linking existing career development activities
- Planned expansion of job profiles, prototype development, and succession planning

Background

NCR develops, produces, markets, and supports information systems and services for worldwide markets. An AT&T company, NCR employs 55,000 people.

NCR's most recent career development efforts began in 1987 as a way of enhancing the careers of internal information systems (IS) personnel, who were often spending their careers in one part of the company. There was a perception that these employees had narrow business experience and had worked only in a marketing or development and production organization. The belief was that high-level IS personnel needed a broad business background; however, it was also difficult for them to move laterally within the IS function, and this created a kind of

Catch-22 for these employees. In addition, IS roles and job requirements for the 1990s needed to be defined.

At the time that an effort was launched to foster the internal movement of IS personnel, NCR was already offering the following career development programs:

- A career development workshop
- A workbook for employees
- Succession planning and high-potential programs
- Management development
- Job posting
- Performance management
- Tuition reimbursement
- Training and development programs (especially for sales positions, systems engineers, and field engineers)

The existing career development workshop focused on career and life planning; it lacked a formal linkage to the organization and its business goals. Gradually, NCR defined a new career development process, identifying necessary tools and practices and how to integrate them.

Many managers were interviewed individually about their needs, and a task force of IS managers and personnel staff was formed to serve as advisers. Needs or issues identified included communication across the organization about jobs and opportunities; movement of people; and redefinition of IS jobs, functions, and roles for the 1990s. Facilitated job modeling (using a research model) helped the redefinition effort within the three functional areas of IS.

In the late 1980s, a career development process and workshops were designed for managers and employees. The focus was on career discussions. A one-day manager workshop was first piloted and revised, and pre- and post-evaluations (and "smile sheets") showed that it was successful. The existing employee workshop was then revamped to complement the manager workshop. Later, executive officers approved a proposal to link existing development tools to the new career development system and to implement the process across the company.

System Components

Currently, almost all NCR business units in the United States have someone trained to deliver workshops and work with employees on career issues. Training of trainers is offered to HR people in the field; they then make presentations to managers regarding developmental tools and career discussions. In many organizations, upper management endorses a policy stating that it is mandatory for managers to attend workshops; the program is then rolled out for employees, whose workshops are voluntary. Employees are encouraged to take responsibility for their own career development, and managers are expected to support the process.

Managers' concerns initially centered on lack of know-how and the availability of information. Over time, their concerns have been related mainly to organizational information, which is now being better integrated into the process. For example, the IS and finance and administration areas offer job modeling and job profiles; engineering, sales, and systems engineering do the same, and they also create prototypes for development information. For example, for high-level job series, prototypes include information on skills, requirements, progression requirements, and measurement criteria.

The career development workshops are designed to change the corporate culture with respect to the manager's role and also to prepare managers for career discussions. An acknowledged missing piece is a system of accountability and rewards, which NCR is now trying to implement.

Results

In addition to accountability, system designers say that evaluation also needs more attention. Although divisions are encouraged to administer pre/post surveys, there has not yet been much followup.

Several functional areas (such as personnel, finance, and administration) have begun a management review process in which upper-level directors review information about all employees in their area (not just high-potentials). This information is used for planning and development. The process may be expanded to other areas of the company.

While job posting is a helpful tool for providing organizational information, NCR managers feel that it works best if it is linked to other career development interventions. The company is currently implementing an electronic job posting system that will make information about job openings available to managers and individuals at their personal computers. It is hoped that this ready availability will broaden the use of the job posting system.

The links between career development and the high-potential program and succession planning are strong. Executive-level managers review succession for all officers and their direct reports. Development plans are sent out directly to high-potentials, and they and their managers fill them out. The reaction to this process has been extremely positive, and it will eventually be put into practice for all employees. Another linkage is the integrated personnel process, through which job modeling (similar to competency analysis) is used to link all HR systems.

BAXTER HEALTHCARE PTY. LTD.

- Local fine tuning of corporatewide systems
- Career development for selection, retention, and maintenance of competitive advantage
- Managers as target group, based on needs assessment
- Expansion of performance appraisal to focus more on development
- Workshops, counseling, and other resources
- Outcomes: enhanced recruitment and retention, improved communication

Background

Baxter Healthcare Pty. Ltd. is an Australia-based subsidiary of the Baxter World Trade Corporation. The corporation's major business is the manufacture, supply, and distribution of products and services for healthcare providers; it is a leader in this market. The Australian business services New Zealand and various other areas within the South Pacific basin. Its current workforce is 530 (150 salaried and 380 nonsalaried employees).

Baxter (Australia) has a career development and performance management system that is firmly established with its culture; much of it originated in the larger Baxter Corporation. The success of the Australian company's career development system is due in part to the skills and efforts of local Australian staff in innovating and fine tuning available system tools, such as the Performax performance profile, various HR programs, and total quality management.

The impetus for career development in Baxter Healthcare was the recognition that to be both competitive and attractive to high-calibre professionals, the company needed to provide a system that would meet employees' career needs. Desired outcome was an improvement in entry standards coupled with retention of key staff.

Implementation

Structured and unstructured discussions were held with employees of all levels and disciplines. Baxter made use of counseling sessions, performance reviews, an informal grapevine, and ad hoc feedback during recruitment and training activities.

During the needs analysis, begun in 1985, data were gathered by members of the HR group with the support of junior, middle, and senior managers. As a result of this analysis, Baxter decided to introduce a wider and more relevant career development program for supervisory, junior, and middle managers. This group represented the most important target, and expectations of the individual employees were greatest.

System Components

The career development program system was launched in 1989 with the introduction of a revised performance appraisal system. The previous system, in use since the early 1980s, had involved an annual review of performance by the employee's managers. Managers prepared their performance reviews in isolation from employees; reviews were delivered to each employee with his or her salary recommendation. Many employees thought that the program was of interest only for its salary outcomes and commented on the weakness of the program and the failure of the Australian organization to consider career issues.

Thus, an initial change was bringing in the Baxter corporate HR group to implement the performance management and career development (PMCD) program and the employee development review (EDR), which encouraged greater employee and manager involvement. Pilot programs as such were not used, as the group size of 150 employees was seen as manageable and there was a clear organizational expectation that the implementation process should not be seen as selective.

Baxter's career development system now includes the following:

- An annual performance management and career development review
- A biannual employee development review
- Career assessment workshops (as required)
- Individual counseling by both internal and external consultants (as required)
- Resources such as books and testing instruments

These components have produced a system with structure but without unnecessary formality. Employees can enter the process at any point, first getting oriented to the resources and options and gradually developing confidence in the system. By the time a salaried staff member is recruited, he or she can have a career development plan for the first twelve months' service that has been developed in conjunction with the employee's manager.

All facets of the system are linked to broader HR and business systems (see Figure 7.4). For example, the performance

Figure 7.4. Baxter Healthcare's HR System.

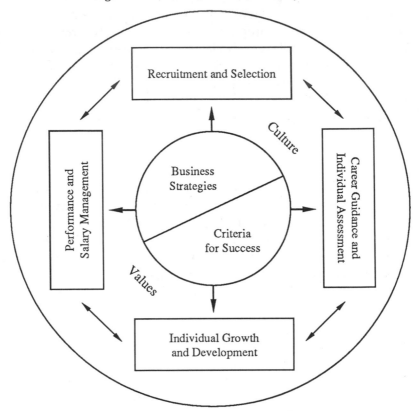

Source: Baxter Healthcare Pty. Ltd. Reprinted with permission.

review produces outputs that are linked to specific components of the career development system, as does the employee development review process. Because the system provides increased control for employees, a wide range of individually designed career development plans has been implemented.

Publicity for the various components was provided largely through training courses. Resistance to implementation was reduced by stressing that career development is much more than promotion and that Baxter provides a wide range of services to employees who are prepared to accept responsibility for their own development.

Results

The effects of career development at Baxter have included:

- Low turnover (the lowest in this industry segment)
- Reduction in complaints about the career development system
- Improved communication between employees and managers on career issues
- Increased awareness and ongoing positive reinforcement that employees are responsible for their own career development
- Increasing level and range of sponsorship by senior management of career development and other HR activities
- Positive labor-market feedback that Baxter's ability to compete for and attract applicants is tied to the career development program

Baxter has yet to begin a substantial evaluation of the program. A current concern is that the validity of the evaluation will be reduced by blurred boundaries between career development and other HR systems.

One of Baxter's key goals is to continue serving internal customers with a flexible program. A large challenge is to increase the publicity and visibility of career development to key opinion leaders by improving its linkage with other HR and business systems.

Notwithstanding this challenge, Baxter's system provides evidence that career development can generate a cooperative partnership between the individual employee and the organization. With its career development system, Baxter has achieved a lower staff turnover and increased sales and profitability while simultaneously increasing customer loyalty.

GAO

- Multiservice, on-site career center staffed by professional counselors

- Separate from but linked to counseling and consultation services
- Carefully positioned as a positive, practical resource
- Growing visibility and usage
- Services available to regional offices nationwide

Background

The U.S. General Accounting Office (GAO) has long been a leader among federal agencies in providing career counseling and job-search assistance services to employees. Services are provided by highly credentialed counselors and psychologists, and the GAO has remained a much sought-after internship site for counseling professionals in training.

One issue that has challenged this agency has been positioning and marketing its services to its employees. The career counseling function is attached to a unit that provides personal counseling on anything from substance abuse to marital problems. For many years, the two functions were linked physically by a common entrance and also shared a common name: the Office of Counseling and Career Development (OCCD). While this linkage provided certain significant advantages—the ability to address often interrelated personal and career issues through interstaff referrals, peer training, and other sharing of resources—it also raised some problems. Many employees were unwilling to seek needed career assistance because of the stigma attached to personal counseling; they were afraid to come for help with a job search, for example, because they were concerned that others would think they had emotional problems. Moreover, many employees were confused or put off by the term "career development," believing it had little relevance to their practical career exploration or job-search needs.

System Components

In 1991 the agency's career services were repositioned as a separate entity and named after one of the most popular components, the career resource center (CRC). The CRC is still part of the OCCD, but it has a completely separate entrance and a separate phone number. This has eased the stigma of counseling. At the same time CRC services have been actively marketed to promote the idea that career development is a positive and normal activity. Posters and brochures advertise the wide range of CRC services throughout GAO:

- Individual confidential career counseling for career exploration, assessment, or job-search assistance
- Noontime seminars and ongoing workshops on self-assessment, career exploration, and job-search techniques
- A career resource library, including books, catalogues, cassettes, videos, and career guidance software
- A job information station with job announcements and listings, a GAO alumni referral network, and a computer program for resume and Form 171 (the application form for federal employment) preparation.

This range of services accommodates diverse learning styles and approaches, from stand-alone to group work to one-on-one interaction. Professional CRC counselors market the center's services through word of mouth, bulletins, and ongoing networking with managers and regional offices throughout GAO.

Results

The CRC opened its doors in July 1991 with a widely publicized ribbon cutting. Usage has grown steadily since then, with participants from all staff units and levels. Seven new, well-attended two-hour workshops have been particularly useful in familiarizing employees with CRC services. Clients served range from lower-wage clerical staff to high-level evaluators and auditors. More managers are taking advantage of the center to get help in coaching their employees on career issues. Employees bring concerns ranging from plateauing to preretirement planning to making a lateral career move. User data are now being collected formally to permit tracking the use and evaluation of specific services. Future plans and priorities include linking career ser-

vices to total quality management and other agency HR initiatives, building closer links with managers, strengthening
relationships with other government agencies, and developing
full-service career centers in the regional offices.

The expansion of GAO's career counseling and development services has enabled the agency to provide varied, practical assistance to many employees while promoting the notion
of career development as a positive, healthy activity.

- Addressing the career development concerns of a changing
  workforce
- Advisory group assessment and focus groups
- Multiple tools and strategies
- Innovative approaches such as development triads, career
  development clinics, and slogans
- Survey evaluation showing strong program support

Background

Bechtel Group is a professional engineering and construction
organization headquartered in San Francisco. It is a worldwide
organization of 32,500 manual and nonmanual employees. In
1987, Bechtel conducted an employee survey that revealed a
strong desire on the part of employees for career development
programs and services. Even earlier, the directors' advisory
group (a high-level leadership committee) had sensed that development was an issue that needed to be dealt with. Bechtel was
facing several HR problems: low retention of college hires, the
anxiety caused by massive downsizing during the mid 1980s,
and an aging workforce.

Implementation

The human resources career development and training unit was
charged with devising a program to address those problems.

The first step was to conduct a series of focus groups with approximately 100 employees and managers around the country. (The resulting program now serves all 22,000 Bechtel employees worldwide.) Also, a career devleopment advisory group (CDAG) was formed, including about twenty line managers and HR people from different geographical and operational areas.

The CDAG, working with two consultants, designed a self-assessment process and workshops for managers and employees. The program, named Building Our Future: Partners in Career Development, emphasized a three-way partnership among employees, managers, and the organization.

One issue was whether workshops should occur on the company's or the employee's time. This was a particular concern for Bechtel because of the contract nature of most of its work; charges to the client are limited. Employee workshops were ultimately designed to occur either during lunch or on the employees' own time.

In 1989, a one-day managers' workshop and training-the-trainer workshops were piloted. The plan was to offer manager workshops monthly; initially, however, there was some skepticism to overcome, and the level of interest in the workshops was not high. Senior management and the HR group played a large role in bolstering involvement; after six months, the interest level had increased.

Next, the company focused on employee materials, developing a popular in-house video. This fifteen-minute video includes an endorsement piece (featuring Riley Bechtel, president and CEO, at a managers' workshop, along with several other top executives), a discussion of the workforce issues that prompted the career development system, and a publicity piece outlining the various tools and components of the system.

System Components

Bechtel's career development system contains various tools as well as several interventions designed to sustain the system. All employees are invited to a one-hour orientation at lunchtime. This session is introduced by a senior manager. The video is shown, and employees are guided through five career development questions. At the end of the hour, they decide whether they want to enroll in the career development process.

Those who decide to enroll have several options. Some choose self-study methods, using a workbook, accompanying audio tape, job aid, and self-assessment cards (which are extremely popular). Those who prefer a more guided process use the same materials in two ninety-minute workshops three weeks apart. The sessions take place half on employees' time and half on Bechtel's. In the first workshop, a trainer takes employees through several exercises, and the self-assessment cards are used. Next, "development triads" of three employees are formed. These three people meet during the three-week period (often at lunch or after work) to do additional exercises. The second session is for debriefing. In response to employee feedback that more time is needed, Bechtel now plans to hold the two sessions four weeks apart.

Because employees also indicated the need for more support, several sustaining efforts were launched. A walk-in, lunch-hour career clinic was offered to answer employee questions, but because it was not heavily used, it was discontinued. Now being designed is a career development forum in which several employees and senior managers will share success stories. Finally, a quarterly newsletter is being developed to discuss future trends, pressing issues and needs, and so on.

The system is publicized through a brochure (which includes an endorsement letter from Riley Bechtel), numerous flyers, posters, and bulletins featuring slogans such as "There's nothing magic about career development" and "Have you caught CD fever yet?"

The system is linked with other HR initiatives at Bechtel. Development is discussed during supervisory training, for example, and in quality training, a clear link is made to career development. When managers coach their employees on career issues, they discuss Bechtel's job-posting system. Throughout, employees are strongly encouraged to tie their own development with the overall strategic direction of the company.

Results

Survey data and comments from both managers and employees show that Bechtel's system has been strongly accepted. Individuals have commented that few programs at Bechtel have lasted so long and been so well received. A telephone survey of participating managers and employees, conducted in August 1991, yielded comments such as "excellent managers' program," "extremely motivating," "excellent materials," and "great for self-analysis."

While it is still too early to assess specific results, the Bechtel workforce is beginning to talk the same language about careers. More people have realistic career plans and are acting on them. Some employees, however, feel they are getting mixed messages from the company, in that Bechtel heavily endorses the system but then provides insufficient time off for using it.

As of mid 1991, 1,500 managers had attended workshops, and 2,200 employees had attended orientations. Over 650 employees had enrolled in guided study, 800 in self-study. Based on current demand in the San Francisco area (where Bechtel has 4,000 employees), bimonthly workshops are being scheduled for managers and employees.

The success of the system has been attributed to the strong need for career development, the high level of senior managerial support for it, and the tenacity of HR staff in pushing the system even when participation was low. The materials themselves also make the program an easy sell.

- Driven by future business needs
- Steering-team approach
- Core models, with decentralized implementation
- Internal career centers with a variety of tools and techniques
- Integration with company HR and quality initiatives

Background

A major impetus for Kodak to create career development systems was to meet future needs of the organization, such as keeping up with new technology and employee retention. In addition, the Kodak opinion trends survey (KOTS), which uses a cross-company sample of employees, showed dissatisfaction over career issues. A review of earlier programs revealed that they lacked systemization and were functioning mostly as training programs.

Kodak's philosophy of career development holds that there are three main participants in the process — the employee, the supervisor (coach), and the organization — and that all three need to be involved collaboratively if the effort is to succeed. When designing and implementing new initiatives, Kodak uses steering teams wherever possible. These teams act as advisory groups for the process before, during, and after implementation. The steering teams are used because they can assess and customize the process to address unique needs of their organizations. They also provide in-house "experts" to help sustain the process beyond the initial rollout.

Often, steering teams become involved in needs assessment through the use of focus groups or a survey process to obtain ideas and commitment from a larger sample of managers and employees within their organizations. In one particular effort, approximately forty people were brought together and asked their views on career development. This approach requires a major commitment of time and resources; the payoff is broader knowledge gained and a greater sense of ownership by employees.

The focus of Kodak's career development efforts has changed. In the early days, career development was targeted mainly at specific groups: high-potentials, exempt employees, women, and minorities. Today, programs usually involve all employees, not just select individuals.

Implementation

Kodak uses a core process and set of principles to define career development and then leaves it up to individual divisions to implement the process in a way that makes sense for them. In addition, Kodak uses a pilot approach during implementation; in fact, early efforts served as pilots themselves.

Generally speaking, this decentralized approach has worked well. There are, however, several barriers to system implementation. Past experience (as well as the KOTS) showed that employees and managers do not always trust the concept of a formal approach; they were wary of the "program of the day" mentality surrounding some past initiatives, and they lacked faith that a new program would last. To overcome this, Kodak attempted to educate everyone who was to be involved in the process; managers were visibly and actively committed through their participation on steering or focus teams.

Another barrier was the level of coaching skills needed. Many managers were often uncomfortable with or unable to perform their "new" role as career coaches. Changing business conditions and organizational priorities caused many divisions to put career development on hold. It is now essentially staggered throughout the organization; some units have discontinued its use or are holding off, while others are starting or improving their systems.

Two final barriers surfaced. First, some employees wanted their career plans to be confidential because of a lack of trust between their managers and themselves. Second, for some employees, a lack of basic skills in math, computers, and language prevented their using traditional career development materials. These obstacles were addressed through the features of the system outlined below.

System Components

Kodak's career development system has the following features:

- Employee and manager (coach) workshops
- Software and workbooks
- Three internal career centers, known as Kodak Career Services, with professional career counselors, career libraries

(including books, tapes, and software), and staff to orient individuals to career development and the use of the centers
- An internal career development network: representatives of units that are exploring or building career development efforts meet monthly to exchange ideas
- Links to other internal resources such as basic skills programs, learning centers, and tuition aid
- Links to other HR processes such as training and development, staffing and selection, expectations, and performance appraisals

Kodak Career Services (KCS) and a resource guide for facilitators were outgrowths of a corporate study team formed in 1987. Orientations to KCS provide an employee with an overview of the career development process and the centers' resources to support them in that process. There is also formal training for employees and managers (coaches) that focuses on the overall process and the interpersonal skills needed to participate in an effective career discussion.

Professionally trained career counselors are available in the career centers to talk with employees about their career plans. This, however, is not intended to circumvent the interactions of employees and managers in career discussions. Counselors are also available to help managers in their role as career coaches.

Today, the overall Kodak CD effort has evolved from a set of separate programs to a more systematic approach. There is a push toward integrating career development with other aspects of employee development and business issues. For example, selection and staffing are linked through Kodak's job-posting system and selection criteria. There is also a conscious effort to link career development to the organization's quality and continuous improvement efforts. The philosophy is communicated that career development consists of growing in the current job as well as looking toward future career moves. Finally, trained peer coaches are increasingly used to help make a shift from traditional to self-directed teams.

Results

While certain quantitative evaluations can be conducted early on, the longer-term, qualitative impact of career development at Kodak will take longer to assess. Nevertheless, in units where career development has been in place consistently, certain effects can be substantiated. These units have clearly witnessed improved relationships between employees and managers. Selection processes now include career development plans and goals as criteria for selection. Future plans include a formal employee network that will enable everyone undertaking a career development process to network throughout all business organizations at Kodak, using predetermined key contacts.

AT&T

- Top-leadership endorsement of companywide career development in response to changing business realities
- Crossfunctional advisory team for needs assessment and implementation
- Autonomous approach with business-unit participation
- Line manager involvement
- Variety of career development tools and activities linked to other HR structures
- Increasing awareness of development; understanding of and satisfaction with career issues

Background

In 1987, AT&T created a division called the corporate career systems group. It consisted of fifteen people who developed career materials and acted as internal consultants to the rest of AT&T. This group identified several factors driving career development at AT&T:

- Management concern that downsizing was affecting employee morale
- A perceived lack of advancement opportunity or attention to career development (revealed in exit interviews and in a 1987–1988 employee survey)
- Turnover of high-potential and middle managers
- A new succession planning process, in which career development played a central role

The first step was a needs assessment, conducted with the help of a career development advisory committee (CDAC). This group, consisting of middle-management HR staff from each business unit, continues to function today. It also has task forces or subgroups, one of which developed a career reference guide.

While line managers are not on the CDAC, they are often asked for their input. Part of the shifting culture of AT&T involves a move toward greater autonomy on the part of individual units. At the same time, one element of the corporate career systems group's mission is to promote a companywide philosophy of career development. Thus, the career systems staff make it a point to deal with line people directly as well as through the CDAC.

Implementation

The needs assessment was done using focus groups of all levels of employees, surveys, and individual interviews with upper management. Several target groups and specific needs emerged. Corporate finance, for example, needed career development tools for the new succession planning process.

As a result, a career development workshop was created. Guides on holding career discussions were developed for supervisors and employees, and a resume writing guide was prepared. These materials were piloted in several business units, and revisions were made using instructional systems designers and subject-matter experts from outside the company.

Career development tools were ready for unveiling by May 1988. Because career development was a corporate initiative, people knew that the company's leadership supported it and thus that it was "the thing to do." Bulletins, an article in the company magazine, and a video with statements by the senior vice president of HR all reinforced the message. A one-day train-the-trainer session was held to orient the heads of HR in the business units to the career development system and tools, so that they could then train the HR representatives in their subunits. Currently, all HR staff have been trained; periodic retraining is available when materials are updated, newcomers arrive, or pockets of people who have not been exposed to the program are discovered.

A growing number of employees have written career plans. A recent survey showed that if written career plans were in place, 83 percent of those involved employee/supervisor discussions and 82 percent of those written career plans were acted on. There are still some employees who for one reason or another did not receive the career development materials. While the corporation has effectively communicated that employees are responsible for their own careers, the cultural shift toward autonomy also means that corporate human resources cannot mandate career development programs to all 320,000 employees.

Changing the traditional view of career development as only job promotion and movement rather than continuous skills improvement has been another communication challenge. There is still limited movement, but the present thrust is the development aspect of career planning. Also, sometimes career planning has arrived on the scene at the same time as a downsizing situation. Such situations have tended to cause employees to perceive career planning in a negative light. Even the resume guide has had to be introduced with a careful explanation that a resume is useful during an internal as well as external job search, but not for the purpose of downsizing.

System Components

AT&T's career development system includes these features:

- A widely publicized statement of twenty-five guiding princi-ples (essentially a vision statement).
- Workshops for both supervisors and employees (super-visory training is currently being strengthened, as em-ployees were not getting adequate followup support from their supervisors).
- Career development guides.
- A career development package (a self-assessment tool, essen-tially a self-paced version of the workshop) with supporting materials.
- A very popular career reference guide that lets all employees know what the various business units do and offers specific examples of job descriptions along with two informational matrices — one with business units by business field, the other with business field by skills.
- A process for the HR planning and development (HRPD) process, which helps users connect career plans with busi-ness plans (managers at all levels discuss with HRPD the summaries of career plans, how they relate to future plans, and what actions are needed).
- Several versions of job posting, including an on-line system, a print-based service from Bell Labs, and a workshop geared toward those at risk for losing their jobs.
- A career center for at-risk people and external outplacement for those who have lost their jobs.
- *The Right Match*, a magazine geared toward line managers that offers a candid look at career issues; it has been so well received that it is hard to keep it in print.

The career development system is closely connected to other HR initiatives: For example, performance appraisal is used as a form of reality checking, and one part of the perfor-mance management cycle is a separate development discussion that is the tactical "playing out" of the strategic career plan. In fact, the entire appraisal process at AT&T is now more focused on development—a major shift. Supervisors are now going to be held accountable for coaching and development through the appraisal process, as employees have been suggesting for some time.

Results

AT&T's district manager of career systems observed that it takes a long time to implement a career development system, and maintaining it requires a great deal of persistence and patience. To "make it contagious," the number of program champions needs to increase.

The career development program was designed as a three-legged stool; employees, supervisors, and the organization each play an essential role. In 1988, the message was clear that individuals were responsible for their own careers. But supervisors and the organization need to give constant support to the process and "walk the talk." In the culture shift away from paternalism and toward employee empowerment, employees may perceive that they have been abandoned. Fortunately, the HRPD process and the expansion of supervisory training are expected to increase significantly the involvement of both organizations and supervisors.

Individual employees are now aware of their responsibilities; that is to the good. Also, awareness of the importance of development is now widespread, and people recognize that the traditional upward movement is no longer the norm.

Proof of line management support of the career development system came in the early 1990s, when its funding mechanism shifted: it went from a service automatically provided by the corporation to one that had to be sold to each business unit. After a great deal of marketing, the service was bought by all units except those that faced serious cost cuts—persuasive proof of its value. The shift in funding may be related to the fact that when the program was introduced in 1988, some people perceived career development as something of a fad; when it was no longer the "concept of the week," it had to justify its value all over again. It is now obvious, however, that career development is not going away; people need to plan more than ever for the uncertain future that has become a reality.

AT&T's career development system has been evaluated through two surveys and an audit of the workshops. Results of the past few annual employee attitude surveys have indicated steadily increasing satisfaction about career programs and tools. Future plans include PC-based assessment tools and resumé guide and workshops to help organizations implement career plans (the HRPD process).

- Continuous improvement as a guiding principle
- Line manager "ownership" of the career development process
- Rigorous design process and systematic, not piecemeal, approach
- Successes publicized

Background

In aerospace, retaining market share amounts to much more than simply offering a complete family of aircraft. The Boeing Company's 1992 annual report is refreshingly frank about the industry, calling it a "difficult business environment." Yet chairman Frank Shrontz ends his message to stockholders with an unambiguous and very upbeat statement of the organization's mission: "to be the number one aerospace company in the world." Boeing's executive team has definite ideas about how to fulfill this ambitious mission. One of the top goals for the year, Shrontz writes, is to make "continuous improvements in the way we design, build, and support our products."

How does this diversified company of more than 140,000 employees intend to reach this goal? "Partnership" is a significant concept in Boeing's strategic plan. Top managers believe that new design and manufacturing processes require a broadened skills base and, just as important, a new corporate culture: one that is more participatory and that encourages all employees to take responsibility for their own career development. To this end, Boeing has identified roles for employees, their managers, and the company itself: employees are "managing partners," managers are "facilitating partners," and Boeing itself is a "resource partner."

In the 1980s, Boeing began shifting its corporate culture away from a "direct and control" style toward a more team-oriented, participative approach. The move toward career development evolved in this context. Also, after conducting an employee attitude survey in 1987, Boeing's management became convinced of the need to offer an improved career development process to its employees and to continue down the path toward a more participative culture.

Several factors complicated this passage; for example, seniority gaps in the engineering staff made a cultural change problematic. By the late 1980s, engineering supervisors had served an average of twenty-one years; in sharp contrast, the people they oversaw had been with Boeing on average less than five years. Obviously, this disparity affects work-group dynamics; the attitudes and expectations of long-term and newer employees differ sharply. In addition, the question of how to fill supervisory job vacancies (as older supervisors retired) began to loom large. Employees with less seniority required training so they would be ready to step in; however, delivering such training itself required trained managers.

In the latter half of the 1980s, Boeing's senior managers decided to deal head on with these internal and external challenges. They began a series of special meetings (held offsite to encourage creative thinking) to discuss and refine their view of Boeing's future. The corporate direction statement that resulted from these meetings was communicated throughout Boeing via fliers, posters, and newsletters. It now helps the company's operating divisions link their individual business plans to clearly stated corporate goals and objectives, many of which focus on human rather than material resources.

System Components

In 1988, Boeing piloted, revised, and then launched a multi-faceted career development program called CAREERS. Initiated by the corporate HR organization and linked with other HR initiatives (such as Performance Management), CAREERS has the following features:

- A briefing for all employees in divisions that offer CAREERS
- A brochure, slides, and videotapes (including success stories) to publicize the program
- Employee and manager training
- Learning centers throughout the company, containing: CareerPoint, a self-assessment and planning system that leads users through a self-paced computer program; organizational information; job descriptions; job population data; training options; a career resources directory; and a directory of local educational resources.

Together, these resources enable individual users to set realistic goals and create viable action plans.

The CAREERS design process, facilitated by a consultant, was unusually rigorous. It involved a six-month literature review and a study of fifty companies and more than fifty vendors. A pilot version was implemented, critiqued, and revised before CAREERS took off. Although division HR staff now support divisional implementation, trained line managers actually carry the ball. They sponsor orientation, schedule and assign workshops and classes, and address implementation issues.

Employees attend a CAREERS orientation session and can elect to participate in a voluntary, three-hour, off-hours "roadmap" workshop. New-employee orientations are being planned that will include an introduction to CAREERS. Management development training supports implementation of CAREERS in those organizations that have introduced it. It is the responsibility of the line organizations, however, to implement it. The idea is eventually to expose everyone at Boeing to the many career development resources available.

The tools offered in CAREERS are designed to help employees assess their skills, interests, and values, all of which help create a good fit between the individual and the job. CAREERS also helps employees find and pursue job enrichment opportunities in their current positions or helps them identify other potential moves within Boeing. The ultimate purpose is to help people create and enact realistic plans for achieving their career goals.

The CAREERS system includes diverse tools and techniques to meet varying employee needs and learning styles. The learning centers offer useful information on jobs, salaries, merit systems, and training; they also highlight career development successes.

Significantly, CAREERS remains a voluntary program. Boeing management strongly believes that individuals should define their own objectives for career success and should take responsibility for meeting those objectives. Through the various learning vehicles offered in CAREERS, users are encouraged to cultivate their skills as their competitive edge.

The performance management system, divisional operating plans, and the career development process are integrated to support individual initiative and ownership of action plans. Employees pursue a variety of options; some, for example, have arranged job rotations; others have taken courses outside their areas of expertise but still related to the company's mission.

As with other HR initiatives, the CAREERS program is powered by the overarching strategic goals and objectives of the company. Those corporate aims are routinely articulated not only through internal advertising for CAREERS but also in the company's employee newsletters and managers' magazine. Repeatedly reminded of the larger context in which they work, individual employees and managers are encouraged to think about where and how their capabilities fit into that context—or need to be developed. Information has thus become a crucial feature of CAREERS.

Boeing's managers have large responsibilities when it comes to employee development. All managers, including vice presidents and directors, are expected to have the ability to develop their people. Many managers have already been trained in career development as well as in coaching and advising employees. Most report positive feelings about this training because it has given them techniques and a structure for helping people with career-related questions and has boosted their confidence level.

The operating styles of line managers participating in CAREERS have undergone impressive changes. Many of these managers report that they now have at their fingertips the information they need and are more clear on what the company expects of them with regard to people development.

Another issue concerns middle managers. Despite the careful planning that preceded the implementation of Boeing's career development system, this layer of managers has not been given a real home within the career development system as a whole. The problem appears to be that because middle managers interact less frequently with nonmanagement employees, they have fewer chances to use the skills they learned in training.

Many middle-level managers have volunteered to act as advisers to employees, offering a global view of the company and performing in effect as a referral network. In this way they are able to use skills that might otherwise grow rusty. And because these managers often have good connections throughout Boeing, they can facilitate informational interviewing, rotational assignments, and so on.

Results

How does Boeing assess its multifaceted career development system? Using employee climate and opinion surveys, focus groups, course evaluations, and a pre- and post-survey, the company has gained a fairly good sense of the effects of its system.

In a one-year period (from June 1990 to July 1991), total usage of CAREERS software increased over 60 percent, and the total time spent by users of the software more than doubled. Interestingly, usage tends to drop off between six and seventeen months after an organization launches the system and to pick up again after about eighteen months — perhaps because skeptical employees see the positive results experienced by others and decide to participate.

Of the organizations that have implemented CAREERS, nearly half their employees have used the system over a two-year period. Of these, roughly 60 percent have used CareerPoint (the self-assessment and development software), and about 40 percent have used the equivalent in the CAREERS workbook.

Although hard data are not available for all aspects of the system, the soft data are compelling. Overall, evaluations indicate that many new lines of communication have been opened between employees and managers. Boeing's most recent employee opinion survey, which contained roughly eighty questions, revealed employee perceptions of improvement in two areas in particular: training and career development. In one of the divisions where CAREERS is used, the 1991 survey showed marked increases since 1989 in availability of guidance for career growth and encouragement by supervisors.

Education matters to Boeing employees; the company's tuition reimbursement program is considered very successful. Many CAREERS survey respondents expressed a desire for on-hours training, for more time to work on their careers, and for even more career-related information. Survey respondents also stated that manager commitment, involvement, and follow-through are the main ingredients of a successful career development program—a clear signal that Boeing is on the right track in encouraging its managers to make more time for employee development.

Significantly, survey respondents have indicated that they seek rotational assignments. They are excited about experiencing different jobs and tasks and learning more, on the job, about the right fit between their own skills and interests and Boeing's needs.

Clearly, the CAREERS program is a far cry from business as usual in the aerospace industry. Boeing still faces lots of challenges. Company executives understand that the real test comes when the level of business changes. The hope is that because of the various development programs, more people will be sufficiently multiskilled to be moved around in the company, either to avoid layoff or to handle increased levels of business.

At present, Boeing is attempting to stabilize its workforce to avoid large or sudden labor cuts. A long-term indicator of CAREERS's success will be the system's ability to aid in this stabilizing process. As CAREERS continues to be implemented, Boeing's emphasis is on developing solid performers: workers motivated from within and ready for the long haul. Training is of course important; so is a definition of "winning" that encompasses not only being at the top but also increasing one's expertise, flexibility, and self-esteem.

There is the sense within the organization that if an adaptable culture is to take root, its managers at every level have to be given the skills and resources to develop a flexible, many-talented workforce. Training employees is only half the picture; managers, too, need development. More than ever, modes of learning will need to reflect real-world learning styles, which for many employees are experience based.

In 1990 Boeing won the prestigious American Society for Training and Development Award for Organizational Career Development. This is not, however, a company that rests on its laurels. Plans are under way to ensure that continuous improvement remains just that: continuous. By building on early successes in workforce development, Boeing intends to keep its sights high and to make sure its performance follows suit.

CORNING

- Career development in response to climate survey data
- Implementation linked to specific business needs
- Conditions of success established
- Work-team development planning process
- Multiple tools: briefings, workbook, software, and manager-employee training
- Measures, evaluation, and continuous improvement
- Accountability mechanisms
- Systems integration

Background

Corning is a major supplier of products and services in specialty glass and ceramic materials, consumer housewares, laboratory sciences, and telecommunications. No newcomer to the realm of employee development, Corning has provided training for over a decade as a means of enhancing the company's skills base. Along with changes in the marketplace, Corning has witnessed a transformation of its workforce. A growing number of its diverse employees are two-career couples. Corporate climate surveys have revealed that Corning's workforce knows about and expects career development assistance; the concepts of being members of a collaborative "partnership" and of being valued for their contributions are not new to these employees. And because many of them are moving into middle-management positions, they exert a strong influence on corporate culture, policies, and practices.

Corning's aim, articulated formally and informally to all employees, is to be one of the ten most admired American companies in terms of performance, quality, and diversity. Acknowledging that versatility requires development, Corning's management has chosen to communicate a standard for everyone, without stipulating right or wrong ways to reach it. Each business division is mandated to meet or exceed the company's criteria in performance, quality, and diversity. Significantly, divisional business strategies (which are presented to the operating company's management) must incorporate plans for people development.

This orientation represents a distinct departure from old norms. In the past, top management communicated its vision by distributing policy booklets throughout all divisions and by holding policy meetings for senior divisional managers. Some units then formed working groups to decide how to implement the corporate vision in their own context and to initiate "change planning"; others simply circulated the booklets to their teams without actually linking the big picture, in practical and visible ways, with their daily operations. The company's employee development programs reflected the problems inherent in this top-down approach.

Then business realities — downsizing, a new pay-for-performance compensation system, financial stresses — forced a reconsideration of the traditional approach. What Corning discovered, through its real-world experience, is that development is an essential ingredient of its business success.

System Components

In the mid 1980s, with the support of top management, Corning's HR staff launched a career development and information program for administrative and technical employees (A&Ts) who had expressed concern in climate surveys that they were undervalued by the company. That program, quickly deemed effective, has become the foundation for an integrated career development system for salaried management and professional employees (M&Ps) that now reaches roughly 70 percent of all M&Ps. Its key features include:

- A generic workbook that also has specialized functional sections for different groups of employees, so that career development can be tailored to divisional strategies.
- Executive briefings for divisional managers and their staff, facilitated by an HR manager or an outside consultant, which give an overview of employee and workforce development.
- Manager training in the career development process and in coaching and counseling skills.

The M&P program is deliberately integrated with other HR tools and activities, including performance appraisals and quality improvement; in fact, the language of quality improvement is being used in career development workshops to reinforce both initiatives. The results of such a systems approach have been quite positive.

The cornerstone of Corning's effort to create what it calls a "world-class workforce development planning process" is its requirement that managers at all levels play a key role. Each supervisor is expected to learn what skills his or her employees need to acquire, what their interests and values are, and how these might be merged with corporate needs. Solid communication between managers and their teams is, of course, central to the development process. Through dialogue and feedback managers find out what they need to know about the capacities and limits of their employees and what can be done to improve each person's contribution and level of job satisfaction.

Some managers at Corning have had trouble relinquishing control and practicing two-way communication. To help them incorporate new ways of thinking, Corning encourages managers to take a close look at their own career development, experiencing the process in the same way that employees do.

Certain business units are beginning to tie employee development to rewards for managerial performance, and this trend is encouraged by the central HR department. The need for a reward system — a tangible means of keeping the managerial team on track — is evident. To begin with, many of the company's managers, a large number of whom have highly technical backgrounds, may be reluctant to change their behavior without incentives. Daily operational firefighting, as one HR staffer calls it, absorbs most managers' attention. In addition, the company's move to a system of 100 percent chargeout of staff groups means that business units are increasingly competing with outside vendors for in-house work — and finding themselves at a disadvantage.

Corning now promotes the notion of an organizational change process, urging managers to think about workforce development as a set of behaviors and attitudes whose benefits are long term. A statement of ten "conditions for success" is currently used as a kind of conceptual roadmap in executive briefings. These success indicators, listed below, are also beginning to serve as the basis of an organizational assessment — a measurement instrument focused on workforce development that the HR department has administered to some individual managers and groups of supervisors.

1.   Management sets expectations.
2.   Supervisors learn new skills.

3.   Employees use career development tools.
4.   Supervisors are held accountable for employee development.
5.   Career information is available.
6.   Leadership demonstrates and models workforce development.
7.   Measures track effectiveness.
8.   Workforce development is integrated with other HR systems.
9.   Approaches are in place to sustain workforce development.
10. Ongoing updates are given for employees and supervisors.

Connected with the issue of rewarding managers for "people development" are the thorny questions of credibility and accountability: ensuring that the workforce development process does what it is supposed to do and is implemented appropriately. Like other companies pioneering new means of linking development with business strategy, Corning has discovered that these questions have no ready answers. The company does, however, stake its claims on interrelated development tools:

•   A strong review process for all employees
•   Skills training in supervising and coaching for managers
•   Career development
•   Succession planning
•   Job assignments and training programs

Results

Corning's central HR department views its role as one of facilitating companywide change. The idea is to present nonnegotiable roles and models for the development process but then to step back and let individual people and business units find their own ways and means of undertaking successful development. HR managers accept that the change process may take several years, and they are working hard to enlist the ongoing support of line managers. The central HR department routinely reviews business plans, checks the match between business needs and skills requirements, and keeps everyone informed of development options and programs.

Thus far, employees appear gratified to find that management cares about their development and their views. Overall, productivity has improved and turnover is down.

Corning experienced some problems gaining managerial acceptance of the M&P career development program. In particular, the workbook was not well introduced: managers were given insufficient notification and instruction on its use, and the workbook was not linked clearly enough to divisional strategies. In hindsight, system designers feel that division-by-division implementation would have been more fruitful than a companywide pilot program.

Experience shows that holding career discussions in a work-group setting is difficult for some managers, and Corning now offers training in this area. Some divisions are thinking about following the lead of the information services unit, which publishes a quarterly newsletter featuring employee-authored success stories.

At Corning there are few preconceived notions about proper career paths; volunteering, temporary assignment, job redesign, and other career options are all possible. This lack of structure can be difficult for employees who are less confident in their ability to manage their own development, which is where the company's training and career development programs come into play. The idea is to give people tools for diagnosing their own strengths and weaknesses and plenty of opportunities to explore how best to merge their needs with Corning's.

Corning's current emphasis on high-performance, self-managed work teams also raises new questions about career development and the team leader's role. But by keeping the focus on a process in which employees and supervisors share the responsibility and benefits of thoughtfully planning development, the company is fulfilling its desire to be a full-time "renewal" organization.

CHAPTER 8

Best Practices: Practical Approaches for Achieving Career Development Objectives

By now it is amply clear that career development systems do not develop overnight—they evolve. Sometimes, however, a particular tool or intervention spearheads a larger career development effort. This chapter profiles six such innovative programs. Some exist essentially on their own; others are part of a larger effort. All highlight the positive ripple effects that can result from one successful undertaking.

These six examples of best practices are drawn from large organizations where rich data and in-depth interviews of HR staff allowed us to gain an accurate and stimulating picture of what can be done, on a "micro" level, to enhance organizational career development. The interview guide used to conduct the best-practice interviews is contained in Appendix B.

Three of the "best practices" deal with aspects of career development for employees: job posting as a career information and development tool, a reward and development program for individual technical contributors, and a labor-management partnership as a career development system for hourly employees. The other three focus on the role of managers in career development and their development as leaders. Honing in on examples of success in these areas seems important, in view of our survey findings that the position of managers is often a weak link in career development systems. Perhaps these profiles can

signal ways to enhance and strengthen the crucial role of managers as people developers.

Job Information System

- Begun in 1989 in response to employee survey data and
  managerial information needs
- Nearly all jobs posted electronically, up to the director level
- Linked to HR review process
- Emphasis on feedback and ties to development
- Pilot process and extensive publicity
- Nearly half of all applications are for nonpromotions
- Benefits include better employee skill identification and
  expanded career information

Background

In late 1989 3M began piloting a job-posting system as part of a
larger effort to provide resources that would enable employees
to take responsibility for their own careers (see Chapter Seven).
The job information system (JIS) was prompted by the diversity
of the company, which made it hard for any one manager to have
information about available jobs, and by opinion surveys under-
scoring employees' desire for information on job opportunities.
The initial objectives of the JIS were to enable 3M's hiring
managers to identify internal candidates and to help employees
identify skills and qualifications needed to prepare for different
job requirements.

Before the JIS was established, the company's job prefer-
ence system required employees to complete a form noting their
preferences. Managers used this form for internal searches, but
employees themselves had no immediate access to specific job
requirements as vacancies occurred. In addition, an HR review
process (still in existence) allowed managers to nominate indi-

viduals for a job on the basis of potential and suitability, whether or not they had applied for the job. (Significantly, many 3M employees are satisfied where they are; they have not tended to apply on their own for other jobs within the company.) Inputs to this process are made annually during performance appraisals.

There are clear advantages to having both the JIS and the HR review process. The JIS covers only self-nominators, while the HR process covers everyone; also, the JIS data are often more current than the annual HR data. The systems complement each other.

System Components

All jobs through management, up to the director level, are posted; only the top 1.5 percent of jobs are not posted. Any approved vacancy is listed, except in the rare circumstance that a vice president or president allows for an exception, such as when an individual is clearly in line for a position as part of succession planning.

Vacancies are listed for ten working days. Jobs are listed electronically; employees access them through their computers. Sales representatives and others working in the field obtain job information by calling a telephone number. There is also a phone hotline for people with questions about the posting system.

Employees can apply for any listed job for which they feel qualified. They must have spent twenty-four months in their current assignment before applying, unless their supervisor waives this requirement. They fill out applications manually; these go directly to the hiring manager for screening. The hiring manager calls the manager of any applicant he or she wishes to interview and then calls the applicant directly.

Feedback is an essential part of the system. The hiring manager responds to all candidates; those not interviewed receive, at minimum, a form letter. All candidates who interview for but do not get a job receive either a memo or a phone call. The program is coordinated by the career resources department.

The company plans to link job posting to a general career

development system, although efforts to coordinate different career-related tools are still fairly new. Currently, a career resource manual is being distributed that includes job posting as one of many resources. Also an optional section of a workshop called "Career Directions" focuses on internal job seeking; this is designed to tie in with the JIS.

Implementation

The system started with a task force that included HR, line, and staff personnel who spent many months gathering information internally and externally and then planning. The pilot began with the engineering function (nationwide) because management felt that the pilot would work best if it started with a specialized group. The pilot then extended to two operating groups that were eager to be involved, later adding several other groups with a particular interest in participating. As of February 1991, the JIS had been implemented corporatewide in the United States; there is interest in expanding it internationally.

The system was publicized through various communications to all employees: letters, articles in company publications, and a manual that walks people through the JIS process.

Introducing the JIS involved a change in management process, which did not happen quickly; for their part, people have needed to see clear benefits before their comfort level increases. Initially, managers had concerns about the process affecting their authority to select among candidates. To ease these concerns, the HR department repeatedly emphasized that the process was for information-sharing purposes; managers would retain the right to select whomever they wished for a given vacancy. Their only obligation was to review all JIS paperwork and respond to applicants. Some managers also feared that everyone would seek a promotion through the JIS — including people who were not qualified. The HR department pointed out that if managers specified job qualifications accurately and in sufficient detail, employees would be able to do a good job of self-nominating. Another concern of managers was that they would lose good people and that employees would spend a lot of time on the system.

Results/Assessment

Employee reactions to the JIS have generally been extremely positive. Managers' reservations disappeared quickly; indeed, many of their concerns proved to be groundless. For example, an initial evaluation revealed that 48 percent of applications have been for nonpromotions; clearly, many employees are thinking developmentally — an intended outcome. Also, the average time an employee spends accessing job listings is only two minutes.

A number of managers have contacted the career resources department with very positive reports of successes. Because of the JIS, the company is doing a much better job of identifying employee potential and providing career opportunities, and employees understand their career options much more clearly and realistically.

System designers say that there is nothing that 3M would have done differently if it were starting over. That is because the company took a lot of time in the pilot stage and made sure to obtain plenty of line and staff input.

AT&T/CWA/IBEW NEW ENGLAND REGIONAL ALLIANCE LEARNING CENTER

Labor-Management Partnership

- National negotiated labor-management program
- Formal on-site center serving over 8,500 employees
- Variety of components, plus training over three shifts
- Ongoing needs assessment and publicity
- Positive feedback and high participation
- Plans for increased manager involvement and evaluation

Background

The Alliance for Employee Growth and Development is a nationwide program negoitated in 1986 through a collective bargaining agreement between AT&T and the Communications Workers of America (CWA) and the International Brotherhood of Electrical Workers (IBEW). The mandate of the Alliance is to provide training, retraining, and career development opportunities for union members of AT&T so as to enhance individual employment security.

Most Alliance programs are run through local teams of volunteers via joint labor-management committees. In North Andover, Massachusetts, however, 5,000 people needed to be served, and an informal volunteer arrangement was inadequate. Instead, an on-site, ten-person Alliance office was set up: the Alliance Learning Center (ALC). It has been so successful that the ALC is now serving roughly 3,500 employees throughout the New England region in addition to its primary focus — the 5,000 employees in the North Andover area.

System Components

A forty-five-minute orientation was developed to acquaint people with the Alliance and its services. Supervisors were the first group to be oriented. Each employee now has an orientation on company time; after that, any use of the Alliance services is on the employee's time. Services include various educational and training offerings and career development components.

- A prepaid tuition program covers area schools.
- On-site classes are held for all three shifts. Some are for full college credit; others, taught by staff members, are not for credit. Still others, such as a popular Spanish class, are taught by employees.
- Individual career counseling is available for self-assessment of interests, values, and so on.
- Individual assistance is available to people selecting a school or college and applying for the Alliance's prepaid tuition program.
- A twelve-hour career development course meets one afternoon a week for six weeks. The objective is for participants to set goals and to do short- and long-term planning to

achieve them. The course was created and is highly recommended for people who want prepaid tuition, but it is open to all, regardless of whether they are going back to school.

The course includes job enrichment; often, one-third to one-half of the participants decide that they want to stay where they are. They are encouraged to hold a career discussion with their supervisors, and the course helps increase their self-confidence. Other focuses of the course are local labor-market information and information on other AT&T training options (including internal training and the company tuition refund plan). Educational credentials are emphasized, as almost any opportunity, even a lateral move, will involve the need for some further training.

- Career discussions with supervisors, while not required, are encouraged as a means of reality checking. Steps and guidelines for such discussions are covered in the career development course. Employee reactions have varied; some were already talking to their supervisors, others have wanted to keep their career development private.

- AT&T sponsors coaching training for supervisors, and although the ALC does not currently offer such training, it has made sure that its materials blend with those of AT&T for consistency.

- A career library offers an extensive collection of materials on career development, job searching, the labor market, and so on.

Implementation

Setting up the ALC as a formal on-site center was very significant. Having a visible, high-profile yet nonthreatening place on site where people could go to discuss career plans made a big impact. The center was staffed with counseling professionals, most of whom had advanced degrees, who were not employed by AT&T. This reassured many people about confidentiality, although some still had fears that had to be overcome.

Additional barriers included some inertia and a fear that the Alliance existed mainly to deal with layoffs. Unfortunately, a layoff did occur during the first year of the program, 1987. However, the Alliance was able to assure people that it was here to stay and that its mandate extended far beyond dealing with layoffs.

The ALC has had top-management support from the beginning. The level of support of the 250 first-line supervisors initially varied greatly. However, since orientations for all supervisors were held in 1991, full support is now apparent. While most employees refer themselves, some supervisors refer their employees to the center, and it is hoped that this will increase.

Initially, an "Alliance Day" was held in the cafeteria (for all three work shifts) to promote the program. Employees filled out a survey about their program preferences, and were given ice cream in return! There have also been "college days," with twenty-two area schools and many employees participating. "Return to school" panels, which feature employees who have used the center's services to gain education and training, are held annually.

Another effective method of getting the word out has been a network of teams of Alliance representatives, who are esesntially peer publicity agents. These teams have five members each across ten plant divisions. Team representatives distribute surveys, solicit feedback, and serve as an informal advisory group. They distribute the center's monthly calendar of activities and schedules for fall, spring, and summer courses.

Results/Assessment

Regular surveys assess individuals' interest in various course offerings. Subjective informal feedback — from employees, union presidents, and management — has been very positive. As an example, students have come to the ALC to show staff members their grades or projects. A local union president has stated that when it comes to the Alliance, there is no trace of any of the adversarial feeling often associated with labor-management relations. The number of referrals and the level of participation are also positive indicators: as of the winter of 1991, 2,500 people had participated in ALC classes and 1,000 in the career development course or individual career counseling, several hundred using prepaid tuition. ALC staff believe that the most important measure is how people feel about themselves and how they have changed—both of which are positive.

There are plans for an employee input survey to be incorporated into the regular course-offerings survey. It will explore knowledge ("do you know about the ALC?"), behavior ("have you used it?"), and attitude ("how would you evaluate the services?"). Responses will be anonymous, and it is hoped that the survey will be administered on company time.

In the past, several unsuccessful career development efforts were launched in response to AT&T corporate surveys, where lack of career development was cited. Because of those earlier failures, it is important that the current effort be successful. Although AT&T technical managers often do not like to address "soft areas," the Alliance is a very attractive service to them and they rely heavily on it. For one thing, it does not reduce their line budgets, and they value the HR services provided by outside sources.

In addition, while the ALC is mainly staffed by "outsiders," its director was an AT&T employee for thirty-two years (in personnel and training), and this gives the program added credibility. The advantage of having a non-AT&T, degreed professional staff is that employees feel comfortable and safe with these staffpeople because they are outsiders; employees also respect the fact that they have degrees. On the negative side, some employees initially doubted whether these professionals would understand or be able to relate to their problems, as they were not part of the culture of AT&T. This latter worry has dissipated, however, as the staff has become more familiar with AT&T and thus more accepted.

Another issue is the link between the ALC and AT&T's HR organization. The HR unit does not offer career counseling; referrals are made back and forth. The ALC meets with HR to discuss assessment, promotion, and movement of personnel. Also, the ALC has a close working relationship with the tuition refund staff.

Finally, the national agreement specifies that Alliance

programs (other than the forty-five-minute orientation) take place on employees' own time. ALC staff feel that it would probably be better if the time commitment were split between the company and the employee; having the company commit some time would send a strong message of support.

One area in which that commitment is clear is the English as a Second Language program run by the ALC. The program offers five levels of instruction; the first four, each for four hours a week, are taught on company time, and the fifth (also four hours) is split between company and employee time.

Efforts are under way to fill a gap in the Alliance program relating to the role of supervisors. Nearly 200 first-line supervisors have gone through training on how to hold a career discussion. In this training they also learned how to do their own career development. The training manual, which will include a chapter on the Alliance, will facilitate supervisory referrals of employees. These steps enabled the ALC to close the loop in what had been an employee-driven program. When this happened, however, the client load of the ALC increased significantly because of more referrals.

Another area under discussion is whether Alliance services should be extended to cover management employees. This expanded service, known as Alliance Plus, is currently under review by the company, and a number of managers have expressed interest in it. This planned program is an interesting reversal of the norm in which career development programs are initially designed for managers and then may filter down to others.

Technical Excellence Program

- Goal is to retain high-level technical contributors in information systems services
- Task force studied unique needs and motivations of technical population

- Three system components, including annual allowance and cash awards
- Evaluation and continuous improvement

Background

The impetus for the Technical Excellence Program (TEP) was a 1987 job review process within Nationwide's property and casualty division. Members of the information systems services (ISS) management team were concerned that technical employees were not being amply rewarded; high-level technical contributors were seen as indispensable, yet as people moved up the salary scale, increases were smaller and less frequent. Turnover was not yet a problem, but there was concern about taking steps to prevent it.

A task force was assembled of several technical contributors, managers who supervised them, personnel staff, and a consultant. The consultant helped task force members understand the characteristics and motivations of technical employees so that a reward and development program could be designed around their specific needs.

There were three goals for this program:

1. To retain and recognize talented technical employees, keep them motivated and challenged, and prevent turnover.
2. To encourage technical specialists to share their knowledge with other people, rather than simply being recognized as experts in their particular area.
3. To encourage them to expand, update, and broaden their knowledge rather than staying in a narrow specialty area.

The latter two goals constituted a change for many technical employees, who often are more comfortable as experts in a specialized area. Moreover, in many cases these employees had been obtaining funding to attend conferences only if these events were related to their particular specialty.

Because of some staffing shifts, the task force went through a significant though temporary hiatus; however, it regrouped, and a pilot program was designed. The program was announced in January 1991; it was explained to all employees initially and then, in more detail, to managers of those people who were accepted into it.

A second group did not start as projected in May 1992. This was because an evaluation was done in April 1992 that included surveys of current TEP participants as well as of those who did not apply. A decision was made to recommend some changes to the program (based on the evaluation findings) and to wait to start a second group until those changes that get approved are actually implemented. The feedback suggested a need for changed selection criteria and process, as well as a broadening of the possible usages of the budget allowance to provide a stronger incentive for people to apply. Another recommended change will be to eliminate the cash award for independent accomplishment due to lack of interest. Current TEP participants have been involved in designing the recommendations for change.

System Components

The TEP is a two-year program open to two high-level but non-supervisory grades of technical employees. Participants may reapply to continue in it. The first group started in May 1991. Twenty-two people applied for the first group; ten were accepted. Candidates were selected on the basis of attributes such as technical expertise, high performance, initiative, commitment to continuing education, and communications skills.

There are three main components:

1. *Budget allowance.* Participants receive a $2,500 annual allowance to be used on any items that further their technical development—conferences, seminars, software, printers, publications, or a second phone line at home so they can use a modem. Participants' managers sign off on use of the allowance.

2. *Cash awards for educational accomplishments.* This feature contains two components. One is a monetary award of $30 per class hour paid to participants who design and teach in-house classes; this is intended to promote knowledge sharing. The

other is a $200 annual cash award to recognize the achievement of a personal development objective related to formal education (some of the technical contributors do not have a bachelor's degree, for example).

3. *Cash award for independent accomplishment.* A variable cash award is given to individuals who complete an assignment, independent of their regular job duties, which results in dollar savings for the company. The award is based on 20 percent of the accrued savings in the first twelve months of implementation, not to exceed $5,000.

Results/Assessment

Most of the first ten participants used the TEP program for the $2,500 allowance, and 80 percent of them turned in expenses under this budget allowance. They commented that they see this as their money, and it allows them to do things they would not otherwise be able to do.

Only two people have designed in-house classes so far, and none have used the other cash award components. Some have said that $30 per hour is not sufficient financial incentive to offset the time involved in designing classes. The amount of money involved, however, is bounded by other corporate policies and programs. A possible reason for the lack of use of the cash award for independent accomplishment is that Nationwide has a similar companywide program (the improved methods plan) that is based on expected rather than actual hard-dollar savings.

Part of the informal evaluation has also involved soliciting feedback from people who were expected to apply for the program but did not. Some of those who were expected to apply for the program but did not stated that the TEP design and implementation process was so lengthy that they had become skeptical and lost interest by the time it became a reality. They said they would see how the first round went and perhaps apply for the next round. Those who applied and were not accepted generally understood the decision once they saw the ten people who were accepted.

Another initial hurdle was the reaction of the applications personnel who work in ISS. Although they are eligible for the program, the selection criteria are so specialized that generally they lack experience or exposure to qualify. Their resentment of this has been largely overcome by explaining to them that this pilot program was designed to address the most pressing need area first.

After the first ten participants started, they were invited to a luncheon with the ISS vice president and director of ISS personnel. The program belonged to the participants, they were told, and they had the opportunity to influence it. The participants had several meetings to look at the program, almost as if they were consultants to it; program designers had this in mind as a goal for the program, although they decided not to formalize it.

Also, an evaluation was done in April 1992 that included surveys of current TEP participants as well as of those who did not apply. A decision was made to recommend some changes to the program (based on the evaluation findings) and to wait to start a second group until those changes that get approved are actually implemented. The feedback suggested a need for changed selection criteria and process, as well as a broadening of the possible usages of the budget allowance to provide a stronger incentive for people to apply. Another recommended change will be to eliminate the cash award for independent accomplishment due to lack of interest. Current TEP participants have been involved in designing the recommendations for change.

Another possible change would be to make the program more objectives driven by requiring action plans and discussions with managers about these plans. (The consultant recommended this, but internal personnel staff feared that it might discourage technical contributors from applying.) Some of the participants have in fact set objectives for personal development and knowledge sharing.

System designers say that they would have liked to have more individual contributors on the task force and to have set more parameters for how it was to operate. Nonetheless, the TEP has met one of its major objectives: to provide the opportunity for technical experts to continue to develop in diverse and exciting ways.

Leadership Education and Development

- Recognition of middle managers' needs for training to respond to a changed environment
- Executive advisory committee needs assessment and benchmarking
- Customized program in partnership with University of Michigan
- Focus on on-the-job applications
- Residential program involving functional and crossfunctional teams
- Emphasis on adult learning principles
- Documented program success

Background

In the 1980s, Ford went through major organizational changes. The transformation involved a move toward empowerment and participation of employees at all levels and a recognition that employee development was fundamental to business success. Prior to this transformation, middle management operated traditionally, implementing directives issued by others. Developing managers was considered unnecessary; the prevailing notion was that "cream rises to the top." In fact, in the early stages of the company's transformation, change efforts focused mainly on senior management and those on the shop floor. Then middle managers alerted company leaders to the fact that they also needed training to adjust to a dramatically changing environment.

Thus began a one-year process of determining middle managers' needs and designing and promoting a program to meet those needs. The program, called Leadership Education and Development (LEAD), is intended to develop and empower 3,000 middle managers from all over the company, including overseas.

The LEAD program was launched in late 1988; as of mid 1992, 2,400 people had gone through it. Managers attend LEAD on company time. Each operation pays for it; so far, it has been reapproved by top management each year.

System Components

In each LEAD program session, approximately fifty participants meet together for five days, usually at the University of Michigan's Executive Education Center. The group is designed to represent a crossfunctional perspective while also including people from within the same functional units. Crossfunctional learning teams of approximately seven people go through experiential exercises; sometimes they meet with others in their functional area.

The five-day core session covers such areas as individual learning styles, the role of middle management at Ford, the competing values model, keeping a customer focus, quality issues, systems thinking, change and continuous improvement, personal and functional leadership, and action planning. At the end of the session, participants videotape themselves explaining how they will apply the session's learnings in their workplace. The focus during the week is strongly on teamwork, moving people from "a relay race to a rugby team," as two LEAD program faculty members described it. And while the program is aimed at awareness and understanding, its major benefits are intended for application on the job.

After an interim period of six to eight months, participants come back for a three-day followup session, where they discuss their application of LEAD concepts and their plans for the future. Achievements, frustrations, and learnings are shared and incorporated in these plans.

Implementation

Initially, an advisory committee was set up that included executives at the highest levels of the company. The committee researched needs internally through focus groups and employee attitude surveys and conducted an extensive study of what other companies were doing in the area of executive education. What it found was that almost no one focused on middle managers even though they represented the majority of the managerial population. Furthermore, few programs integrated the study of leadership and management. These findings underscored the need for Ford to develop its own customized program.

The committee encountered significant internal differences of opinions about such a program, however. Some company leaders saw no need for one, or their ideas on what was needed were in conflict. Many worried about the commitment of time and resources involved. Even some members of the committee were not convinced that a program was necessary. Ultimately, several occurrences turned these opinions around.

- The focus groups involved advisory committee members interviewing middle managers within their own organizations. The consensus from the groups about the need for such a program was so convincing that previously doubtful members of the committee became enthusiastic champions.
- The employee attitude survey showed that the one area of middle management dissatisfaction was training and that the level of dissatisfaction was increasing.
- Several in-depth, one-on-one meetings were held with company leaders; these meetings helped persuade them of the value of a program.

Once the program had a green light, the advisory committee focused on finding a theoretical model that would address the leadership and managerial dilemmas of organizational life and finding an educational institution that would partner with Ford to sponsor the program.

The competing values model, devised by Robert Quinn (1988), was chosen because it provides a practical framework for explaining the dilemmas and paradoxes of organizations rather than attempting to lay out solutions. Furthermore, it provides for the development of company-specific applications to be used on the job—another important element desired by the committee.

Over a six-month period, Ford worked out a partnership arrangement with the University of Michigan to jointly develop, sponsor, and teach the LEAD program. The arrangement provided for every class to be taught by both a university faculty member and a Ford senior executive. Executive trainers are rotated, as teaching is a good developmental experience. The development of this unusual partnership between business and academia was a learning experience for both parties. It has resulted in a win-win situation: the company benefits from the university's research base and broad analytical perspective and the university benefits from working with Ford's real-world population.

Results and Assessment

The LEAD program was designed to make use of key principles of adult learning. It emphasizes the empowerment of learners, enabling them to reflect on their learning, using experiential techniques, applying what is learned in a real-world setting, and doing comprehensive followup. The process is designed to be replicated so that managers can take what they learn and apply it with their subordinates, thereby empowering their work groups.

The success of the program has been demonstrated in several ways. Not only has the program received continued support, but there is ample evidence that managers have undertaken new projects as a result of LEAD, projects that have led to direct improvements and significant financial savings for the company. These projects, which directly support Ford's business purposes, have been performed above and beyond the managers' regular duties.

Senior managers have interviewed program participants with no LEAD program representatives present to get their candid feedback on the program. In addition, the university is collaborating with Ford on followup activities and has developed an instrument to measure degrees of empowerment. The LEAD program has generated a huge data base that the university will use for longitudinal research on a variety of workplace issues. Overall, the program has shown itself to be an innovative way of empowering people to serve as successful and effective managers.

Westpac Banking Corporation

Succession Planning and Career Development

- Career development with a strategic focus
- Competency-based succession planning for replacement and development
- Corporate executive development group with four career development programs
- Key executive group program for senior executive development

Background

Westpac, Australia's oldest bank, operates in twenty-seven countries, with global assets totaling over A\$106 billion and a total of 39,576 employees. In June 1991, *Euromoney* ranked Westpac as the thirty-first largest bank in the world in terms of shareholders' funds.

Westpac has long championed the importance of people development. Since the mid 1980s, the company's approach to career development has assumed an increasingly strategic focus. Its objective has been to integrate HR strategy with business strategy and to generate career development programs that help achieve two basic business objectives: maintaining executive continuity and improving executive quality.

The first goal—maintaining continuity—has these specific objectives:

- Identifying and placing the talent required to lead the organization as it evolves.
- Obtaining the requisite number of high-quality managers needed to manage the organization and deliver its future.

- Reducing turnover of high-potential managers.
- Improving mobility and deployment across business units.

The second goal—improving quality—involves these objectives:

- Developing future leaders with experience across a range of functions and businesses.
- Helping individuals design more satisfying and better-managed career plans.
- Developing the competencies required to lead the organization as it grows.
- Inculcating a keen sense of responsibility and accountability for creating the organization's future.

Career development at Westpac is a joint responsibility of both the individual and the organization. Individuals are expected to participate actively in development activities, and managers are expected to support their efforts. A range of development opportunities is currently available, including targeted management development programs, a study assistance scheme, cooperative education programs, and extensive internal and external training.

System Components

Westpac's approach to career development centers on its succession planning system. This system is competency based and designed to develop levels of management competence across the organization. Essentially, Westpac views succession planning as a business activity driven by the line. The system includes:

- Methods for assessing potential, such as career development interviews and use of the career path appreciation (developed by Gillian Stamp of the University of West London).
- Special programs to select and develop high-potentials.
- Appropriate career development for the corporate executive development group.

- Training, education, and development activities to enhance relevant management and technical competencies.

Westpac's aim is to identify the competencies required for all positions included in the succession planning system. Potential candidates can then be assessed against an ideal competency profile. Ultimately, the system will deliver people skilled in the way and to the levels that the business requires at any given time.

Westpac's succession planning system has three main components:

1. *Replacement planning.* For Westpac, succession planning and replacement planning are not mutually exclusive; they are different aspects of the continuum that is HR planning. What differentiates the two is their time frame. Replacement planning tends to focus on the best available candidate in the coming twelve to eighteen months, whereas succession planning looks to the longer term, generating critical competencies across all levels of the organization.

The replacement plan, then, centers on the extent, nature, and timing of short-term staffing changes. Some of the issues addressed are competencies required to achieve desired business outcomes; new positions; and mobility and individual potential.

2. *Executive resource review.* A key element of the succession planning system is the executive resource review (ERR), an annual meeting between senior management and senior HR managers. The objective is to review the performance and quality of critical human resources across particular business units, divisions, or departments. The ERR addresses the following core areas: business review and planning, HR planning, individual development planning, and the corporate executive development group.

The ERR process specifically links people to the business strategy as it solidifies the relationship between human resources and the delivery of business goals. HR managers consult with line managers on the following critical issues:

- Overall performance in light of the business plan
- Emerging business needs
- People to meet present and future requirements
- Required resources
- Overall performance of people
- Ongoing business planning.

3. *Corporate executive development group.* This group has emerged as a crucial component of Westpac's succession planning system. Its management principles can be summarize as follows:

- The group is "owned" by line management and managed by HR staff in conjunction with the line.
- Development of program participants is the joint responsibility of the individual, the reporting manager, and the relevant development program manager.
- Cross-unit movement, training, education, and other development opportunities are to be managed in terms of business requirements but with support from the line.
- Managers of development program participants are consulted and involved at all times in their development planning. The support, cooperation, and involvement of managers are essential for development programs to work effectively.

Although it could be argued that various elements and outcomes of the broader HR and succession planning systems at Westpac have career development implications, it is under the umbrella of the corporate executive development group that four career development programs exist.

1. The management development scheme for new high-performing graduate entrants and current employees who are solid performers, willing to undertake formal education (if they do not already possess a degree or diploma), and have expressed interest in a management career.

2. The senior development program for junior to middle managers.
3. The executive development program for middle to senior managers.
4. The key executive group for senior executives and general (or higher) managers.

The key executive program, established in the late 1980s, is the culmination of Westpac's career development effort. It consists of individuals who have been assessed as Westpac's most critical resources with the potential to move into the senior executive positions. Participation in this program provides the ultimate development opportunity for those with general management and senior executive potential.

Linked to the succession planning process through the corporate executive development group, key executive development focuses on a framework of generic management competencies that both reflect and anticipate Westpac's changing business requirements.

Participants are selected through the ERR process. All recommendations are referred to the general manager of the HR division and the chief manager of executive resources, who then make final recommendations to the managing director. A range of assessment tools may be used to determine suitable applicants, including management competency ratings by individual and nominating managers, structured panel interviews, career path appreciation, career development interviews, psychological tests, and assessments undertaken earlier during tenure in the executive development program.

The central development strategies for the key executive group are:

*   Providing individual, broadly based development plans for all participants.
*   Ensuring that these plans are structured to provide development opportunities that further develop or enhance competencies in areas deemed essential.
*   Providing crossfunctional experiences.

- Planning development opportunities in at least two or three major business units.
- Providing work experiences that stretch and test individual potential.
- Providing international experience (preferably offshore assignments with emphasis on developing crosscultural understanding).
- Ensuring that equal employment opportunity principles are embraced.
- Emphasizing education and training to encourage lifelong learning.

Participation covers a three- to five-year cycle, with development plans reviewed at the end of each cycle. At this time, a review is conducted to determine whether participants remain in the program. This review may be conducted during the ERR or through a separate review of the corporate executive development group. Its outcome is communicated to the participant immediately and confidentially. Generally, along with past information provided through the ERR process, this review considers the following issues:

- Work performance as assessed through annual appraisals.
- Input from the reporting executive and other senior executives.
- Further development needs that have surfaced.
- Management competencies.
- The participant's own views of his or her career and continuation in the program.

Success is measured against program objectives. To date, the program has succeeded in meeting short-term replacement planning needs and is slowly but consistently enhancing the management competencies required to steer the organization through its evolution. The real success of this program will be seen over a longer period. It is hoped that in five to ten years, future leaders will be supported by sufficient reserves of talent developed across all functions of the business.

A MAJOR TELECOMMUNICATIONS COMPANY

Managers as People Developers

- Program driven by results of employee survey and manager needs for skill building
- Three-part initiative includes required development discussion, manager documentation of direct reports' activity, and employee survey for "360-degree" feedback
- Managers held accountable for people development on performance appraisal
- Focus on development and skill building
- Highly positive manager reactions

Background

An employee survey in the late 1980s revealed widespread manager dissatisfaction in this large telecommunications company. Managers felt that their mobility within the organization was being blocked if they were good at what they did. They also said they were not being given enough assistance and skill-building opportunities to support their role as people developers, despite the existence of tuition reimbursement and other supports.

  The company instituted a program focusing on the development of management employees, including a guaranteed mobility plan or "releasability policy" and a three-part development initiative for managers and their subordinates.

System Components

The core of the program is the three-part process:

1. A required development discussion between managers and their employees.
2. A form that enables managers to document the development opportunities they offered their subordinates during the year.

3. A survey form asking subordinates to describe what actually happened with regard to development.

The development discussion is a mandatory beginning-of-year conversation in which the employee's development goals for the year are mutually agreed upon. Both the manager and the employee keep a copy of the resulting plan, which may be updated as needed.

Along with this, managers' performance appraisals include a "development of people" objective. Results from the employee survey are a mandatory component of this; another piece is management observation. The survey is currently being revamped so as to eliminate unnecessary detail, focus more on upward appraisal, and serve as a tool for "360-degree" feedback—that is, feedback from multiple sources. Its scope will also be broadened to include leadership support for empowerment, communication, and corporate values. Senior management has provided a great deal of support for this initiative.

To ensure confidentiality, a minimum number of respondents is required before a survey report is generated for an individual manager; if this minimum is not reached, the results are aggregated up the line and included in a larger group report.

In addition to these elements, the program now includes an updated skills data base and a resource guide for both internal and external training and for development options. The program as a whole is geared toward development and skill building.

Results and Assessment

The goal of the program is to have a well-developed and trained management group to meet the challenges of the 1990s. Various other company management development programs, such as the core curriculum for newly promoted supervisors, tie in with this program.

Managers' reaction to the notion of upward appraisal, evidenced by focus-group findings, has been very positive. Notwithstanding possible anxiety about being evaluated by their own subordinates, managers seem to be pleased with the idea of being able to provide input for their own managers' development. In the future, consideration will be given to extending the survey to include the company's nonmanagement personnel.

CHAPTER 9

Career Development Successes: What Works and Why

Experience, as we all know, teaches us what theory cannot; fortunately, experience can be vicariously meaningful. Current organizational career development practice — the experience chronicled in this book — has much to teach practitioners as they design, put into place, and improve their own career development systems in organizations large and small.

In any endeavor, of course, success can be defined in part by its opposite: by what does *not* work. In this regard, our survey findings are worth recalling. The American respondents generally did not rate their career development systems very highly. They focused on upward mobility, saw the role of managers as weak, and were doing very little formal evaluation of their career development efforts — all of which complicated the design of viable systems. Moreover, when asked what they would have done differently and what they planned for the future, they repeatedly cited the need to increase systemization and accountability and to better support and train managers. These findings revealed to us some of the more problematic aspects of career development, things that so far have not worked as well or as predictably as practitioners might have hoped.

Yet we were struck, as we looked closely at state-of-the-art systems and best practices, by the existence of strong models for career development, systems that work well and give every ap-

---

Practical Tips from the Field

- Start off by making sure you understand the organizational culture and business needs.
- Focus on business objectives and drive everything from them.
- Involve top management early, and ensure that the system has champions.
- Develop a central philosophy or set of guiding concepts, but have the line implement the system and allow it to unfold on a business-unit basis.
- Always involve line managers and employees in design as well as implementation processes; ask them what they need and then use their feedback.
- Communicate consistently and constantly throughout the process.
- Look at the entire system and process, not just pieces.
- Start small, build ownership, pilot extensively, and build on successes.
- Allow for diverse learning styles and tools.
- Develop supporting structures and accountabilities.
- Continuously evaluate, revise, and improve.
- Expect system development to take time.
- Stay current in the field, read widely, and don't be afraid to seek assistance from others.

---

pearance of being able to meet future business requirements. These models share certain common success themes, which we explore in detail in this chapter.

How can practitioners build on these useful suggestions? Stepping back to look at the big picture, we can delineate two important realms of action: taking a systems approach to change and keeping career development alive.

Taking a Systems Change Approach

It has become abundantly clear that a systematic approach is needed if any organizational change effort, including career development, is to have a genuine, long-lasting impact. But what does this mean in practice?

One approach (Beckhard and Harris, 1977) identifies three elements that must be in place: (1) a *need* or opportunity for change, (2) a *vision* or picture of how the organization will be different as a result of the change, and (3) an *action plan* or first steps toward making the change happen. To these three elements, Leibowitz, Farren, and Kaye (1986) have added a fourth: *maintenance of the change.* In our view—amply confirmed by our survey findings—if any of these elements is not present, the organization will lack the energy to offset the difficulties and costs of making significant changes.

Our nine success themes (see Figure 9.1) fit into this framework. The first two relate to the element of need or opportunity; the next two, to vision; the next pair, to action; and the final three, to maintenance of change.

1. *Link development to business strategy.* As we have seen again and again, a career development system is much more likely to be effective if it is shaped by the business needs of the organization. Increasing acceptance of career development as a business necessity rather than a "nice-to-have" activity has come from recognition of its direct relevance to competitive advantage and the bottom line. Westpac, for example, developed succession planning as a competency-based means of achieving its core business objectives, and Kodak's business priority was to develop employees so they could keep up with new technologies. Nationwide Insurance faced the threat of losing some of its key technical talent, and OTC needed to build the international marketing capability of its sales force. Each of these organizations had a clear business need that drove career development and helped system designers keep their sights on what really mattered—meeting present and future requirements with a well-trained, motivated workforce.

Figure 9.1. A Systems Approach to Change.

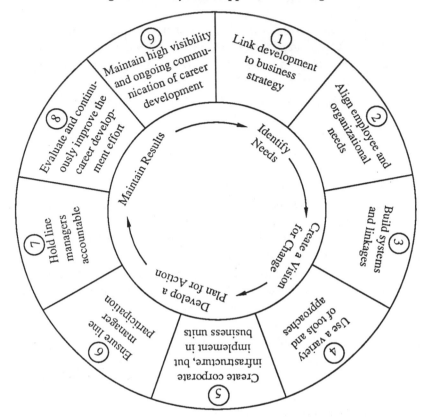

Source: Adapted from Z. B. Leibowitz, C. Farren, and B. L. Kaye, *Designing Career Development Systems* (San Francisco: Jossey-Bass, 1986).

2. *Align employee and organizational needs.* When individuals plan their careers in concert with overall business strategy and direction, the resulting win-win alignment can produce significant gains for both parties. Amoco created its career development system both to improve profitability and competitiveness and to help employees define and seek career success. Similarly, 3M found that its job information system was a way of making more internal talent available to hiring managers while simultaneously building employee awareness of opportunities within the organization. And BPX used career develop-

ment to respond to strong employee interest while also supporting the organization's strategic plan.

3. *Build systems and linkages.* Career development system
planning should start with a vision of how the organization will
operate differently as a result of the system. What will success
look like, and what will it mean for the everyday life of the
organization? This involves asking both how career development inteventions will tie together and how they will interact
with other HR systems and activities.

Both NCR and 3M connected already existing career
development tools and activities for maximum benefits. Corning and Boeing integrated their career development programs
with other HR initiatives such as performance management and
total quality. Corning found, for example, that using the language of quality in its career development activities reinforced
both initiatives. And Baxter Healthcare's career development
program began with the revision of its performance appraisal
system.

4. *Use a variety of tools and approaches.* Adults have varying
learning styles and preferences, and different work sites require
different approaches. A good career development system takes
this into account and offers an array of tools and activities.

Bechtel designed approaches ranging from self-study
courses to workbooks and audio tapes to development sessions
and a walk-in clinic for hands-on assistance. Kodak has internal
career centers with professional career counselors and libraries
as well as software, workbooks, and workshops; Boeing has a
similar range of tools. Baxter's system of performance and employee review and career self-assessment is designed as an interrelated and flexible set of activities; employees can enter the
system at any point.

5. *Create a corporate infrastructure, but implement career development systems in individual business units or divisions.* Kodak, Corning, BPX, and AT&T all found that the most effective way of
building a career development system is to lay out a guiding
philosophy and then to let implementation occur throughout
separate business units. When systems develop locally and vol-

untarily, they fit better with specific business needs and thus gain more buy-in, ownership, and commitment.

6. *Ensure line manager participation.* Because managers are a critical link in a career development system, it is essential to get their buy-in and participation early in the process. In fact, Ford and the telecommunications company we studied focused their interventions specifically on the needs of middle managers, who saw the need for their own development in the face of a changing business environment. Clearly, if managers are to develop their employees, they in turn need to be developed so they can perform this role effectively. Boeing managers, for example, go through mandatory career development training.

7. *Hold line managers accountable.* To put teeth in the system, accountability mechanisms have to be built in so that the effects are sustained over time. AT&T, Corning, Boeing, and the telecommunications company have made "people development" an important part of the manager's performance appraisal; the latter three organizations also introduced upward appraisals or subordinate feedback as part of this process.

8. *Evaluate and continuously improve the career development effort.* Ongoing evaluation, revision, and refinement—a central feature of total quality management—occurs in most state-of-the-art systems. Corning and Boeing have done pre- and post-surveys to measure the impact of career development interventions, and Corning has developed conditions of success against which local organizations can benchmark their activities. Similarly, APC's comprehensive four-phase planning and implementation process used a continuous improvement approach even though the system was still in the development stage. And AT&T has done a number of employee surveys and workshop audits to track the progress and effects of its career development system.

9. *Maintain high visibility and ongoing communication of career development.* To become institutionalized, career development needs to be a high-profile, well-publicized undertaking. Boeing, Bechtel, and AT&T ensured this by using videos, bulletins, posters, and brochures that featured top leaders' endorsements of their systems. The ALC held publicity events on site. The U.S. General Accounting Office announced the opening of its career

center with a ribbon-cutting ceremony and has continued to publicize it through posters, brochures, bulletins, and meetings with managers.

Keeping Career Development Alive

The process of sustaining a change effort is always very challenging. Even the best career development systems lose their edge and effectiveness, and may even fade completely, if they are not carefully cultivated for longevity. Many pressures — competition, fast-moving technological advances, and shifting workforce demographics, to name just a few — can weaken even the most thoughtfully conceived change initiatives.

However, there are ways of keeping career development alive. Here are some strategies that we consider very effective (Leibowitz and Kaye, 1991).

1. Follow up implementation with hard-hitting activities and offerings such as these:
    a. "Learning while doing" projects to help individuals gain specific competencies and enrich their jobs.
    b. Mentoring (in groups or one on one) and career action teams (ongoing support and talent-sharing groups for employees and managers).
    c. Coaching clinics (often with a skill or problem orientation).
    d. Manager/staff meetings for information trading.
2. Connect the system with other HR structures wherever possible, as in these examples:
    a. *Performance appraisal:* Make the distinction between development for current requirements and for future needs.
    b. *Total quality management:* Keep the focus on a shared goal of continuous improvement.
    c. *Competencies:* Make these real — and urgent — for employees in all their career planning efforts.
    d. *Orientation:* Streamline and strengthen the joining-up process to retain good employees.

    e.   *Succession planning:* Make sure people are trained and ready to replace exiting managers.

    f.   *Compensation:* Reward people not just for being in place but for value-added performance.

3.   Communicate and plan constantly.

    a.   Rely on planning teams with cross-organizational representation.

    b.   Build strategic alliances with others in the organization.

    c.   Use public reviews and other open forums for information sharing, motivation, and celebration of successes.

    d.   Use one initiative to publicize another.

4.   Make managers accountable for people development.

    a.   Define critical skills and standards for people development.

    b.   Give managers feedback on their skills.

    c.   Provide opportunities for skill development.

    d.   Link development of employees with rewards and possible sanctions.

5.   Continuously monitor, evaluate, and revise.

    a.   Use multiple evaluation measures: of attitudes, behaviors, and knowledge.

    b.   Collect data on needs up front, for benchmarking purposes.

    c.   Offer rewards.

    d.   Keep the process positive, open, and nonthreatening.

A Final Word

The nine success themes reported here were culled from our case studies and examination of best practices, and from advice offered by interviewees who evaluated their own experiences. One of the most striking features of these themes is that they all demonstrate that career development should be considered a work in progress. As many interviewees noted, it takes considerable time to develop a viable system and to assess its effects. It also takes a great deal of work to sustain it.

    Most of the people we talked with said they were still "in

process" and had a long way to go before they could proclaim their efforts successful. Yet in our view, their commitment to constant evaluation, revision, and improvement definitely earns them the title of "success models." Our hope is that readers will view their experiences as something to strive for in a spirit of continuous improvement, as did the dedicated practitioners we studied.

CONCLUSION

Challenges and Recommendations for the Twenty-First Century

> The predictable conditions of the transitional decade of the 1990s, including the unpredictability of events, will require more fundamental change efforts involving large organizations than at any time in the past. . . .
> A paradox is that the more uncertain the environment, the more there is a need for a well-designed and -managed organization that is purposeful and energized to thrive in such uncertainty.
> —Richard Beckhard and Wendy Pritchard,
> *Changing the Essence*

> Today the success of businesses is directly linked to the development, commitment, and full participation of all employees. . . . The challenge for business in the 1990s will be to liberate the creativity and win the full commitment of all employees.
> —Charles Garfield,
> *Second to None*

Change is a continuum. The career development systems and practices we profiled in this book exemplify, in many ways, the future directions predicted by our survey respondents, who were themselves experimenting with many of the issues raised by respondents in the 1978 survey. These shifting career directions, however, should be set in the broader context of changes affecting the workplace as a whole, changes that have serious implications for development.

196

The Context of Development

Several important trends and issues already in evidence will have a dramatic impact on the workplace of the twenty-first century.

The link between business strategy and people development. More and more companies recognize that developing people is central to organizational effectiveness. Leaders of organizations increasingly view the HR division as a member of the strategic team. Now that technology advantages are lessening, what differentiates organizations and provides the competitive edge are the skills, commitment, and talent of the workforce. More organizations are seeing the link between big-picture strategic planning and the development needs of individual employees.

Organizational downsizing, reorganizing, and restructuring. A variety of factors, from increased economic pressures to the problem of overstaffing, have led many organizations to become leaner and meaner. Whether called downsizing or rightsizing, the reduction of management layers and permanent layoffs of employees are frequent occurrences. Organizations once known for providing long-term job security no longer offer such promises as they remove literally thousands of employees from their rolls. In short, the constant threat of changes and concomitant insecurity have become facts of organizational life in the 1990s.

Reshaping of the workforce. Another facet of organizational restructuring is a shift in the shape of the existing workforce. More and more workforces are moving to a model in which a small group of core or essential workers is surrounded by a contingent group of temporary and part-time employees and independent contractors; all nonessential functions are outsourced. In some cases, workers become part of the contingent workforce by choice; in many others, it is their only alternative to being unemployed.

The changed psychological contract between organizations and employees. One major effect of organizational restructuring and the core-contingent workforce model has been a rewriting of the unspoken rules and expectations that exist between individuals and the organizations that hire them. The old rules of the game were that in exchange for hard work and loyalty, employees were rewarded with a paycheck and the implicit promise of job security for years to come. However, with few of today's organizations able to make this promise, there is a new currency: organizations now offer opportunities for employees to grow and develop during their tenure and they exact employees' commitment for the duration of that tenure. Where employee loyalty exists, it is often to a profession rather than to an organization.

Work-life balance. The loyalty shift also involves realms outside the workplace. In the 1980s, there was frequent talk of "new-value" employees, who looked to their work to fulfill their needs for growth and personal development. While this is often still true of the baby-boomers, the baby-bust generation that has followed operates on the basis of a different set of constructs. Having seen baby-boomers' investment in work often rewarded with stress, burnout, or layoffs, many in this new generation have vowed to invest more heavily in other areas of life, such as family, community, or religious activities. A number of organizations, motivated by enlightenment or necessity, have taken steps to accommodate these shifting priorities through flexible schedules and leave policies.

Workforce diversity. An even more pressing reason for organizations to address the work-life balance is the change in the demographics of the workforce, which is composed increasingly of women, minorities, and disabled and older workers. Organizations are faced with a variety of employee needs, including time for child rearing and elder care, literacy, and accessible working conditions and schedules. Recruitment and retention of workers are clearly related to how effectively organizations can meet these concerns.

Focus on quality. Total quality management (TQM) is a dominant concern of many organizations. Heralded as a new way of business, TQM, with its themes of customer service, excellence, and continuous improvement, is seen as essential to gaining and maintaining a competitive advantage.

Empowerment of employees. TQM happens as employees are empowered to make decisions and take responsibility for delivering error-free products and services. Many organizations have developed self-manged work teams as the structure through which work is done. Increasingly, these work teams emphasize participation — a significant departure from the old-style model of "direct and control," where employees simply executed the directives of managers. In this newer model, managers spend much more time coaching, providing resources, and championing change efforts than administering, directing, and monitoring task completion.

Changed competency and skill requirements. Another outgrowth of empowerment is that effectiveness requires different competencies. This is true for both managers and employees. Central to success in management is an ability to lead and to motivate others to become change agents. Managers need to be comfortable empowering others to make decisions and coaching them through the process. They also need a big-picture focus that takes into account the business strategy of the organization as well as how different divisions, units, or work groups fit into that strategy. Employees, too, need to think big and to work comfortably and effectively in team settings. Communication skills — listening, speaking, and writing — are essential for team participation. The abilities to think ahead, to plan for contingencies, to be proactive, and to maintain a customer focus are also crucial. Flexibility and adaptability to change are necessary for both managers and employees.

The creation of "learning organizations." With the increased awareness of the importance of the new competencies for competitiveness, organizations are focusing on creating atmospheres of learning and continual development. There is a new emphasis on how people learn and develop most effectively and what the organization can do to foster this process.

Technology. Rapid changes in technology have transformed every aspect of the workplace. New skills and learning are required to adjust to new ways of doing business. Moreover, the pace of technological change continues to speed up.

The global context. Modern technology has, among other

things, created communications vehicles that have brought the world closer together. Competition occurs in a global rather than a national context, and success in business requires an understanding of the rest of the world. This global, multi-cultural focus becomes increasingly important as we near the next century.

Implications

The broad context outlined above has significant implications for organizational career development on the brink of the twenty-first century. Some are quite positive. The culture shift toward empowerment of employees and new roles for managers is very much in line with two central emphases of organizational career development—that employees take responsibility for their own development and that managers play an important coaching and facilitation role in the process. The greater acceptance of the link between business strategy and development and the need for new competencies in learning organizations both underscore the crucial importance of organizational support for career development systems and processes. TQM's emphasis on evaluation, measurement, and improvement should create a greater commitment to (and experience with) the concept of evaluating career development. Organizational restructuring and the changed psychological contract both suggest a broadened definition of career development away from traditional notions of moving up a career ladder toward a focus on fostering growth, challenge, and job enrichment.

Even some negatives such as reduced job security have positive implications, as they underscore the importance of continual employee cross training and retraining. This, as well as the need for a global and big-picture focus, suggests that workers should develop portfolios of transferable skills. Technological change is likely to lead to more and better innovations in career development activities. And the needs and opportunities related to employee diversity clearly mandate attention to the varied developmental requirements of diverse populations.

There are some negative implications, however. Downsizing and economic pressure can lead to a focus away from development, as organizations become frozen in concerns about immediate survival. Decreases in loyalty and job security can engender employee cynicism, fear, or lack of interest in the considerable work involved in undertaking career development processes. Norms governing careers and employee-manager relationships differ across diverse cultural groups and can potentially create difficulties in obtaining buy-in to the process.

These issues and implications, as well as the research presented in this book, have prompted us to offer a set of recommendations for the future of organizational career development.

Recommendations

To enhance the progress of organizational career development, we recommend that organizations adopt the following strategies.

1. *Integrate development planning and strategic planning.* Make the link explicitly at all levels of the organization. Involve managers and employees in a process of examining the direction of the business and then assessing the implications for development needs and strategies.

2. *Strengthen linkages between career development and other HR systems.* With the increased sophistication of career development systems comes a recognition of the ways in which they interact with other areas of human resources. For example, job posting, performance appraisal, compensation, and succession planning all affect and are affected by career development. Enlightened HR planning involves a collaboration among representatives of all these systems to address their interaction. This kind of systems thinking maximizes the benefits from all HR areas.

3. *Move career development systems toward greater openness.* Organizations can no longer afford to be closed with respect to control and information. While managers must support career development efforts, they cannot control them; employees have primary responsibility for their own careers. In the same vein, a

free flow of information is crucial to ensure that everyone involved in a career development system has access to vital resources, feedback, and information on new opportunities. The
question of how employees are seen by supervisors—which
naturally relates to feedback as an "open-system" feature—
also affects other HR planning processes, such as performance
appraisals.

4. *Enhance the role of managers in career development through
both skill building and accountability.* It is essential to hold managers accountable for the development of their employees—but by
itself not sufficient. They must also be amply supported in this
process. To be effective coaches and facilitators, managers must
be trained in these skills and then receive ongoing support and
followup as they use these skills on the job. In essence, they need
coaching in their role as coaches. Also, part of training managers for this role involves clarifying the standards or dimensions
of developing employees, offering examples of what is involved
in being a developer of people.

5. *Develop and expand peer-learning methodologies and other
team-based development approaches.* With increased employee empowerment and participation and with managers playing a less
traditional role, the impetus and responsibility for development
will lie more and more in the hands of self-managed teams. Peer-
learning models should be actively explored and developed; as
teams are more involved in linking development needs to business realities, team development needs will become more apparent. Methodologies for addressing those needs should be
expanded.

6. *Stress on-the-job development; deemphasize traditional training approaches.* Research has underscored the value of learning
on the job as well as the importance of practice, reinforcement,
and followup. If learning is to stick, it must be an ongoing
process instead of a one-shot event. In many cases, the ongoing
approach is also the most cost effective. This is not to say that
employees and managers should not go to training sessions;
however, such sessions should be carefully leveraged for maximum benefits and effectiveness.

7. *Emphasize enrichment and lateral movement.* The defini-

tion of success needs to be uncoupled from the traditional notions of upward mobility and job change. There will be fewer and fewer opportunities for promotions, and career development should emphasize the strong value of growing and learning in one's current job as well as maintaining challenge by exploring other areas within an organization.

8. *Identify and develop transferable competencies.* Restructuring inevitably brings increased job change, either within an organization or outside it. Career development should include a common language — that of competencies — for talking about the skills, attributes, and knowledge needed for success in today's workplace. This language can then be used in everything from recruiting through job descriptions, development, and performance management. One competency that should be highlighted is adaptability to change.

9. *In career development activities, including values and lifestyle assessments.* Decisions that employees make about leaving or staying at organizations, as well as how committed they are to their jobs, are related (often subconsciously) to the degree of fit between their values and those of the organization. It is important to bring these values to the surface so that they can be addressed and good employees can be retained. With the increased prominence and relevance of issues surrounding work-life balance, career development activities can and should be a forum for addressing these issues as well.

10. *Implement a variety of career development approaches to accommodate different learning styles and the needs of a diverse workforce.* What works for one employee may be problematic for another. A workshop may be the ideal setting for one person to learn; another person may be uncomfortable in a workshop and prefer a workbook. A work group in a distant location may learn best through computer instructional programs. Part of the business of a learning organization is accommodating different approaches and needs. Part of the mission of effective career development is to help people understand their own learning styles so they can pick the best approach.

11. *Tie career development directly to quality initiatives.* The two processes are very much related and complement each

other. A workforce will not be a high-quality workforce unless it is developed; continuous learning and improvement are central to quality. A career development system works best by focusing on stakeholder (internal customer) needs and by emphasizing continual measurement and improvement of the system. The quality focus on employee empowerment should be linked to the need for employees to take responsibility for their own development.

12. *Expand career development measurement and evaluation.* Build measurement and continuous improvement into all phases of career development system implementation. Also, organizations should explore "macro" evaluation to assess the impact of development on overall business performance. This moves a step beyond most current career development evaluation approaches, which examine only career development outcomes, not how they affect the larger organization.

13. *Continue to study best practices and organizational career development in a global context.* Whether organizations do their own exploration or study the work of independent researchers, it is important to begin a tradition of benchmarking in a global context. Practitioners should continue to learn from success stories, and the sphere of inquiry should no longer be confined to a few countries. This study has made clear the worldwide reach of innovative efforts. It is indeed true — and important — that we all learn from each other.

We can expect to see development grow and flourish in the twenty-first century as a genuine partnership between individuals and organizations. This partnership will be essential to maintaining a committed, talented, and productive workforce. The promising evolution of this partnership, showcased in this book, has pointed all of us in new directions for continued success.

Appendixes

APPENDIX A:
ASTD SURVEY QUESTIONNAIRE AND RESULTS

ASTD Survey of Organizational
Career Development Practices

In many organizations, career development is a relative new-comer to the human resource planning and development process. Practices differ from organization to organization, and little hard information on organizational experience with formal career development programs has been available. In an attempt to change that, a survey of organizational career practices was conducted in 1978. Much has happened since then, and this survey is an effort to capture some of these changes. We hope the results will guide organizations in their decisions on new policies and practices in career development.

Please respond to the questions on the attached survey concerning career planning and development practices in your organization. Please respond even if you do not have a formal career development program. If you work in a subsidiary of a larger, parent company, please address all of your answers to the subsidiary company environment.

Every respondent will receive a summary of the survey results.

Directions: For most items you need circle only the number of the most appropriate response. Unless noted otherwise, circle only one response per question.

1. Which of the following best describes your organization?
   1. Manufacturing (consumer)
   2. Manufacturing (industrial)
   3. Retail/wholesale trade
   4. Banking, finance, insurance, real estate
   5. Energy (public utilities, petroleum, chemicals)
   6. Education/nonprofit
   7. Government/military
   8. Services (business services, food and hospitality, recreation, repairs)
   9. Medical/health care

10. Diversified/conglomerate (explain): _____

_____

11. High tech
12. Other: _____

2. Your organization's annual sales or annual budget:
   1. Under $25 million
   2. $25 million to $49 million
   3. $50 million to $99 million
   4. $100 million to $499 million
   5. $500 million to $999 million
   6. $1 billion or over

3. How many employees are there in your entire organization?
   1. Fewer than 500
   2. 500 to 999
   3. 1,000 to 4,999
   4. 5,000 to 9,999
   5. 10,000 to 24,999
   6. 25,000 to 49,999.
   7. 50,000 or more

   Of these, how many are salaried?
   1. Fewer than 500
   2. 500 to 999
   3. 1,000 to 4,999
   4. 5,000 to 9,999
   5. 10,000 to 24,999
   6. 25,000 to 49,999
   7. 50,000 or more

4. Where is your organization headquartered?
   1. Northeast
   2. Mid-Atlantic
   3. Southeast
   4. Midwest
   5. Northwest
   6. West Coast
   7. Southwest
   8. Outside the U.S. (specify): _____
   9. Other: _____

5. Which of the following best describes your organization in terms of markets served and scope of operations?
   1. Local
   2. Regional
   3. National
   4. International

6. Is there currently an organizational career development system in your organization?

    By "organizational career development system," we mean a system of processes and practices designed to link an individual employee's career goals with the organization's human resource needs. Examples of career development programs and activities would include workshops, manager-employee career discussions, resource centers, career planning software, and succession/replacement planning:

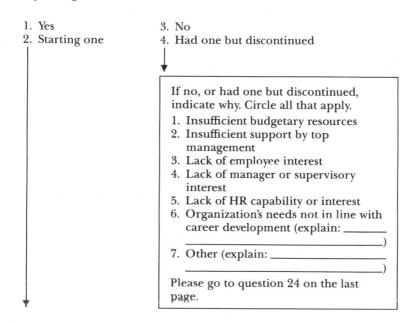

1. Yes
2. Starting one

3. No
4. Had one but discontinued

If no, or had one but discontinued, indicate why. Circle all that apply.

1. Insufficient budgetary resources
2. Insufficient support by top management
3. Lack of employee interest
4. Lack of manager or supervisory interest
5. Lack of HR capability or interest
6. Organization's needs not in line with career development (explain: _____ _____)
7. Other (explain: _____ _____)

Please go to question 24 on the last page.

7. If yes, or starting one:

    Some career development systems emphasize the individual employee, while others focus on the organization. Indicate on the continuum below where you would place your organization's career development efforts in terms of this focus:

    Individual |_____|_____|_____|_____| *Organization*
    0   25   50   75   100

    Please explain your response: _____
    _____

8. How long have you had a career development system in place?
    1. Less than a year
    2. One to two years
    3. Three to four years
    4. Five to six years
    5. More than six years

9. Where does the responsibility for your career development system reside?
   1. Centralized
   2. Decentralized
   3. Both

10. Is there a particular unit or function assigned responsibility for career development?

   1. No   2. Yes

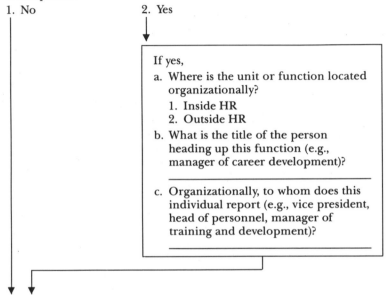

If yes,
a. Where is the unit or function located organizationally?
   1. Inside HR
   2. Outside HR
b. What is the title of the person heading up this function (e.g., manager of career development)?

_____

c. Organizationally, to whom does this individual report (e.g., vice president, head of personnel, manager of training and development)?

_____

11. How many human resource staffpersons, if any, are there in your organization devoted full time to career development, including yourself?
   0. Less than one
   1. One
   2. Two
   3. Three or four
   4. Five or more

12. Organizational career systems vary in their view of who is responsible for career development—the employee, the manager, or the organization. Please assign percentages of responsibility to these three parties as reflected in your organization's system, adding up to 100%.
   Employee _____% Manager _____% Organization _____%

13. Which groups are covered by your career development system? Circle all that apply.
    1. Exempt salaried employees
    2. Nonexempt salaried employees
    3. Hourly employees

Please respond to the remaining questions as they apply to exempt salaried employees only. If your career development system does not cover exempt salaried employees, please go to question 24 on the last page.

---

14. Please indicate those salaried employee groups for whom you have targeted career development programs. Please circle all that apply.
    1. Preretirees
    2. Women employees
    3. Minority employees
    4. Management trainees
    5. "Fast-track" management candidates or high-potentials
    6. Handicapped employees
    7. Older workers
    8. Plateaued employees
    9. New employees
    10. Other (specify): _____

15. From the list below, please indicate the top three factors that influenced the development of your organization's career planning or development programs.
    Write in the number of the

    | ☐ Most important | ☐ Second most important | ☐ Third most important |

    1. Organizational commitment to career development
    2. Shortage of promotable talent
    3. Concern about turnover
    4. Equal employment opportunity program commitments
    5. Desire to motivate employees under conditions of limited organizational growth
    6. Desire to develop or promote from within
    7. Desire to keep up with competitors
    8. Strong expression of employee interest in career planning
    9. Survey or needs assessment findings
    10. Shift in skill mix or human resources planning needs
    11. Development of organization's strategic plan
    12. Desire to improve worker productivity
    13. Need to encourage early retirement
    14. Desire for positive recruiting image
    15. Desire to avoid unionization
    16. Other (specify): _____

16. Have you used a task force, advisory group, or consultative committee in the design or implementation of your career development system?

    1. Yes   2. No

    If yes, how would you rate its effectiveness? Circle the number of the appropriate response:

    Very   *Very*
    Ineffective 1.................2.................3.................4.................5 *Effective*

17. For the career development practices listed below, please indicate their status in your organization. If a practice currently exists, please rate its effectiveness. Circle the appropriate response for each item:

	Never did this	Discontinued this	Planning this	Doing this	If you are currently doing this, please rate its effectiveness:				
					Very Ineffective				Very Effective
A. *Employee self-assessment tools*									
1. Career planning workshops	ND	DIS	P	Doing	1	2	3	4	5
2. Career workbooks (stand-alone)	ND	DIS	P	Doing	1	2	3	4	5
3. Preretirement workshops	ND	DIS	P	Doing	1	2	3	4	5
4. Computer software	ND	DIS	P	Doing	1	2	3	4	5
B. *Organizational potential assessment processes*									
5. Promotability forecasts	ND	DIS	P	Doing	1	2	3	4	5
6. Psychological testing	ND	DIS	P	Doing	1	2	3	4	5
7. Assessment centers	ND	DIS	P	Doing	1	2	3	4	5
8. Interview process	ND	DIS	P	Doing	1	2	3	4	5
9. Job assignment	ND	DIS	P	Doing	1	2	3	4	5
C. *Internal labor-market information exchanges*									
10. Career information handbooks	ND	DIS	P	Doing	1	2	3	4	5
11. Career ladders or dual-career ladders	ND	DIS	P	Doing	1	2	3	4	5
12. Career resource center	ND	DIS	P	Doing	1	2	3	4	5
13. Other career information formats or systems	ND	DIS	P	Doing	1	2	3	4	5
D. *Individual counseling or career discussions*									
14. Supervisor or line manager	ND	DIS	P	Doing	1	2	3	4	5
15. Senior career advisers	ND	DIS	P	Doing	1	2	3	4	5
16. Personnel staff	ND	DIS	P	Doing	1	2	3	4	5
17. Specialized counselor a) internal	ND	DIS	P	Doing	1	2	3	4	5
b) external	ND	DIS	P	Doing	1	2	3	4	5

	Never did this	Discontinued this	Planning this	Doing this	If you are currently doing this, please rate its effectiveness:				
					Very Ineffective				Very Effective
E. *Job-matching systems*									
18. Informal canvassing	ND	DIS	P	Doing	1	2	3	4	5
19. Job posting	ND	DIS	P	Doing	1	2	3	4	5
20. Skills inventories or skills audit	ND	DIS	P	Doing	1	2	3	4	5
21. Replacement or succession planning	ND	DIS	P	Doing	1	2	3	4	5
22. Staffing committees	ND	DIS	P	Doing	1	2	3	4	5
23. Internal placement system	ND	DIS	P	Doing	1	2	3	4	5
F. *Development programs*									
24. Job enrichment or job redesign	ND	DIS	P	Doing	1	2	3	4	5
25. Job rotation	ND	DIS	P	Doing	1	2	3	4	5
26. In-house training and development programs	ND	DIS	P	Doing	1	2	3	4	5
27. External seminars or workshops	ND	DIS	P	Doing	1	2	3	4	5
28. Tuition reimbursement	ND	DIS	P	Doing	1	2	3	4	5
29. Supervisor training in career discussions	ND	DIS	P	Doing	1	2	3	4	5
30. Dual-career couple programs	ND	DIS	P	Doing	1	2	3	4	5
31. Mentoring systems	ND	DIS	P	Doing	1	2	3	4	5
32. Employee orientation programs	ND	DIS	P	Doing	1	2	3	4	5

If you discontinued any of the practices listed in Question 17 above, please indicate which practices were discontinued, approximately how long they were in effect, and why they were abandoned.

Practice discontinued	How long it was in effect	Reason for discontinuing
_____	_____	_____
_____	_____	_____
_____	_____	_____

18. Please check all of the personnel systems below that you have in your organization and indicate whether they are linked with career development (Y = yes, N = no).

	Have it?		Linked to career development?	
a. Performance appraisal (planning and review)	Y	N	Y	N
b. Recruitment practices	Y	N	Y	N
c. Promotion and transfer practices	Y	N	Y	N
d. Salary administration	Y	N	Y	N
e. Job description or evaluation	Y	N	Y	N
f. Human resource planning	Y	N	Y	N

	Have it?	Linked to career development?
g. Organizational strategic planning	Y N	Y N
h. Employee assistance programs	Y N	Y N
i. Organization design	Y N	Y N
j. Equal employment opportunity or affirmative action	Y N	Y N
k. Other (specify): _____	Y N	Y N

19. In your opinion, how would your organization view the following statements regarding career development? Circle the appropriate response for each item.

	Strongly agree	Agree	Disagree	Strongly disagree
1. Career development programs must be tied in with the organization's strategic plan.	SA	A	D	SD
2. Senior management believes career development raises employee expectations.	SA	A	D	SD
3. Senior management feels that career development is a fad.	SA	A	D	SD
4. Senior management believes that career development is an important part of employee development.	SA	A	D	SD
5. Managers believe career development is not really anything new.	SA	A	D	SD
6. Managers believe career development is not needed.	SA	A	D	SD
7. Career development means an increased burden for supervisor.	SA	A	D	SD
8. Few supervisors are equipped to hold employee career discussions.	SA	A	D	SD
9. Supervisors feel that employee career development is not part of their job.	SA	A	D	SD
10. Turnover increases as a result of employee participation in career development programs.	SA	A	D	SD
11. Only a small percentage of employees are really interested in career development.	SA	A	D	SD
12. Career development enhances the job performance of employees.	SA	A	D	SD
13. Career development increases personal anxiety for many employees.	SA	A	D	SD
14. Career development allows improved utilization of employee talents.	SA	A	D	SD
15. Career development strains the capacity of other human resources systems such as job posting, employee training, tuition reimbursement, etc.	SA	A	D	SD
16. Career development equips employees to use personnel systems more effectively.	SA	A	D	SD
17. Career development generally disrupts an organization.	SA	A	D	SD
18. Career development is best introduced on a pilot, experimental basis.	SA	A	D	SD
19. Job requirements and career information need not be provided in a career development program.	SA	A	D	SD
20. Employees' participation in a career development program should be voluntary.	SA	A	D	SD

Strongly agree Agree Disagree Strongly disagree

21. Employees should be able to keep confidential their records or other outputs of career planning activities.   SA A D SD
22. Career development helps employees deal with a stable, low-growth environment.   SA A D SD

20. How are your career development programs or practices evaluated? Circle all that apply.
    1. No evaluation is done
    2. Informal verbal feedback from participants
    3. Interviews of focus groups to measure attitudes, learning, or behavior
    4. Questionnaires to measure attitudes, learning, or behavior
    5. Data analysis re: productivity, performance, mobility, costs, etc.

    6. Other (specify): _____

    _____

21. Overall, how effective is your career development system?
    1. Very ineffective
    2. Somewhat ineffective
    3. In between
    4. Somewhat effective
    5. Very effective

    Please elaborate: _____

    _____

    _____

    _____

    _____

    _____

22. What in your opinion has been the major impact (positive or negative) of your organization's career development effort?

    _____

    _____

    _____

    _____

    _____

    _____

23. What, if anything, would you have done differently with your organization's career development system?

_____

_____

_____

_____

_____

_____

24. What are your organization's plans for future career development practices?

_____

_____

_____

_____

_____

_____

25. In your view, how has organizational career development changed (if at all) in the last ten years?

_____

_____

_____

_____

_____

_____

We invite you to attach copies of any materials that may be useful in our interpretation of the information you have provided. If we may identify your organization by name in relation to your practices, please indicate here □. Otherwise, all answers will be kept strictly confidential and will be presented only as part of the aggregated statistics.

Organization name _____

Name of individual to contact _____

Title _____

Address _____

City _____ State _____ Zip _____

Phone: (   ) _____ Ext. _____

Thank you for your participation!

Survey Results: U.S. Corporate Sample

Noted in parentheses after each question is the number of valid cases. Total N = 256.

1. Which of the following best describes your organization?
   - 7.5%   Manufacturing (consumer)
   - 22.9   Manufacturing (industrial)
   - 4.7   Retail/wholesale trade
   - 24.5   Banking, finance, insurance, real estate
   - 18.6   Energy (public utilities, petroleum, chemicals)
   - .4   Education/nonprofit
   - .4   Government/military
   - 4.0   Services (business services, food and lodging, recreation, repairs)
   - 2.0   Medical/health care
   - 4.3   Diversified/conglomerate
   - 5.1   High tech
   - 5.5   Other
   - (253)

2. Your organization's annual sales or annual budget:
   - 2.9%   Under $25 million
   - 1.3 $25 million to $49 million
   - 2.9 $50 million to $99 million
   - 22.7 $100 million to $499 million
   - 16.8 $500 million to $999 million
   - 53.4   Over 1 billion
   - (238)

3. How many employees are there in your entire organization?

4.3%	Fewer than 500
7.1	500 to 999
35.3	1,000 to 4,999
18.0	5,000 to 9,999
17.3	10,000 to 24,999
9.8	25,000 to 49,999
8.2	50,000 or more
	(255)

Of these, how many are salaried?

15.2%	Fewer than 500
15.7	500 to 999
42.2	1,000 to 4,999
10.3	5,000 to 9,999
9.4	10,000 to 24,999
4.9	25,000 to 49,999
2.2	50,000 or more
	(223)

4. Where is your organization headquartered?

25.2%	Northeast
9.8	Mid-Atlantic
6.3	Southeast
38.2	Midwest
2.0	Northwest
8.7	West Coast
7.9	Southwest
.4	Outside the U.S.
1.6	Other
	(254)

5. Which of the following best describes your organization in terms of markets served and scope of operations:

7.1%	Local
29.1	Regional
21.3	National
42.5	International
	(254)

6. Is there currently an organizational career development system in your organization?

47.0% Yes   30.9 No
20.5 Starting one   1.6   Had one but discontinued
      (249)

36.5%	Insufficient budgetary resources
54.0	Insufficient support by top management
9.5	Lack of employee interest
23.8	Lack of manager or supervisor interest
27.0	Lack of HR capability or interest
23.8	Organization's needs not in line with career development
19.0	Other (63)

7. Some career development systems emphasize the individual employee, while others focus on the organization. Indicate on the continuum below where you would place your organization's career development efforts in terms of this focus:

Mean = 50.4   SD = 22   Median = 50   Mode = 50   (169)

Individual |————————|————————|————————|————————| Organization
          0   25   50   75   100

8. How long have you had a career development system in place?

25.5% Less than a year
20.6   One to two years
16.4   Three to four years
12.7   Five to six years
24.8   More than six years
       (165)

9. Where does the responsibility for your career development system reside?

37.5% Centralized
10.2   Decentralized
52.3   Both
       (176)

10. Is there a particular unit or function assigned responsibility for career development?

23.3% No   76.7% Yes
        (180)

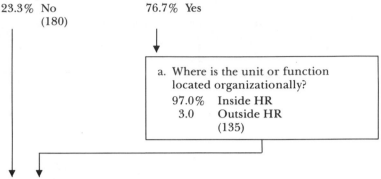

a. Where is the unit or function located organizationally?
97.0%   Inside HR
 3.0   Outside HR
        (135)

11. How many human resource staffpersons, if any, are there in your organization devoted full time to career development, including yourself?

54.1%   Less than one
21.0   One
 9.4   Two
 5.5   Three or four
 9.9   Five or more
        (181)

12. Organizational career systems vary in their view of who is responsible for career development — the employee, the manager, or the organization. Please assign percentages of responsibility to these three parties as reflected in your organization's system, adding up to 100%.

Employee	*Manager*	*Organization*
Mean = 51.9 SD = 22	Mean = 25.4 SD = 13	Mean = 24.3 SD = 16
Median = 50	Median = 25	Median = 20
Mode = 50	Mode = 25	Mode = 25

13. Which groups are covered by your career development system?

98.8%   Exempt salaried employees
58.7   Nonexempt salaried employees
35.5   Hourly employees
        (172)

14. Please indicate those salaried employee groups for whom you have targeted career development programs.

18.1%   Preretirees
49.4   Women employees
50.6   Minority employees
56.0   Management trainees
74.1   "Fast-track" management candidates or high-potentials
16.9   Handicapped employees

16.9   Older workers
28.9   Plateaued employees
36.1   New employees
29.5   Other
        (166)

15. From the list below, please indicate the top three factors that influenced the development of your organization's career planning/development programs.

[Items cited as most important]

12.6%   Organizational commitment to career development
13.8   Shortage of promotable talent
2.3   Concern about turnover
2.3   Equal employment opportunity program commitments
8.0   Desire to motivate employees under conditions of limited organizational growth
23.0   Desire to develop or promote from within
4.0   Desire to keep up with competitors
6.3   Strong expression of employee interest in career planning
5.2   Survey or needs assessment findings
3.4   Shift in skill mix or human resources planning needs
12.1   Development of organization's strategic plan
1.7   Desire to improve worker productivity
0   Need to encourage early retirement
.6   Desire for positive recruiting image
0   Desire to avoid unionization
4.6   Other
        (174)

16. Have you used a task force or advisory group in the design or implementation of your career development system?

49.1% Yes   50.9% No
    (175)

↓

> If yes, how would you rate its effectiveness? Circle the number of the appropriate response:
>
> *Very*   *Very*
> *Ineffective* 1 ....2................3................4................5 *Effective*
>
> Mean = 3.6   SD = .9   Median = 4   Mode = 3   (83)

17. For the career development practices listed below, please indicate their status in your organization. If a practice currently exists, please rate its effectiveness. Circle the appropriate response for each item:

	Never did this	Discontinued this	Planning this	Doing this		If you are currently doing this, please rate its effectiveness:				
						Very Ineffective			Very Effective	
A. *Employee self-assessment tools*										
1. Career planning workshops	39.3%	8.4%	18.0%	34.3%	(178)	0.0%	5.1%	45.8%	30.5%	18.6% (59)
2. Career workbooks (stand-alone)	63.2	3.5	15.2	18.1	(171)	0.0	9.7	41.9	35.5	12.9 (31)
3. Preretirement workshops	36.4	6.4	11.0	46.2	(173)	2.5	5.0	20.0	48.8	23.8 (80)
4. Computer software	67.4	2.3	16.9	13.4	(172)	0.0	17.4	34.8	21.7	26.1 (23)
B. *Organizational potential assessment processes*										
5. Promotability forecasts	37.1	3.4	13.7	45.7	(175)	1.3	13.9	35.4	43.0	6.3 (79)
6. Psychological testing	50.0	9.3	7.0	33.7	(172)	1.7	5.2	36.2	50.0	6.9 (58)
7. Assessment centers	66.3	9.3	10.5	14.0	(172)	0.0	4.2	8.3	54.2	33.3 (24)
8. Interview process	23.7	1.2	6.9	68.2	(173)	0.0	5.2	37.9	42.2	14.7 (116)
9. Job assignment	18.7	1.8	14.6	64.9	(171)	1.8	5.5	32.7	48.2	11.8 (110)
C. *Internal labor-market information exchanges*										
10. Career information handbooks	65.7	4.0	11.4	18.9	(175)	0.0	6.3	43.8	37.5	12.5 (32)
11. Career ladders or dual-career ladders	48.0	4.0	13.7	34.3	(175)	1.7	20.7	43.1	26.7	6.9 (58)
12. Career resource center	63.2	4.0	13.2	19.5	(174)	3.1	12.5	31.3	43.8	9.4 (32)
13. Other career information formats	64.5	0.0	13.6	21.9	(169)	0.0	11.1	38.9	41.7	8.3 (36)
D. *Individual counseling or career discussions*										
14. Supervisor or line manager	8.0	.6	8.5	83.0	(176)	2.8	26.8	48.6	19.7	2.1 (142)
15. Senior career advisers	69.8	.6	7.6	22.1	(172)	0.0	7.9	44.7	39.5	7.9 (38)
16. Personnel staff	11.9	0.0	5.6	82.5	(177)	.7	18.3	50.0	28.2	2.8 (142)
17. Specialized counselor										
a) internal	72.0	0.0	4.2	23.8	(168)	0.0	7.7	41.0	28.2	23.1 (39)
b) external	79.1	1.9	1.9	17.1	(158)	0.0	3.7	40.7	40.7	14.8 (27)
E. *Job-matching systems*										
18. Informal canvassing	43.5	.6	3.5	52.4	(170)	0.0	24.7	46.1	25.8	3.4 (89)
19. Job posting	9.6	1.7	5.6	83.1	(178)	.7	10.8	27.7	38.5	22.3 (148)
20. Skills inventories or skills audit	38.1	3.4	21.6	36.9	(176)	1.6	12.5	34.4	45.3	6.3 (64)
21. Replacement or succession planning	15.3	2.3	17.0	65.3	(176)	1.8	14.3	35.7	39.3	8.9 (112)
22. Staffing committees	73.1	.6	2.3	24.0	(171)	2.4	7.3	48.8	31.7	9.8 (41)
23. Internal placement systems	34.1	1.2	9.2	55.5	(173)	2.1	9.5	37.9	44.2	6.3 (95)
F. *Development programs*										
24. Job enrichment or job redesign	45.1	0.0	14.3	40.6	(175)	1.4	5.6	47.9	39.4	5.6 (71)
25. Job rotation	29.5	1.7	14.8	54.0	(176)	2.2	17.2	43.0	25.8	11.8 (93)
26. In-house training and development programs	1.7	1.1	5.6	91.6	(178)	.6	6.1	31.3	44.8	17.2 (163)
27. External seminars or workshops	5.6	1.1	2.2	91.0	(178)	0.0	10.5	38.9	44.4	6.2 (162)
28. Tuition reimbursement	2.2	1.7	1.1	95.0	(181)	1.8	4.1	22.8	37.4	33.9 (171)
29. Supervisor training in career discussions	30.5	3.4	22.0	44.1	(177)	2.6	9.0	43.6	26.9	17.9 (78)
30. Dual-career couple programs	85.8	1.7	4.5	8.0	(176)	6.7	0.0	53.3	40.0	0.0 (15)
31. Mentoring systems	59.9	3.4	15.8	20.9	(177)	0.0	18.9	37.8	35.1	8.1 (37)
32. Employee orientation programs	5.0	2.2	6.7	86.1	(180)	.7	13.8	36.8	36.8	11.8 (152)

18. Please check all of the personnel systems below that you have in your organization and indicate whether they are linked with career development.

	Have it? Yes		Linked to career development? Yes	
a. Performance appraisal (planning and review)	97.2%	(182)	82.9%	(175)
b. Recruitment practices	97.8	(183)	49.2	(177)
c. Promotion and transfer practices	99.5	(182)	82.6	(178)
d. Salary administration	98.9	(184)	44.6	(177)
e. Job description or evaluation	97.3	(182)	48.6	(173)
f. Human resource planning	75.6	(180)	70.0	(150)
g. Organizational strategic planning	84.8	(178)	46.5	(157)
h. Employee assistance programs	86.2	(181)	16.0	(163)
i. Organization design	59.4	(175)	36.1	(133)
j. Equal employment opportunity or affirmative action	95.1	(183)	60.6	(170)

19. In your opinion, how would your organization view the following statements regarding career development?

	Strongly agree	Agree	Disagree	Strongly disagree	
1. Career development programs must be tied in with the organization's strategic business plan.	31.6%	48.9%	13.9%	1.1%	(180)
2. Senior management believes career development raises employee expectations.	12.2	67.2	19.4	1.1	(180)
3. Senior management feels that career development is a fad.	1.1	15.1	62.6	21.2	(179)
4. Senior management believes that career development is an important part of employee development.	14.4	65.6	18.9	1.1	(180)
5. Managers believe career development is not relay anything new.	3.4	71.0	23.9	1.7	(176)
6. Managers believe career development is not needed.	2.2	11.7	71.7	14.4	(180)
7. Career development means an increased burden for supervisor.	11.7	62.6	23.5	2.2	(179)
8. Few supervisors are equipped to hold employee career discussions.	28.2	56.4	13.8	1.7	(181)
9. Supervisors feel that employee career development is not part of their job.	5.0	47.2	45.6	2.2	(180)
10. Turnover increases as a result of employee participation in career development programs.	.6	12.8	65.4	21.2	(179)
11. Only a small percentage of employees are really interested in career development.	1.7	18.3	61.7	18.3	(180)
12. Career development enhances the job performance of employees.	21.7	66.7	11.7	0.0	(180)
13. Career development increases personal anxiety for many employees.	3.4	26.4	62.9	7.3	(178)
14. Career development allows improved utilization of employee talents.	23.5	68.7	7.8	0.0	(179)
15. Career development strains the capacity of other human resources systems such as job posting, employee training, tuition reimbursement, etc.	3.4	20.1	62.6	14.0	(179)
16. Career development equips employees to use personnel systems more effectively.	9.7	73.9	14.8	1.7	(176)

	Strongly agree	Agree	Disagree	Strongly disagree	
17. Career development generally disrupts an organization.	1.1	11.7	67.8	19.4	(180)
18. Career development is best introduced on a pilot, experimental basis.	4.0	55.1	34.1	6.8	(176)
19. Job requirements and career information need not be provided in a career development program.	1.7	15.6	46.9	35.8	(179)
20. Employees' participation in a career development program should be voluntary.	28.5	54.7	13.4	3.4	(179)
21. Employees should be able to keep confidential their records or other outputs of career planning activities.	22.6	55.4	20.3	1.7	(177)
22. Career development helps employees deal with a low-growth environment.	13.0	68.9	15.8	2.3	(177)

20. How are your career development programs or practices evaluated?

   24.0% No evaluation is done
   63.7   Informal verbal feedback from participants
   21.6   Interviews of focus groups to measure attitudes, learning, or behavior
   32.7   Questionnaires to measure attitudes, learning, or behavior
   11.7   Data analysis re: productivity, performance, mobility, costs, etc.
    7.6   Other
          (171)

21. Overall, how effective is your career development system?

   10.7% Very ineffective
   17.9   Somewhat ineffective
   41.7   In between
   23.2   Somewhat effective
    6.5   Very effective
          (168)

Survey Results: U.S. Government Sample

Noted in parentheses after each question is the number of valid cases. Total N = 27.

1. Which of the following best describes your organization?

          Manufacturing (consumer)
          Manufacturing (industrial)
          Retail/wholesale trade
          Banking, finance, insurance, real estate
          Energy (public utilities, petroleum, chemicals)
          Education/nonprofit
   100%   Government/military
          Services (business services, food and lodging, recreation, repairs)

Medical/health care
Diversified/conglomerate
High tech
Other
(27)

2. Your organization's annual sales or annual budget:

20.0%   Under $25 million
 8.0 $25 million to $49 million
 0.0 $50 million to $99 million
32.0 $100 million to $499 million
 4.0 $500 million to $999 million
36.0   Over 1 billion
        (25)

3. How many employees are there in your entire organization?

18.5%   Fewer than 500
 7.4   500 to 999
29.6   1,000 to 4,999
18.5   5,000 to 9,999
 7.4   10,000 to 24,999
 3.7   25,000 to 49,999
14.8   50,000 or more
        (27)

Of these, how many are salaried?

19.2%   Fewer than 500
 7.7   500 to 999
38.5   1,000 to 4,999
 7.7   5,000 to 9,999
 7.7   10,000 to 24,999
 3.8   25,000 to 49,999
15.4   50,000 or more
        (26)

4. Where is your organization headquartered?

11.1%   Northeast
77.8   Mid-Atlantic
 3.7   Southeast
 0.0   Midwest
 0.0   Northwest
 0.0   West Coast
 0.0   Southwest
 0.0   Outside the U.S.
 7.4   Other
        (27)

5. Which of the following best describes your organization in terms of markets served and scope of operations:

    3.7%   Local
    0.0   Regional
    63.0   National
    33.3   International
           (27)

6. Is there currently an organizational career development system in your organization?

    59.3% Yes   29.6   No
    3.7   Starting one   7.4   Had one but discontinued
           (27)

    50.0%   Insufficient budgetary
            resources
    87.5   Insufficient support by top
            management
    0.0   Lack of employee interest
    37.5   Lack of manager or
            supervisor interest
    25.0   Lack of HR capability or
            interest
    12.5   Organization's needs not in
            line with career development
    25.0   Other
            (8)

7. Some career development systems emphasize the individual employee, while others focus on the organization. Indicate on the continuum below where you would place your organization's career development efforts in terms of this focus:

    Mean = 50.9   SD = 22   Median = 50   Mode = 50   (17)
    Individual |_____|_____|_____|_____| *Organization*
              0   25   50   75   100

8. How long have you had a career development system in place?

    11.8% Less than a year
    11.8   One to two years
    23.5   Three to four years
    5.9   Five to six years
    47.1   More than six years
           (17)

9. Where does the responsibility for your career development system reside?

   33.3%   Centralized
   22.2   Decentralized
   44.4   Both
           (18)

10. Is there a particular unit or function assigned responsibility for career development?

    10.5% No   89.5% Yes
           (19)

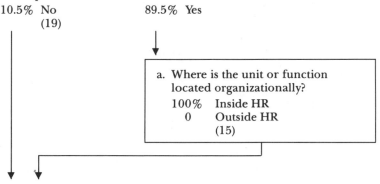

a. Where is the unit or function located organizationally?

   100%   Inside HR
     0   Outside HR
          (15)

11. How many human resource staffpersons, if any, are there in your organization devoted full time to career development, including yourself?

    44.4% Less than one
     5.6   One
    11.1   Two
     5.6   Three or four
    33.3   Five or more
           (18)

12. Organizational career systems vary in their view of who is responsible for career development—the employee, the manager, or the organization. Please assign percentages of responsibility to these three parties as reflected in your organization's system, adding up to 100%.

Employee	*Manager*	*Organization*
Mean = 45.9 SD = 16	Mean = 27.9 SD = 14	Mean = 25.0 SD = 15
Median = 40	Median = 25	Median = 20
Mode = 40	Mode = 20	Mode = 20
(17)	(17)	(17)

13. Which groups are covered by your career development system?

    94.4% Exempt salaried employees
    88.9   Nonexempt salaried employees
    44.4   Hourly employees
           (18)

14. Please indicate those salaried employee groups for whom you have targeted career development programs:

    50.0% Preretirees
    75.0   Women employees
    56.3   Minority employees
    68.8   Management trainees
    68.8   "Fast-track" management candidates or high-potentials
    25.0   Handicapped employees
     6.3   Older workers
    43.8   Plateaued employees
    75.0   New employees
     6.3   Other
           (16)

15. From the list below, please indicate the top three factors that influenced the development of your organization's career planning/development programs.

    [Items cited as most important]
    33.3% Organizational commitment to career development
     0.0   Shortage of promotable talent
     6.7   Concern about turnover
     0.0   Equal employment opportunity program commitments
     6.7   Desire to motivate employees under conditions of limited organizational growth
     0.0   Desire to develop or promote from within
     6.7   Desire to keep up with competitors
    26.7   Strong expression of employee interest in career planning
     0.0   Survey or needs assessment findings
     6.7   Shift in skill mix or human resources planning needs
     0.0   Development of organization's strategic plan
     0.0   Desire to improve worker productivity
     0.0   Need to encourage early retirement
     0.0   Desire for positive recruiting image
     0.0   Desire to avoid unionization
    13.3   Other
           (15)

16. Have you used a task force or advisory group in the design or implementation of your career development system?

62.5% Yes   37.5% No
  (16)

↓

If yes, how would you rate its effectiveness?

Very   *Very*
Ineffective 1..................2..................3..................4..................5 *Effective*
Mean = 3.5   SD = .9   Median = 3.5   Mode = 3   (8)

---

17. For the career development practices listed below, please indicate their status in your organization. If a practice currently exists, please rate its effectiveness. Circle the appropriate response for each item:

	Never did this	Discontinued this	Planning this	Doing this		If you are currently doing this, please rate its effectiveness:				
						Very Ineffective				Very Effective
A. *Employee self-assessment tools*										
1. Career planning workshops	18.8%	18.8%	6.3%	56.3%	(16)	0%	0%	33.3%	66.7%	0%	(9)
2. Career workbooks (stand-alone)	38.5	15.4	7.7	38.5	(13)	0	0	80.0	20.0	0	(5)
3. Preretirement workshops	0.0	0.0	12.5	87.5	(16)	0	0	7.1	57.1	35.7	(14)
4. Computer software	37.5	6.3	12.5	43.8	(16)	0	0	14.3	57.1	28.6	(7)
B. *Organizational potential assessment processes*										
5. Promotability forecasts	93.8	0.0	0.0	6.3	(16)	0	0	0	100	0	(1)
6. Psychological testing	81.3	12.5	0.0	6.3	(16)	0	0	0	0	0	(0)
7. Assessment centers	43.8	12.5	0.0	43.8	(16)	0	0	28.6	57.1	14.3	(7)
8. Interview process	42.9	7.1	7.1	42.9	(14)	0	16.7	16.7	50.0	16.7	(6)
9. Job assignment	33.3	6.7	13.3	46.7	(15)	0	0	14.3	57.1	28.6	(7)
C. *Internal labor-market information exchanges*										
10. Career information handbooks	28.6	7.1	7.1	57.1	(14)	0	12.5	62.5	0	25.0	(8)
11. Career ladders or dual-career ladders	25.0	0.0	6.3	68.8	(16)	0	9.1	45.5	9.1	36.4	(11)
12. Career resource center	46.7	6.7	13.3	33.3	(15)	0	0	100	0	0	(4)
13. Other career information formats	38.5	0.0	23.1	38.5	(13)	0	0	40.0	60.0	0	(5)
D. *Individual counseling or career discussions*										
14. Supervisor or line manager	13.3	0.0	20.0	66.7	(15)	0	10.0	50.0	30.0	10.0	(10)
15. Senior career advisors	30.8	7.7	23.1	38.5	(13)	0	0	40.0	40.0	20.0	(5)
16. Personnel staff	12.5	0.0	6.3	81.3	(16)	0	0	58.3	25.0	16.7	(12)
17. Specialized counselor										
a) Internal	23.5	11.8	17.6	47.1	(17)	0	0	37.5	37.5	25.0	(8)
b) external	46.2	0.0	15.4	38.5	(13)	0	0	60.0	20.0	20.0	(5)
E. *Job-matching systems*										
18. Informal canvassing	40.0	0.0	6.7	53.3	(15)	0	25.0	37.5	25.0	12.5	(8)
19. Job posting	0.0	0.0	5.9	94.1	(17)	0	0	33.3	26.7	40.0	(15)
20. Skills inventories or skills audit	41.2	11.8	5.9	41.2	(17)	0	0	42.9	42.9	14.3	(7)
21. Replacement or succession planning	31.3	6.3	12.5	50.0	(16)	0	12.5	62.5	25.0	0.0	(8)
22. Staffing committees	37.5	12.5	6.3	43.8	(16)	0	0	28.6	57.1	14.3	(7)
23. Internal placement systems	20.0	6.7	0.0	73.3	(15)	0	0	36.4	45.5	18.2	(11)
F. *Development programs*										
24. Job enrichment or job redesign	33.3	13.3	20.0	33.3	(15)	0	0	20.0	60.0	20.0	(5)
25. Job rotation	11.8	0.0	5.9	82.4	(17)	0	0	35.7	28.6	35.7	(14)

	Never did this	Discontinued this	Planning this	Doing this		If you are currently doing this, please rate its effectiveness:					
						Very Ineffective				Very Effective	
26. In-house training and development programs	0.0	0.0	5.9	94.1	(17)	0	0	18.8	37.5	43.8	(16)
27. External seminars or workshops	5.9	0.0	5.9	88.2	(17)	0	0	20.0	53.3	26.7	(15)
28. Tuition reimbursement	5.9	0.0	5.9	88.2	(17)	0	0	46.7	20.0	33.3	(15)
29. Supervisor training in career discussions	31.3	6.3	18.8	43.8	(16)	0	0	42.9	42.9	14.3	(7)
30. Dual-career couple programs	93.8	0.0	6.3	0.0	(16)	0	0	0	0	0	
31. Mentoring systems	29.4	5.9	17.6	47.1	(17)	0	12.5	25.0	50.0	12.5	(8)
32. Employee orientation programs	0.0	0.0	18.8	81.3	(16)	7.7	0	30.8	46.2	15.4	(13)

18. Please check all of the personnel systems below that you have in your organization and indicate whether they are linked with career development.

	Have it? Yes		Linked to career development? Yes	
a. Performance appraisal (planning and review)	100.0%	(17)	62.5%	(16)
b. Recruitment practices	100.0	(17)	50.0	(16)
c. Promotion and transfer practices	100.0	(17)	68.8	(16)
d. Salary administration	100.0	(16)	26.7	(15)
e. Job description or evaluation	100.0	(17)	46.7	(15)
f. Human resource planning	70.6	(17)	83.3	(12)
g. Organizational strategic planning	82.4	(17)	38.5	(13)
h. Employee assistance programs	94.1	(17)	25.0	(16)
i. Organization design	88.2	(17)	35.7	(14)
j. Equal employment opportunity or affirmative action	100.0	(17)	56.3	(16)

19. In your opinion, how would your organization view the following statements regarding career development?

	Strongly agree	Agree	Disagree	Strongly disagree	
1. Career development programs must be tied in with the organization's strategic business plan.	25.0%	62.5%	12.5%	0.0%	(16)
2. Senior management believes career development raises employee expectations.	17.6	70.6	11.8	0.0	(17)
3. Senior management feels that career development is a fad.	0.0	11.8	70.6	17.6	(17)
4. Senior management believes that career development is an important part of employee development.	26.7	46.7	26.7	0.0	(15)
5. Managers believe career development is not really anything new.	6.3	81.3	12.5	0.0	(16)
6. Managers believe career development is not needed.	0.0	6.3	93.8	0.0	(16)
7. Career development means an increased burden for supervisor.	6.3	68.8	25.0	0.0	(16)
8. Few supervisors are equipped to hold employee career discussions.	31.3	56.3	12.5	0.0	(16)
9. Supervisors feel that employee career development is not part of their job.	14.3	42.9	35.7	7.1	(14)

	Strongly agree	Agree	Disagree	Strongly disagree	
10. Turnover increases as a result of employee participation in career development programs.	0.0	37.5	56.3	6.3	(16)
11. Only a small percentage of employees are really interested in career development.	0.0	12.5	50.0	37.5	(16)
12. Career development enhances the job performance of employees.	37.5	56.3	6.3	0.0	(16)
13. Career development increases personal anxiety for many employees.	14.3	35.7	42.9	7.1	(14)
14. Career development allows improved utilization of employee talents.	17.6	76.5	5.9	0.0	(17)
15. Career development strains the capacity of other human resources systems such as job posting, employee training, tuition reimbursement, etc.	0.0	31.3	62.5	6.3	(16)
16. Career development equips employees to use personnel systems more effectively.	11.8	70.6	17.6	0.0	(17)
17. Career development generally disrupts an organization.	0.0	6.3	81.3	12.5	(16)
18. Career development is best introduced on a pilot, experimental basis.	6.3	25.0	62.5	6.3	(16)
19. Job requirements and career information need not be provided in a career development program.	0.0	5.9	64.7	29.4	(17)
20. Employees' participation in a career development program should be voluntary.	23.5	52.9	23.5	0.0	(17)
21. Employees should be able to keep confidential their records or other outputs of career planning activities.	26.7	33.3	40.0	0.0	(15)
22. Career development helps employees deal with a low-growth environment.	12.5	81.3	6.3	0.0	(16)

20. How are your career development programs or practices evaluated?

    12.5% No evaluation is done
    68.8   Informal verbal feedback from participants
    31.3   Interviews of focus groups to measure attitudes, learning, or behavior
    56.3   Questionnaires to measure attitudes, learning, or behavior
    18.8   Data analysis re: productivity, performance, mobility, costs, etc.
    6.3   Other
           (16)

21. Overall, how effective is your career development system?

    7.1%   Very ineffective
    14.3   Somewhat ineffective
    28.6   In-between
    35.7   Somewhat effective
    14.3   Very effective
           (14)

APPENDIX B:
INTERVIEW QUESTIONNAIRE FOR CASE STUDIES AND BEST PRACTICES

(Note that some interviewees will have filled in the survey prior to the interview.)

Case Studies (Systems)

1. Clarify what portion of the organization your responses will represent.

Implementation

2. What was the impetus for your organization to implement a career development system?
3. What process did you use to implement career development? (describe)
   Advisory group?
   Needs assessment?
4. How did you determine needs and target groups? What need(s) and target group(s) did you decide on?
5. Did you use a pilot approach for implementation? Why or why not? Describe the process.
6. How did you publicize the system?
7. What barriers to implementation did you encounter? How did you address or overcome these barriers?

The System

8. What are the key features or elements of your career development system? How did you select these?
9. What are the pros and cons of the various features or approaches you are using?
10. Describe what makes your career development process a system.

11. How and how closely is the system connected to other aspects of human resources in your organization?

Results and Assessment

12. What has been the effect of career development on employees? Managers? The organization?
13. What kind of surprises or unanticipated impacts did you encounter? How did you deal with these?
14. How visible is career development across the organization? What role does the top leadership play here?
15. Have respondents expand on responses on last page of survey (covers evaluation, impacts, what they would have done differently, future plans, etc.). [*Note:* If they have not filled out the survey, then ask them:]
    a. How are your career development programs evaluated?
    b. How would you rate the career development (CD) system's effectiveness and why?
    c. What in your opinion has been the major impact (positive or negative) of your organization's CD effort?
    d. What, if anything, would you have done differently with your organization's CD system?
    e. What are your organization's plans for future CD practices?
    f. In your view, how has organizational CD changed (if at all) in the last ten years?
16. What advice would you give to others who would like to implement a career development system?
17. Any other comments?

Best Practices

1. Clarify what portion of the organization your responses will represent.
2. What was the impetus for your organization to implement career development?

3. How did you go about implementation and determining needs?
4. How did you decide what practices to use?
5. What barriers to implementation did you encounter? How did you address or overcome these barriers?
6. Describe your best practice or practices.
7. What are the pros and cons of the practice(s)?
8. How systemized is career development?
9. How and how closely is career development connected to other aspects of human resources in your organization?
10. What has been the effect of the career development practice(s) on employees? Managers? The organization?
11. What kind of surprises or unanticipated impacts did you encounter? How did you deal with these?
12. How visible is career development across the organization? What role does the top leadership play here?
13. Have respondent expand on responses on last page of survey (covers evaluation, impacts, what they would have done differently, future plans, etc.). *Note:* If they have not filled out the survey, then ask them the following:
    a. How are your CD practices evaluated?
    b. Overall, how effective are your practices and why?
    c. What in your opinion has been the major impact (positive or negative) of your organization's CD practices?
    d. What, if anything, would you have done differently with your CD practices?
    e. What are your organization's plans for future CD practices?
    f. In your view, how has organizational CD changed (if at all) in the last ten years?
14. What advice would you give to others who would like to implement career development?
15. Any other comments?

APPENDIX C:
AUSTRALIAN SURVEY RESULTS

The AITD Study

Research and analysis of the Australian data were undertaken by a survey team from the career development network of the New South Wales division of the Australian Institute of Training and Development (AITD). Supplementary analysis was conducted by Conceptual Systems, Inc. (in the United States). AITD reported the findings discussed below.

Respondents identified four factors that inhibit the implementation of an effective career development system. These factors were extracted from qualitative questions and subsequent discussions with selected respondents who rated their career development systems highly.

1. *Planning, communication, and attitudinal factors.* Lack of role models of best practices, clear measures for evaluating success, and data on the external labor market all inhibited system implementation. Failure to use past and current data to determine the need for career development was also a factor.
2. *Organizational and systems factors.* Lack of organizational commitment hindered system implementation severely.
3. *Implementation factors.* Short-term business returns were privileged over long-term cultural change. Moreover, those individuals advocating a career development system tended to exhibit their own beliefs rather than to stress what the organization actually needed. Among key staff driving the system, turnover or rotation was common, weakening continuity. Also, the lack of line managerial skill in conducting career counseling was an ongoing obstacle.
4. *Additional factors.* Skepticism about change was a major obstacle in some organizations. Decentralized and large organizations experienced difficulties in communicating, standardizing, and integrating their career development

efforts. Learning for the benefit of both individuals and the organization did not always occur, and the lack of ongoing evaluation was a major problem.

Improvements Resulting from Career Development

Respondents claimed the following improvements as a direct result of their career development systems:

- Retention of key personnel
- Improvement in productivity, gross turnover, and work standards
- Reduced turnover
- Development of a strong, more unified corporate culture
- Increased number of staff nominating career options
- Extension of career development activities to staff not currently targeted
- Increased female representation in senior positions
- Increased level of technical skills

Evaluation Methodologies

Turnover and retention rates were measured so as to link the outcomes of career development with the strategic plan. Program outcomes were measured against outcomes for groups not covered by the program, and success was evaluated by comparing performance against industry and national averages. Among the efficiency and effectiveness indicators used were these:

- The number of people changing career paths or seeking career enhancements
- The number of people seeking career development counseling
- The use of internal resources rather than external recruitment to meet skill needs
- The effective placement of surplus staff
- The number of career development options available

- The number of placements for short-term projects for skill enhancement

Additional Comparative Research

Findings from other recent studies provide additional perspectives on the status of Australian organizational career development. The 1991 Commercial Clearing House and Australian Graduate School of Management National Survey of Training and Development Practices provided the following key findings of 867 organizations:

- The percentage of respondents who were expanding their workforces had decreased from 31 percent in 1986 to 13 percent in 1991, mirroring the deterioration of the Australian economy during the current recession.
- There has been a gradual increase in the use of systematic assessment of training needs by respondents. The five major techniques being used to identify training needs in the 1991 survey were development plans (arising from performance appraisal), corporate or business plans, promotion or transfer decisions, workforce or succession planning, and career counseling interviews.
- Since 1986, increases were noted in the use of development plans arising from performance appraisals.
- Also, since 1989 there has been a strengthening of the link between corporate goal setting and the identification of new HR initiatives and programs. In 1991, 80 percent of respondents drew up formal business plans; 53 percent used them to link corporate goals to training and development activities.
- A significant increase in the involvement of managers in the training and development of staff has occurred over the last five years. However, only 20 percent of organizations reported that rewards or recognition were given for effective involvement. (This occurred more in the private sector than in the public sector.)
- The portion of payroll allocated to structured training ac-

tivities was between 1 and 2.5 percent for nearly half of all respondents; between 2.5 and 5 percent for one-third; and between 5 and 10 percent for a few organizations. (Less than 2 percent of respondents spent either less than 1 percent or more than 10 percent of payroll on training.)

- Most respondents indicated that they actively encouraged their employees to undertake study, and most offered formal training and development for their managers (an increase of 10 percent from 1986). As a group, managers were more likely to receive training in the public sector; however, the private sector was focusing more specifically on high-potentials.

- On-the-job training was widely used; higher duties or acting positions and assignments of special projects received the highest ratings.

The Curtin University of Technology surveyed top executives in its study of HRD in Australian top corporate profit makers in 1985–1986. This study found that Australian organizations' practice was like that of Fortune 500 companies in 1986 in terms of strategic planning, program scope, the design of training programs, evaluation methodology, and the existence of career development programs (63 percent in Australia versus 62 percent in the United States).

With the exception of certain financial and retail institutions, very few Australian organizations had extended their career development initiatives past traditional training courses. Therefore, many Australian organizations are either overestimating the comprehensiveness of their career development programs or keeping them very secret.

The responsibility for developing human resources is best managed, according to this study, through a professional split of 75 percent line management and 25 percent HR staff. Actual practice suggested that less responsibility for career development and on-the-job training rested with the line manager than with the HR department and executive management. Top executives may lack a clear awareness of the importance of the line manager's role in career development.

Finally, greater consultation and mutual understanding are needed between HR development professionals and those in other personnel subfunctions (such as compensation, HR planning, and so on) in order to offer effective career development, award restructuring, and skills formation for all employees.

APPENDIX D:
SINGAPORE SURVEY RESULTS

Table D.1. Industry Types.

Type	Percentage
Manufacturing	22
Retail/wholesale trade	13
Banking/finance, insurance, real estate	11
Energy (petroleum, chemicals)	4
Education/nonprofit	2
Government/statutory board	3
Services (business services, food and hospitality, recreation, repairs)	15
Medical/health care	3
Diversified/conglomerate	2
High technology	6
Others	19
Total	100 (n = 250)

Table D.2. Organizational Sizes.

Number of Employees	Percentage
100 or fewer employees	53
101 to 200 employees	15
201 to 500 employees	11
500 to 1,000 employees	10
1,000 to 5,000 employees	9
5,000 and more employees	2
Total	100 (n = 252)

Table D.3. Organizational Types.

Type	Percentage
Multinationals	51
Local companies	38
Joint-venture companies	7
Government ministries/statutory boards	4
Total	100 (n = 251)

Table D.4. Organizations with a Career Development System.

Industry Type	Percentage
Manufacturing	16
Retail/wholesale trade	14
Banking/finance, insurance, real estate	14
Energy (petroleum, chemicals)	6
Education/nonprofit	1
Government/statutory board	7
Services (business services, food and hospitality, recreation, repairs)	19
Medical/health care	6
Diversified/conglomerate	4
High technology	9
Others*	4
Total	100 (n = 70)

* Includes information systems products and services; engines and parts distribution centers; and trading and distribution or consumer products.

Table D.5. Duration of Career Development Systems.

	<1 Year	1–2 Years	3–4 Years	5–6 Years	>6 Years	Total
Government ministry Statutory board	3	1	1	1	0	6 (9%)
Local company	4	4	5	4	5	22 (31%)
Joint venture	0	1	2	0	4	7 (10%)
Multinational	0	6	8	4	17	35 (50%)
Total	7 (10%)	12 (17%)	16 (23%)	9 (13%)	26 (37%)	70 (100%)

Table D.6. Career Development Practices.

	Doing	Planning	Discontinued	Done	Very Ineffective 1	2	3	4	5 Very Effective
Employment self-assessment tools									
Career planning workshops	24%	13%	3%	60% (63)	0%	7%	40%	40%	13% (15)
Career workbook (stand-alone)	10	10	0	80 (59)	0	17	33	33	17 (6)
Preretirement workshops	5	5	0	90 (57)	0	67	33	0	0 (3)
Computer software	27	5	0	68 (60)	0	14	7	64	14 (14)
Organizational potential assessment process									
Promotability forecasts	70	10	2	19 (62)	0	2	30	61	7 (43)
Psychological testing	26	5	9	60 (55)	0	7	14	64	14 (14)
Assessment centers	23	7	2	68 (56)	0	8	46	38	8 (13)
Interview process	77	5	0	18 (62)	0	2	28	62	9 (47)
Job assignment	84	11	0	5 (62)	0	2	29	54	15 (52)
Internal labor-market information exchange									
Career information handbooks	19	5	2	74 (57)	0	9	46	36	9 (11)
Career ladders or dual-career ladders	34	9	2	55 (56)	0	0	37	47	16 (19)
Career resource center	2	4	2	93 (55)	0	0	0	100	0 (1)
Other career information format or systems	26	6	2	67 (55)	0	8	23	62	8 (13)
Individual counseling or career discussions with:									
Supervisor or line manager	97	0	0	3 (66)	0	2	27	60	11 (63)
Senior career advisers	19	4	2	75 (57)	9	0	18	64	9 (11)
Personnel staff	67	12	0	22 (60)	2	2	43	50	2 (40)
Specialized counselor: internal	16	5	0	79 (56)	0	0	22	56	22 (9)
external	4	6	0	91 (53)	50	0	50	0	0 (2)

Table D.6. Career Development Practices, Cont'd.

	Doing	Planning	Discontinued	Done	Very Ineffective 1	2	3	4	Very Effective 5
Job-matching systems									
Informal canvassing	40	2	0	58 (62)	0	8	40	32	29 (25)
Job posting	68	6	0	26 (66)	0	9	19	63	9 (43)
Skills inventories or skills audit	38	19	2	41 (63)	0	0	44	52	4 (23)
Replacement or succession planning	69	13	0	18 (67)	0	7	24	58	11 (45)
Staffing committee	30	5	0	66 (64)	0	11	26	36	26 (19)
Internal placement system	60	6	0	34 (65)	0	3	37	47	13 (38)
Development programs									
Job enrichment or job redesign	70	17	2	11 (64)	2	7	29	42	20 (45)
Job rotation	60	14	0	26 (66)	5	3	25	53	15 (40)
In-house training and development programs	88	8	0	5 (66)	2	3	28	45	22 (58)
External seminars or workshops	97	0	0	3 (68)	0	5	40	46	9 (65)
Tuition reimbursement	78	2	2	18 (65)	0	8	35	45	12 (51)
Supervisor training in career discussions	30	20	0	50 (60)	0	6	39	44	11 (18)
Dual-career couple programs	13	3	0	84 (62)	0	0	63	25	13 (8)
Mentoring systems	44	18	2	36 (66)	0	3	28	55	14 (29)
Employee orientation programs	78	11	0	11 (65)	2	8	24	43	24 (51)

Table D.7. Evaluation of Career Development Systems.

Method of Evaluation	Percentage
Informal verbal feedback from participants	67
Data analysis re: productivity, performance, mobility, costs, etc.	36
Questionnaires to measure attitudes, learning, or behavior	27
Interviews of focus groups to measure attitudes and learning	21
No evaluation	19
Others*	4 (n = 70)

* Includes reports submitted by officers sent for courses and in-house briefings given to the rest of the employees by staff who have attended a training program (i.e., also rated by all).

Table D.8. Effectiveness of Career Development System.

Effectiveness	Percentage
Very ineffective	1
Somewhat ineffective	7
In between	19
Somewhat effective	65
Very effective	7
No answer	1
Total	100 (n = 70)

APPENDIX E:
READINGS IN ORGANIZATIONAL
CAREER DEVELOPMENT

Books

Bailyn, L. *Living with Technology: Issues at Mid-Career.* Cambridge, Mass.: MIT Press, 1980.

Bardwick, J. M. *The Plateauing Trap.* New York: AMACOM, 1986.

Burack, E. H. *Career Planning and Management: A Managerial Summary.* Lake Forest, Ill.: Brace-Park Press, 1983.

Burack, E. H., and Mathys, N. J. *Career Management in Organizations: A Practical Human Resource Planning Approach.* Lake Forest, Ill.: Brace-Park Press, 1980.

Dalton, G. W., and Thompson, P. II. *Novations: Strategies for Career Management.* Glenview, Ill.: Scott, Foresman, 1986.

Derr, C. B. *Managing the New Careerists.* San Francisco: Jossey-Bass, 1986.

Feldman, D. C. *Managing Careers in Organizations.* Glenview, Ill.: Scott, Foresman, 1988.

Gutteridge, T. G., and Otte, F. L. *Organizational Career Development.* Washington, D.C.: ASTD Press, 1983.

Hall, D. T. *Careers in Organizations.* Glenview, Ill.: Scott, Foresman, 1976.

Hall, D. T., and Associates. *Career Development in Organizations.* San Francisco: Jossey-Bass, 1987.

Jelinek, M. *Career Management for the Individual and the Organization.* Chicago: St. Clair Press, 1979.

Kanter, R. M. *When Giants Learn to Dance: Mastering the Challenges of Strategy, Management, and Careers in the 1990s.* New York: Simon & Schuster, 1989.

Kaye, B. L. *Up Is Not the Only Way.* Englewood Cliffs, N.J.: Prentice-Hall, 1982.

Lea, H. D., and Leibowitz, Z. B. (eds.). *Adult Career Development.* (2nd ed.) Alexandria, Va.: National Career Development Association, 1992.

245

Leibowitz, Z. B., Farren, C., and Kaye, B. L. *Designing Career Development Systems.* San Francisco: Jossey-Bass, 1986.

Leibowitz, Z. B., and Hirsh, S. K. (eds.). *Career Development: Current Perspectives.* Alexandria, Va.: American Society for Training and Development, 1984.

Leibowitz, Z. B., and Lea, H. D. (eds.). *Adult Career Development.* Alexandria, Va.: American Association for Counseling and Development, 1985.

London, M., and Mone, E. M. *Career Management and Survival in the Workplace.* San Francisco: Jossey-Bass, 1987.

London, M., and Mone, E. M. (eds.). *Career Growth and Human Resource Strategies.* New York: Quorum Books, 1988.

London, M., and Stumpf, S. A. *Managing Careers.* Reading, Mass.: Addison-Wesley, 1982.

McCall, M. W., Jr., Lombardo, M. M., and Morrison, A. M. *The Lessons of Experience: How Successful Executives Develop on the Job.* Lexington, Mass.: Lexington Books, 1988.

Merman, S. K., and Leibowitz, Z. B. *Career Development Systems: Questions Worth Asking and Answers Worth Questioning.* Alexandria, Va.: American Society for Training and Develpment, 1984.

Montross, D. H., and Shinkman, C. J. (eds.). *Career Development: Theory and Practice.* Springfield, Ill.: Thomas, 1992.

Otte, F. L., and Hutcheson, P. G. *Helping Employees Manage Careers.* Englewood Cliffs, N.J.: Prentice-Hall, 1992.

Raelin, J. *The Salaried Professional: How to Make the Most of Your Career.* New York: Praeger, 1984.

Roth, L. M. *A Critical Examination of the Dual Ladder Approach to Career Advancement.* New York: Center for Research in Career Development, Graduate School of Business, Columbia University, 1983.

Schein, E. H. *Career Dynamics: Matching Individual and Organizational Needs.* Reading, Mass.: Addison-Wesley, 1978.

Slavenski, L., and Buckner, M. *Career Development Programs in the Workplace.* Columbus, Ohio: ERIC Clearinghouse on Adult, Career, and Vocational Education, 1988.

Sonnenfeld, J. A. *Managing Career Systems: Channeling the Flow of Executive Careers.* Homewood, Ill.: Richard Irwin, 1984.

Souerwine, A. *Career Strategies: Planning for Personal Achievement.* New York: AMACOM, 1978.

West, J. P. *Career Planning, Development, and Management: An Annotated Bibliography.* New York: Garland, 1983.

Williams, R. *Career Management and Career Planning: A Study of North American Practice.* London, England: HMSO, 1981.

Van Maanen, J. (ed.). *Organizational Careers: Some New Perspectives.* Chichester, England: Wiley, 1978.

Articles

Abdelnour, B., and Hall, D. T. "Career Development of Established Employees." *Career Development Bulletin*, 1980, 2, 5–8.

Arthur, M. B. "Career Development and Participation at Work: Time for Mating?" *Human Resource Management*, Summer 1988, 27, 181–199.

Baird, L., and Kram, K. "Career Dynamics: Managing the Superior/Subordinate Relationship." *Organizational Dynamics*, Spring 1983, pp. 46–63.

Bardwick, J. M. "How Executives Can Help 'Plateaued' Employees." *Management Review*, Jan. 1987, 76(1), 40–46.

Bowen, D., and Hall, D. T. "Career Planning for Employee Development: A Primer for Managers." *California Management Review*, 1977, 20, 23–35.

Bratkovich, J. R., Steele, B., and Rollins, T. "Develop New Career Management Strategies." *Personnel Journal*, 1992, 69(9), 98–108.

Brenner, O. C., and Singer, M. G. "Career Repotters: To Know Them Could Be to Keep Them." *Personnel*, Nov. 1988, 55–60.

Brooks, L. "Career Planning Programs in the Workplace." In D. Brown, L. Brooks, and Associates, *Career Choice and Development*. San Francisco: Jossey-Bass, 1984.

Brousseau, K. R. "Career Dynamics in the Baby Boom and Baby Bust Era." Paper presented at the annual meeting of the Society of Industrial and Organizational Psychology, Boston, 1989.

Carulli, L. M., Noroian, C. L., and Levine, C. "Employee-Driven

Career Development." *Personnel Administrator*, March 1989, 67–70.

Chanick, R. "Career Growth for Baby Boomers." *Personnel Journal*, 1992, *71*(1), 40–44.

Charles, E. J. "Where Do I Go from Here?" *High Tech Career Advancement*, May 1986, 16–17, 34.

Chatman, J. A. "Matching People and Organizations: Selection and Socialization in Public Accounting Forms." *Administrative Science Quarterly*, 1991, *36*(3), 459–484.

Cross, Les. "Career Management Development: A System That Gets Results." *Training and Development Journal*, Feb. 1983, 54–63.

Dalton, G. W., and Thompson, P. H. "From 'Apprentice' to 'Director.'" *National Business Employment Weekly*, May 15, 1987, 13–14.

Dalton, G. W., Thompson, P. H., and Price, R. L. "The Four Stages of Professional Careers." *Organizational Dynamics*, Summer 1977, *6*(1), 19–42.

Day-Foley, C., and Balok, R. "When Career Panic Strikes: Motivation Calms the Fears." *Personnel*, 1991, *68*(9), 13.

DeLuca, J. R. "Strategic Career Management in Non-Growing Volatile Business Environments." *Human Resource Planning*, 1988, *11*, 49–61.

Elsass, P. M., and Ralston, D. A. "Individual Responses to the Stress of Career Plateauing." *Journal of Management*, 1989, *15*, 35–47.

Farren, C., and Kaye, B. "The Principles of Program Design: A Successful Career Development Model." *Personnel Administrator*, June 1984, 109–118.

Feldman, D. C. "Careers in Organizations: Recent Trends and Future Directions." *Journal of Management*, June 1989, 135–156.

Feldman, D. C., and Weitz, B. A. "Career Plateaus Reconsidered." *Journal of Management*, 1988, *14*, 69–80.

Ference, T. P., Stoner, J. A., and Warren, E. K. "Managing the Career Plateau." *Academy of Management Review*, Oct. 1977, 602–612.

Getty, C. "Tapping the Power for Career Development." *Training and Development Journal*, Feb. 1986, 36–37.

Grossman, B. B., and Blitzer, R. J. "Choreographing Careers." *Training & Development*, Jan. 1992, 67–68.

Gutteridge, T. G. "Organizational Career Development and Planning." *Pittsburgh Business Review*, March 1987, 8–14.

Gutteridge, T. G., and Otte, F. L. "Organizational Career Development: What's Going On Out There?" *Training and Development Journal*, Feb. 1983, 22–26.

Gutteridge, T. G., and others (eds.). "Conversations with Ed Schein, Tim Hall, and Marlys Hanson." *Training and Development Journal*, Feb. 1983, 66–70.

Hall, D. T., and Richter, J. "Career Gridlock: Baby Boomers Hit the Wall." *Academy of Management Executives*, 1990, *4*(3), 7–22.

Hanson, M. C. "Implementing a Career Development Program." *Training and Development Journal*, July 1981, 80–90.

Hanson, M. C. "Career/Life Planning Workshops as Career Services in Organizations—Are They Working?" *Training and Development Journal*, Feb. 1982, 58–63.

Harvey, E. K., and Schultz, J. R. "Responses to the Career Plateau." *The Bureaucrat*, Fall 1987, 31–34.

Hawkins, M., and Moravc, M. "Career Paths Discourage Innovation and Deflate Motivation." *Personnel Administrator*, Oct. 1989, 111–112.

Hendricks, D. W. "Career Development: If We Know What It Is, Why Don't We Do It?" *Industrial Management*, Jan./Feb. 1990, 13–15.

Jackson, T., and Vitberg, A. "Career Development, Part 1: Careers and Entrepreneurship." *Personnel*, 1987, *64*(2), 12–17.

Jackson, T., and Vitberg, A. "Career Development, Part 2: Challenges for the Organization." *Personnel*, 1987, *64*(3), 68–72.

Jackson, T., and Vitberg, A. "Career Development, Part 3: Challenges for the Individual." *Personnel*, 1987, *64*(4), 54–57.

Jones, P. R., Kaye, B. L., and Taylor, H. R. "You Want Me to Do What?" *Training and Development Journal*, July 1981, 56–62.

Kanter, R. M. "From Climbing to Hopping: The Contingent Job and the Post-Entrepreneurial Career." *Management Review*, April 1989, 22–27.

Kaye, B. L. "Up Is Not the Only Way." *Supervisory Management*, Feb. 1980, 2–9.

Kaye, B. "Career Development: The Integrating Force." *Training and Development Journal*, May 1981, 36–40.

Kaye, B. "Career Development Puts Training in Its Place." *Personnel Journal*, Feb. 1983, 132–137.

Kaye, B., and others. "Whose Career Is It, Anyway?" *Training and Development Journal*, May 1984, 112–116.

Kirkpatrick, D. "Is Your Career on Track?" *Fortune*, July 2, 1990, 38–48.

Kuchta, W. J. "Options in Career Paths." *Personnel Journal*, Dec. 1988, 28–32.

Labich, K. "Take Control of Your Career." *Fortune*, Nov. 18, 1991, 87–88, 92, 96.

Laser, S. A. "Career Development in a Changing Environment." *Journal of Managerial Psychology* (UK), 1988, *3*(3), 23–25.

Leibowitz, Z. B. "Training Managers for Their Role in a Career Development System." *Training and Development Journal*, July 1981, 72–79.

Leibowitz, Z. B. "Designing Career Development Systems: Principles and Practices." *Human Resource Planning*, 1987, *10*(4), 195–207.

Leibowitz, Z. B., Farren, C., and Kaye, B. L. "Will Your Organization Be Doing Career Development in the Year 2000?" *Training and Development Journal*, Feb. 1983, 14–20.

Leibowitz, Z. B., Farren, C., and Kaye, B. L. "The 12-Fold Path to CD Enlightenment." *Training and Development Journal*, April 1985, 28–32.

Leibowitz, Z. B., Farren, D., and Kaye, B. L. "Overcoming Management Resistance to Career Development Programs." *Training and Development Journal*, Oct. 1986, 77–81.

Leibowitz, Z. B., Feldman, B. H., and Mosley, S. H. "Career Development Works Overtime at Corning, Inc." *Personnel*, April 1990, 38–45.

Leibowitz, Z. B., Kaye, B. L., and Farren, C. "What to Do About Career Gridlock." *Training and Development Journal*, April 1990, 28–35.

Leibowitz, Z. B., and Schlossberg, N. K. "Training Managers for

Their Role in a Career Development System." *Training and Development Journal*, July 1981, 72–79.

Leibowitz, Z. B., and Schlossberg, N. K. "Critical Career Transitions: A Model for Designing Career Services." *Training and Development Journal*, Feb. 1982, 12–19.

Leibowitz, Z. B., Schlossberg, N. K., and Shore, J. E. "Stopping the Revolving Door." *Training and Development Journal*, Feb. 1991, 43–49.

Leibowitz, Z. B., Shore, J. E., and Schuman, G. M. "Managers Can Be Developers, Too." *Training and Development Journal*, March 1992, 46–62.

London, M. "Organizational Support for Employees' Career Motivation: A Guide to Human Resource Strategies in Changing Business Conditions." *Human Resource Planning*, 1988, *11*, 23–32.

Louis, M. R. "Managing Career Transition: A Missing Link in Career Development." *Organizational Dynamics*, Spring 1982, 68–77.

Mainiero, L. A. "The Typecasting Trap." *Training and Development Journal*, March 1990, 83–86.

Mainiero, L. A., and Upham, P. "Repairing the Dual Ladder Program." *Training and Development Journal*, May 1986, 100–104.

Meckel, N. T. "The Manager as Career Counselor." *Training and Development Journal*, July 1981, 65–69.

Mirabile, R. J. "Designing CD Programs the OD Way." *Training and Development Journal*, Feb. 1986, 38, 40–41.

Mirabile, R. J. "New Directions for Career Development." *Training and Development Journal*, Dec. 1987, 30–33.

Mirabile, R. J. "Using Action Research to Design Career Development Programs." *Personnel*, Nov. 1988, 4–11.

Moir, E. "Career Resource Centers in Business and Industry." *Training and Development Journal*, Feb. 1981, 54–57.

Moravec, M., and McKee, B. "Designing Dual Career Paths and Compensation." *Personnel*, 1990, *67*(8), 4–9.

Mosca, J. B. "Technology Affects Careers: A Proposal for the Year 2000." *Journal of Employment Counseling*, Sept. 1989, 98–106.

Moses, B., and Chakiris, B. J. "The Manager as Career Counselor." *Training and Development Journal*, July 1989, 60–65.

Nilan, K. J., Walls, S., Davis, S. L., and Lund, M. E. "Creating a Hierarchical Career Progression Network." *Personnel Administrator*, June 1987, 168–183.

Nussbaum, B. "I'm Worried About My Job." *Business Week*, Oct. 7, 1991, 94–104.

Pazy, A. "Joint Responsibility: The Relationships Between Organizational and Individual Career Management and the Effectiveness of Careers." *Group and Organization Studies*, Sept. 1988, 311–331.

Pinto, P. R. "Career Development Trends for the 80's." *Training*, April 1980, 31–33.

Pinto, P. R. "Career Development." In H. Meltzer and W. Nord (eds.), *Making Organizations Humane and Productive*. New York: Wiley, 1981.

Portwood, J. D., and Granrose, C. S. "Organizational Career Management Programs: What's Available? What's Effective?" *Human Resource Planning*, 1986, *9*(3), 107–119.

Raelin, J. A. "Two-Track Plans for One-Track Careers." *Personnel Journal*, 1987, *66*(1), 96–101.

Randolph, B. A. "Managerial Career Coaching." *Training and Development Journal*, July 1981, 54–55.

Raskin-Young, K. "Career Counseling in a Large Organization." *Training and Development Journal*, Aug. 1984, 57–58.

Rosen, B., and Jerdee, T. H. "Middle and Late Career Problems: Causes, Consequences, and Research Needs." *Human Resource Planning*, 1990, *13*, 59–70.

Roth, L. M. "A Critical Examination of the Dual Ladder Approach to Career Advancement." New York: Center for Research in Career Development, Graduate School of Business, Columbia University, 1982.

Russell, J.E.A. "Career Development Interventions in Organizations." *Journal of Vocational Behavior*, 1991, 237–287.

Russell, M. "Career Planning in a Blue-Collar Company. *Training and Development Journal*, Jan. 1984, 87–88.

Schmidt, S. "Career Development Programs in Business and Industry." *Journal of Employment Counseling*, June 1990, 76–83.

Schultz, J. R., and Harvey, E. K. "The Career Plateau: What Is It and What Can We Do About It?" *The GAO Review*, Summer 1986, 24–26.

Settle, M. "Up Through the Ranks at McDonnell Douglas." *Personnel*, Dec. 1989, 17–22.

Sheppeck, M. A., and Taylor, C. "Up the Career Path." *Training and Development Journal*, Aug. 1985, 46–48.

Sheridan, J. E., Slocum, J. W., Jr., Buda, R., and Thompson, R. C. "Effects of Corporate Sponsorship and Departmental Power on Career Tournaments." *Academy of Management Journal*, 1990, *33*, 578–602.

Slavenski, L. "Career Development: A Systems Approach." *Training and Development Journal*, Feb. 1987, 56–60.

Steele, B., Bratkovich, J. R., and Rollins, T. "Implementing Strategic Redirection Through the Career Management System." *Human Resource Planning*, 1990, *13*(4), 241–264.

Stephens, G. K., and Black, S. "The Impact of Spouse's Career Orientation on Managers During International Transfers." *Journal of Management Studies*, 1991, *28*(4), 417–428.

Stump, R. W. "Evaluating Career Development: Fact and Fantasy." *Training and Development Journal*, Dec. 1987, 38–40.

Stumpf, S. A. "Choosing Career Management Practices to Support Your Business Strategy." *Human Resource Planning*, 1988, *11*, 33–47.

Thomas, W. C. "A Career Development Program That Works." *Management Review*, May 1980, 38–42.

Thompson, P., and Hammond, S. "From Career Plateau to Peak Performance." *Executive Excellence*, Oct. 1988, 14–15.

Tucker, R., and Moravec, M. "Do-It-Yourself Career Development." *Training*, Feb. 1992, 50.

Tucker, R., Moravec, M., and Ideus, K. "Designing a Dual Career-Track System." *Training & Development*, June 1992, 55–58.

Von Glinow, M. A., and others. "The Design of Career-Oriented Resource Systems. *Journal of Management Review*, 1983, *9*, 23–32.

Walker, J. W. "Does Career Planning Rock the Boat?" *Human Resource Management*, Spring 1978, 2–7.

Weber, J., Driscoll, L., and Brandt, R. "Farewell, Fast Track." *Business Week*, Dec. 10, 1990, 192–200.

Wilhelm, W. "Helping Workers to Self-Manage Their Careers." *Personnel Administrator*, Aug. 1983, 83–89.

Williamson, B. A., and Otte, F. L. "Assessing the Need for Career Development." *Training and Development Journal*, March 1986, 59–61.

Zenger, J. "Career Planning: Coming in from the Cold." *Training and Development Journal*, July 1981, 47–52.

REFERENCES

Ackoff, R. L. *Creating the Corporate Future*. New York: Wiley, 1981.

Aikin, O. "Development in Equality." *Personnel Management*, 1990, 22(9), 81–83.

American Society for Training and Development. *1990 Membership Directory*. Alexandria, Va.: American Society for Training and Development, 1990.

Atkinson, J. "Four Stages of Adjustment to the Demographic Downturn," *Personnel Management*, 1989, 20–25.

Australian Council of Trade Unions and Trade Development Council to Western Europe. *Australia Re-Constructed*. Canberra: Australian Government Publishing Service, 1987.

Australian Institute of Training and Development. *Career Development Practices in Selected Australian Organisations: An Overview of Survey Findings*. Chatswood: Australian Institute of Training and Development, 1991.

Bailyn, L. "Resolving Conflicts in Technical Careers, or What If I Like Being an Engineer?" *Technology Review*, Nov./Dec. 1982, 38–50.

Beckhard, R., and Harris, R. *Organizational Transitions: Managing Complex Change*. Reading, Mass.: Addison-Wesley, 1977.

Beckhard, R., and Pritchard, W. *Changing the Essence: The Art of Creating and Leading Fundamental Change in Organizations*. San Francisco: Jossey-Bass, 1992.

Berney, K. "Get Ready for the Quality Generation." *International Management*, 1990, *45*(6), 26–31.

Collins, R., and Hackman, K. *National Survey of Training and Development Practices*. Sydney, Australia: Commercial Clearing House and Australian Graduate School of Management, July 1991.

Dalton, G. W., and Thompson, P. H. *Novations: Strategies for Career Management*. Glenview, Ill.: Scott, Foresman, 1986.

Derr, C. B. *Managing the New Careerists*. San Francisco: Jossey-Bass, 1986.

Derr, C. B. "Managing High-Potentials in Europe: Some Cross-Cultural Findings." *European Management Journal*, 1987, *5*(6), 72–80.

Derr, C. B., and Laurent, A. "The Internal and External Career: A Theoretical and Cross-Cultural Perspective." In M. B. Arthur, D. T. Hall, and B. S. Lawrence (eds.), *Handbook of Career Theory*. Cambridge, England: Cambridge University Press, 1989.

Derr, C. B., and others. "The Emerging Role of the HR Manager in Europe." *IMD/European Association of Personnel Management Report*. International Institute of Management Development (IMD), Chemin de Bellerive 23, P.O. Box 915, CH-1001 Lausanne, Switzerland, 1992.

Driver, M. J. "Career Concepts: A New Approach to Research." In R. Katz (ed.), *Career Issues in Human Resource Management*. Englewood Cliffs, N.J.: Prentice-Hall, 1982.

Eurostat. "Unemployment." Luxembourg, Sept. 1990. ISSN 0252-9920.

Evans, P., Farquhar, A., and Landreth, O. "Fostering Innovation Through Human Resources: Lessons from Practice." In P. Evans, Y. Doz, and A. Laurent, *Human Resource Management in International Firms*. London: Macmillan, 1989.

Garfield, C. *Second to None*. Homewood, Ill.: Irwin, 1992.

Gibbons, L. (ed.). *The Corporate 1000*, 1990a, *6*(2).

Gibbons, L. (ed.). *The Financial 1000*, 1990b, *3*(1).

Green, A. E. "Craft and Technical Skill Shortages in Engineering." *International Journal of Manpower*, 1990, *11*(2, 3), 18–22.

Gutteridge, T. G. "Organizational Career Development Systems:

The State of the Practice." In D. T. Hall and Associates, *Career Development in Organizations*. San Francisco: Jossey-Bass, 1987.

Gutteridge, T. G., and Otte, F. L. *Organizational Career Development: State of the Practice*. Alexandria, Va.: American Society for Training and Development, 1983.

Hall, D. T., and Associates. *Career Development in Organizations*. San Francisco: Jossey-Bass, 1987.

Healy, G., and Kraithman, D. "The Other Side of the Equation: The Demands of Women on Re-entering the Labour Market." *Employee Relations*, 1991, *13*(3), 17–28.

Kanter, R. M. "The New Managerial Work." *Harvard Business Review*, Nov.–Dec., 1989, 85–92.

Leibowitz, Z. B., Farren, C., and Kaye, B. L. *Designing Career Development Systems*. San Francisco: Jossey-Bass, 1986.

Leibowitz, Z. B., and Kaye, B. L. "Keeping Career Development Alive." Speech delivered at the ASTD National Conference, San Francisco, 1991.

"Meeting Mothers Halfway." *International Management*, June 1989, 48–52.

Merman, S. K., and Leibowitz, Z. B. *Career Development Systems: Questions Worth Asking and Answers Worth Questioning*. Alexandria, Va.: American Society for Training and Development, 1984.

Moy, J., and Rylatt, A. *Career Development Practices in Selected Australian Organisations: An Overview of Survey Findings*. St. Ives, New South Wales: Australian Institute of Training and Development, 1992.

Naisbitt, J., and Aburdene, P. *Megatrends 2000: Ten New Directions for the 1990s*. New York: Morrow, 1990.

National Board of Employment, Education, and Training. *Progress and Prospects in Improved Skill Recognition*. Canberra: Australian Government Publishing Service, Dec. 1991.

Price-Waterhouse Cranfield. *Price-Waterhouse Cranfield Research Project on International Strategic Human Resource Management*. Bedford, United Kingdom: Cranfield University, 1991.

Quinn, R. E. *Beyond Rational Management: Mastering the Paradoxes and Competing Demands of High Performance.* San Francisco: Jossey-Bass, 1988.

Smith, A. "Training: Waking Up to the Possibilities." *Industrial Society* (UK), Dec. 1990, 24–25.

Storey, W. D. (ed.). *A Guide for Career Development Inquiry: State of the Art Report on Career Development.* ASTD Research Series, no. 2. Alexandria, Va.: American Society for Training and Development, 1979.

Thomason, S. "Utilizing Women's Skills." *Employee Relations,* 1991, *13*(4), 54.

United States Government. *1990 Membership Roster of the Interagency Advisory Group of the Committee on Development and Training.* Washington, D.C. (Photocopied.)

Vandernerive, S. "Youth Consumers: Growing Pains." *Business Horizons,* May/June 1990, 30–36.

Walker, J. W. *Human Resource Planning.* New York: McGraw-Hill, 1980.

Walker, J. W., and Gutteridge, T. G. *Career Planning Practices.* AMA Survey Report. New York: AMACOM, 1979.

Washington Monitor. *Financial 1000.* Washington, D.C.: Washington Monitor, 1990.

"Women at Work: The Politics of the Nursery." *The Economist,* Nov. 1991, 51–54.

The World Competitiveness Report, 1992. International Institute of Management Development (IMD), Chemin De Bellerive 23, P.O. Box 915, CH-1001 Lausanne, Switzerland, 1992.

INDEX

Chapter Seven:

The profile of Amoco Production Company's career development program and their corporate logo are printed with the permission of Amoco Corporation.

The profile of BP Exploration's career development program and its logo are printed with the permission of BP Exploration Operating Company, Ltd.

The profile of Overseas Telecommunications Company's career development program is printed with the permission of Overseas Telecommunications Company.

The profile of 3M's human resources operation and the corporate logo are printed with the permission of 3M.

The profile of NCR's career development program and the corporate logo are printed with the permission of NCR.

The profile of the Baxter Healthcare Pty. Ltd. career development program is printed with the permission of Baxter Healthcare Pty. Ltd.

The profile of the career counseling and job-search assistance services of the U.S. General Accounting Office (GAO) and the GAO logo are printed with the permission of the United States General Accounting Office.

The profile of Bechtel Group's career development program and the corporate logo are printed with the permission of Bechtel.

The profile of the Kodak career development program and the corporate logo are printed with the permission of Eastman Kodak Company.

The profile of AT&T's career development program is printed with the permission of AT&T.

The profile of Boeing's career development program and the corporate logo are printed with the permission of The Boeing Company.

The profile of Corning's career development program and the corporate logo are printed with the permission of Corning Incorporated.

Chapter Eight:

The case study of the 3M Job Information System and the 3M corporate logo are printed with the permission of 3M.

The case study of the Alliance Learning Center's labor-management partnership is printed with the permission of the Alliance Learning Center.

The case study of Nationwide Insurance's Technical Excellence Program and the corporate logo are printed with the permission of Nationwide Insurance.

The case study of Ford's Leadership Education and Development Program and the corporate logo are printed with the permission of Ford Motor Company.

The case study of Westpac Banking Corporation's succession planning and career development and the corporate logo are printed with the permission of Westpac Banking Corporation.

Conclusion:

The first epigraph opening the conclusion to the book is quoted from Richard Beckhard and Wendy Pritchard, *Changing the Essence*, 1992, Jossey-Bass, pp. 93–94. Reprinted with permission.

The second epigraph opening the conclusion is quoted from Charles Garfield, *Second to None: How Our Smartest Companies Put People First*, 1992, Business 1 Irwin, p. 46. Reprinted with permission.